Revolt Against Theocracy

Revolt Against Theocracy

The Mahsa Movement and the Feminist Uprising in Iran

Farhad Khosrokhavar

polity

okhavar 2024

ed as Author of this Work has been
ht, Designs and Patents Act 1988.

y Polity Press

s
eet
UR, UK

ss
reet
030, USA

of short passages for the purpose of
ation may be reproduced, stored in a
r by any means, electronic, mechanical,
ut the prior permission of the publisher.

5095-6449-1
95-6450-7(pb)

available from the British Library.

ol Number: 2024930040

4pt Warnock Pro
td, Cuddington, Cheshire
by CPI Group (UK) Ltd, Croydon

urs to ensure that the URLs for external
ect and active at the time of going to press.
sibility for the websites and can make no
at the content is or will remain appropriate.

ll copyright holders, but if any have been
ed to include any necessary credits in any
eprint or edition.

on Polity, visit our website:
books.com

Contents

Preface viii

Introduction 1

1. **The mindset of the younger generation: the new culture of "joie de vivre" against Islamic theocracy** 5
2. **Protest movements before the Mahsa Movement** 70
3. **The Mahsa Movement: the first sweeping feminist movement in Iran** 85
4. **The new intellectuals** 128
5. **From a theocratic state to a totalitarian one** 172
6. **Secularization counter to the Theocratic State** 203

Conclusion 221

Notes 224
Index 242

Preface

The first thesis presented in this book is that the Mahsa Movement is most probably the first genuine, global, and extensive feminist movement in Iran ever, and perhaps in the Muslim world. This is not to deny that women have played a significant role in social movements in Turkey, Egypt, Syria, Iran, and other Muslim countries since the nineteenth century. But within these movements, women were not in the vanguard, did not become the main actors, did not express their feminist demands in clear antagonism towards the powers that be, and men did not follow them en masse.

In the Mahsa Movement young women played a pioneering role not only in launching the movement, but also in their participation throughout. The protests quickly spread among young men, who showed that they largely shared the women's views on the veil, on equal gender rights, and the rejection of theocratic rule. The movement was, in a sense, the apogee of what had begun the day after the establishment of the Islamic Republic in Iran with the imposition of the veil and, subsequently, the application of Sharia law, which spelled out the structural inferiority of women in terms of rights. But the movement also represents a break with prevailing trends in

Iranian feminism, notably in terms of the explicit and direct rejection of the veil and the Islamic Regime, as well as in the affirmation of a new culture based on the joy of living and the unvarnished, uninhibited secularization expressed throughout the movement without any reference to religion.

What essentially characterizes a global feminist movement is the primordial role played by women, where the major slogans and demands refer explicitly to women. In the Mahsa Movement, these conditions are certainly met: the slogan "Woman, life, freedom" sets the tone, the role of women at the vanguard is undeniable, and in addition, young men participated actively in it. When in March–April 2023 the movement lost its ability to mobilize groups, individual women continued in the struggle, by rejecting the compulsory veil.

While women were the trailblazers in the protest movement, young Iranian men conscientiously played an ancillary role by putting into question their masculine pride founded on patriarchal, traditional Islam – their male "Islamic honor" so-called (*gheyrat* in Persian, *gheyra* in Arabic). The distinctive feature of the Mahsa Movement was not only that young women rebelled against their subaltern role – in many movements throughout the Muslim world women have revolted time and again in the twentieth and twenty-first centuries against their inferior condition – but that the young men joined them without ulterior motive, recognizing their legitimacy and their role as foremost denouncers of the Islamic patriarchy and theocracy.

The Mahsa Movement has two essential characteristics: the quest for gender equality and the denunciation of dictatorship. This book seeks to analyze the mindset of the young men but also, and especially, of the young women within the movement and their conflictual relationship with a patriarchal state that denies them equality and the freedom to own their bodies. The movement began mid-September 2022, called here the Mahsa Movement after the first name of the young Iranian woman, Mahsa Amini, killed by the Vice Squad in Tehran on

September 16, 2022. In cooperation with young men, women challenged the Theocratic Regime for several months.

The second purpose of this book is to depict the political and ideological features of the Islamic State that has ruled the country since 1979 and its distorted relationship to society. I call it a "soft" totalitarian regime: it stifles social protest but is unable to prevent its rise. This book describes the multiple forms of the State's repression through its central organization, the Islamic Revolutionary Guards Corps (IRGC), through the clergy, and through the repressive organizations under their aegis (official and unofficial prisons, militia, the Basij Resistance Force, etc.). Arbitrary arrests according to the formal Iranian Constitution, torture, sequestration, and execution are the arsenal of this state, which acts promptly to stop non-violent protest movements. It survives because it crushes unorganized, leaderless protesters; it prevents their organization and progress by ruthless repression, breaking them through extreme violence.

The book focuses on the emergence of new social activists. First are the women themselves, whose forebears – often leading feminist intellectuals – have raised the awareness of the younger generations, and paid a heavy price through imprisonment and systematic mistreatment, even psychological and physical torture. They have provided the new generations with a body of feminist literature and social movements (for instance, the Campaign for One Million Signatures in 2006) that have left their imprint on the young women who are risking their lives to demonstrate in the streets of Iran.

Meanwhile a new type of intellectual has emerged, comprising hip-hop, rap, and blues singers, who have become the "organic intellectuals" of the latest protest movement. The book points also to the influence of the diaspora, through TV channels and the internet, in shaping the culture of Iranian youth. The latter reject the Theocratic State and its repression and total disregard for their aspirations.

The book also underlines the secular culture of the new generations, which I call "joie de vivre" (zest for earthly life). It is centered on this world's pleasure and daily life, and not on a sacrificial afterlife in the name of martyrdom which underpins the ideology of the Islamic Republic. In this new culture, free and secular relations between men and women, the desire to enjoy life in this world and not in the hereafter, as well as the rejection of the "mournful culture" of the Islamic Regime, are emphasized. The culture of joy is expressed in opposition to the Theocratic Regime's ideology in a festive but also transgressive way, of which dancing, partying, and the ostentatious female unveiling in public are prominent aspects.

In the protest movements that have unfolded in Iran since 2009, the middle classes have played a decisive role. But they have been undermined by the decline in their living standards. The Islamic Regime has debilitated them through its economic policies, and not least the general crisis of the Iranian economy has taken its toll due to its exclusion from the world economy in consequence of the country's nuclear program. A large part of the population could be said to be middle class in terms of culture due to the overall increase in the level of education, but it does not have the economic status corresponding to its expectations as aspiring middle-class members. I call them "would-be middle classes." In this group, their adverse economic status in conjunction with their secular culture pits them directly against the Islamic State, which disapproves of meritocracy and is driven by cronyism, deep-rooted corruption, and prohibitions on bodily freedom and gender mixing in the name of orthodox Islam. Its clash with the young would-be middle classes is head-on.

The would-be middle classes have a half-imaginary, half-real construction of a global, worldwide civil sphere. They take it as witness to the legitimacy of their struggle for freedom and the illegitimacy of a state that denies them the most elementary freedoms. The protagonists in the fight against women's inequality are recognized and awarded for the defense of freedom by the international institutions that represent the global civil sphere. Reference to the wider world is one of the hallmarks of the Mahsa Movement.

This book aims to show the vigor of secularization in Iran despite the Islamic State's unrelenting endeavors to turn its citizens into submissive Muslims through its state apparatus (national education, the official TV and radio networks, the propaganda machine sustained by the government). Secularization has occurred against a rigid form of Shi'ism that I term theocratic Shi'ism, which is the ideological cornerstone of the Islamic Republic. It shows major differences with traditional Shi'ism. Theocratic Shi'ism places special emphasis on martyrdom and mourning in the service of a theocratic state and its purpose is to legitimize the domination of society by the *Velayat faqih* (the absolute rule of the Supreme Leader). It justifies the constraints imposed by the government: the compulsory veil, segregation of men and women, prohibition of alcohol consumption, respect for Ramadan fasting, prohibition of celebration and dancing in public, opposition to the West in the name of a politico-religious conception imposed on society and not open to debate, and so on. In most cases, what was flexible in traditional Shi'ism has become rigid and unyielding under theocratic Shi'ism.

The Islamic Republic has failed to de-secularize society and this book seeks to explain why. The widespread protest movements since 2009 are analyzed in this respect. The Mahsa Movement of 2022–3 has shaken the Islamic Regime but has failed to overthrow it. It has succeeded, culturally and socially, in showing the Regime's illegitimacy, and women continue to reject the mandatory veil by appearing unveiled in public. The book underlines the recurrence of the protest movements, despite the harshness of the repression, leading to the wearing down of the Theocratic State.

Preface

This book highlights the continued action of a predatory state that represses its citizens in everyday life, and whose elite enriches itself by indulging in illegal practices that it forbids to the population. It allows itself every kind of abuse, and its very existence is a denial of dignity to its citizens (and is perceived as such by a large majority of them). It is based on a theocratic version of Shi'ism which is different from the traditional one in many respects, and that are described at length in this book. An increasingly secularized society rejects the Regime's religious and political claim to govern it. But for the time being, citizens do not succeed in overthrowing it for lack of organization and leadership.

A note on terminology and data

In this book, the Islamic Republic in Iran is referred to variously as the Islamic Regime, the Theocratic State, the Islamic Republic, the Regime, and sometimes, the predatory state in reference to its ruthless, violent action against its citizens.

The protest demonstrations, which began in mid-September 2022 and continued up to February/March 2023 and beyond, have been alternately called a movement (*harekat*), an uprising (*khizesh*), a super-movement (*abar-jonbesh*)[1], a female revolution (*enqelab zananeh*), and a peace revolution (*enqelab solh*)[2]. While I have chosen to call it the Mahsa Movement, it has also been called the September 2022 Movement[3] or the Jina Movement (Jina being the Kurdish first name of Mahsa Amini).

Several expressions have been introduced to translate the Persian terms regarding how the veil is worn: "de-veiling" or "unveiling" (*kashfe hejab*), unveiled or "veil-less" (*bi hejab*), "mal-veiled" or "badly veiled" (*bad hejab*), or "loosely veiled" (*shol hejab*).

Translations from Persian and French texts into English are mine, unless stated otherwise.

It should also be noted Iranian statistics have been subject to vigilant censorship since at least 2009 and are not always reliable. Data on human rights in Iran can be found on the websites of Hrana (Human Rights Activist News Agency), https://www.en-hrana.org, Iran Human Rights Society, https://iranhrs.org/, and Iran Human Rights Watch, http://iranhrw.com/

The research for this work ended in July 2023.

Introduction

A new subjectivity characterizes the younger Iranian generation which the Islamic Republic does not understand at all. The Theocratic Regime is the target of their hatred because it is the major obstacle to their self-realization, to their desire to be recognized in their dignity as citizens, and to live their lives to the fullest in a secular, joyful life in this world, disregarding the grim view of life imposed from above in the name of Islam. Paramount is the mandatory veil, which is an assault on the body of the young women who do not want to wear it. There are, of course, economic, political, and social motives that also play an important role in the protest movement of 2022–3. The Regime failed to offer decent living prospects to new generations, whether economically, politically, or culturally. It robbed them of their freedom in the name of a conservative version of Islam. It denied them access to modernity and its inherent desires (deciding what one wears, being able to travel and meet friends without fear of being arrested and abused, recognition of one's competence, having the right to a fair future). The new subjectivity, especially among young women, does not recognize an intangible sacred rule from above, and more generally, rejects any norm that hinders their desire to live their life freely, to be in control of their own personal destiny – in short, to have no religious guardian. There is an unfathomable abyss between the Theocratic Regime and its youth. It deliberately ignores or even despises their demands and believes that it can subdue them through intimidation, repression, and, ultimately, death. However, its capacity for intimidation has limits, and two strategies are available to the youth: either violating on the sly repressive standards that are light years away from their aspirations, or collectively protesting when the opportunity arises.

It should be noted that workers did not play a significant role in the Mahsa Movement. There is a great deal of worker discontent in Iran as a result of wages not keeping pace with inflation and the breaches of economic fairness for the working classes. But precisely because of their poverty and the absence of a culture of radical protest, workers' movements have confined themselves to sectoral demands, and they did not play even a supporting role in the Green Movement in 2009 or in the Mahsa Movement in 2022–3. The many and varied workers' protests, whether at the Sherekat Vahed urban bus company or the Haft Tappeh sugar plant in Khuzestan (southwest Iran), or among oil and steel workers, focused on economic demands, without calling into question the political nature of the Islamic Regime. Meanwhile other types of protest movement played a role in the Mahsa Movement, namely among ethnic minorities (Kurds, Baluchi, Iranian Arabs, etc.), Muslim religious minorities (the Sufi Gonabadi dervishes in Tehran, the Iranian Sunni Muslims, who are discriminated against, especially in the underdeveloped southeastern province of Sistan and Baluchistan), the Baha'is (who are not even recognized as a religious minority and are systematically repressed and denied their elementary rights under different pretexts), citizens exposed to pollution and sandstorms (in the city of Ahvaz in the southwest of Iran, among others) or to the drying up of lakes (such as Lake Urmia in the northwest of the country) or rivers (Zayandeh Rud in Isfahan) or subject to water shortages, and especially students, who are systematically repressed in their desire for freedom of expression and gender equality.

The Mahsa Movement is the crowning achievement of these acts of protest. It has been driven by the will to overthrow the Theocratic Regime and establish a democratic one. But at its heart it is a profoundly cultural revolution, namely against what can be called traditional Shi'ism with its tragic vision of existence that the Islamic Regime has tried to exploit mainly through the cult of martyrdom. The movement has been centered on women because they are the focus of traditional Islam, which targets them as the symbol of fertility that must be desexualized and therefore covered by a veil in public and segregated from men other than husbands and fathers. Juridically, women weigh half as much as men. The movement challenged the inferior status of women, who freed themselves from the mandatory veil and segregation and asserted themselves as equal to men in daily life, by participating in the festivities on the streets where men and women came together and as joyful citizens danced, sang, and feasted. The Mahsa Movement has been therefore in direct conflict with the values of Islamic culture and its theocratic version that has become the ideology of the Islamic Republic.

The Mahsa Movement was marked by the activism of young women and the willingness of young men to follow them in confronting the Islamic Regime. The women's agency, motivated by feminist demands, made them protesters in the vanguard for the first time in Iran's history, and probably in the Muslim world. They believed women should have sovereignty over their clothing, their bodies, and their socialization with men, without the intervention of the state in the name of religion. In the Mahsa Movement, men came second; they backed women and showed their solidarity with them, but the impetus came from women.

On the other hand, men also wanted to free themselves from the constraints of the Theocratic Regime, create new relationships with women, mingle freely with them in broad daylight, and live with them without gender segregation. Male and female youth alike rejected the roles assigned to them by patriarchal Islam and openly engaged in the struggle for secular citizenship. One important difference with the earlier protest movements is that the Mahsa Movement directly challenged the Islamic Regime without any sense of guilt; on the contrary, as we shall see, the protesters had a clear conscience, they had no remorse in trampling the religious norms underfoot. This is the radical novelty of this movement: it seeks to innovate culturally and politically.

1

The mindset of the younger generation: the new culture of "joie de vivre" against Islamic theocracy

Social movements are determined by objective, historical conditions but go beyond them. Activists launch the movement by questioning a social and political order they perceive as repressive and act to end their alienation and their sense of being dominated.[1] In Iran, the main enemy is the Islamic Regime, which denies freedom to the people in the name of a theocratic version of Shi'ism. The Mahsa Movement was distinct from the large movements of 2009 (the Green Movement) and those of 2016–19. It differed from the former in that it unambiguously rejected the powers that be (the leitmotiv of the movement was "Death to the dictator" [*marg bar dictator*]), whereas the Green Movement of 2009 accepted the Islamic Republic and aimed at reforming it from within. It also differed from the latter in that the Mahsa Movement proposed a political system under the slogan "Woman, life, freedom." Like the 2016–19 movements it was marked by a lack of leadership and organization, indicative of its institutional weakness. By cutting off the internet and massively arresting the demonstrators (around 20,000 arrests until end of January 2023), the Islamic Regime stifled the movement, which cruelly lacked organization and leadership, due to the government's repression.

The objective causes of the Mahsa Movement were the increasingly totalitarian character of the political system coupled with the economic decline of the middle and lower classes and the elimination of Reformists (Khatami's presidency from 1997 to 2005 was the apogee of reformism and since then, Reformists have been gradually excluded from the political arena). Iran was experiencing an increase in poverty as a result of the lack of development, government policies, and the duality within the Iranian State (the large organizations under the aegis of the Supreme Leader versus the official government). Furthermore, it was isolated on the international scene, and the withdrawal of the United States under President Trump from the nuclear treaty in 2018 and the application of restrictive clauses made the legal sale of oil extremely difficult for Iran, inducing the depreciation of the Iranian currency and a very high rate of inflation. The middle classes were feeling the effects of impoverishment too.

The subjective rationale for the movement was a youth that was not intimidated by government repression, unlike the older generations.

In the denial of the legitimacy of the Islamic Republic by the protesters, one dimension stood out: the secularization of the youth and the importance of this-worldly life, or what I will call "joie de vivre," with all its pleasures including the unfettered relationship between men and women and full rights and freedoms for women. The extent of the youth's secularization caught the Shi'i theocracy unawares. Foremost, they aspired to a secular life and repudiated mandatory religious values. They rejected the Shi'i theocracy as a killjoy[2] and an agent of social injustice and poverty.[3]

In a sense, the Theocratic Regime has made the lives of young men and women alike unbearable for almost identical reasons: the denial of their subjectivity, of their sense of dignity, of their desire to be full-fledged citizens, of their wish to live in a less religious, more secular society, where each person can decide on their own faith, free from a normative religion imposed from above. In addition to the denial of freedom, high rates of inflation have pushed more than half of the population into poverty, including the middle classes.[4]

The dark view of the future is expressed by the Iranian rapper Emad Ghavidel in his song "My Generation" (*nasle man*), who has recently been put in prison:

Today I regret yesterday
Tomorrow I cry for today
I can't sing with feelings anymore,
I'm from the burnt generation, let me wallow in the ashes.

The feeling of impotence is heightened by a dark despair that the singer eloquently expresses:

When as a young person, your joy of living (zowgh) is dead,
continuing to live makes you nauseous.

It is with this deep sense of a future blocked and the present worse than the past that the movement of general insubordination began in September 2022 – not only as a protest, but also a way to recover the joy of life from the grasp of a killjoy state that epitomizes a combination of cultural oppression, economic injustice, political repression, and government corruption.[5] The new generations are in touch with the outside world through the web and the Iranian diaspora (more than 3 million Iranians live outside Iran). They are aware of what is happening in their country in comparison to the outside world. The conjunction of repression, corruption, and negligence is unacceptable to them. On top of that, the government's antagonistic attitude to the West hurts the new generations in terms of global economic development and, furthermore, does not reflect their views. It makes the Iranians' social and material life difficult. They do not harbor adverse feelings towards the

West, where a few million diasporic Iranians reside and mostly enjoy a middle-class standard of living. The Iranian youth dream of emigrating to the West, for lack of opportunity in Iran, but also to breathe the air of freedom alongside economic progress. One of the slogans of the Mahsa Movement protesters was: "Our enemy is here [the Islamic Republic]/They [the Islamic Regime proponents] lie by claiming it is America" (*dochmane ma haminjast/dorouq migan amrikast*).

A large part of Iranian youth in the 2020s is secular.[6] Above all, often inspired by the Iranian diaspora who have managed to keep close ties with Iranians at home, they aspire to a pluralistic society where freedom of dress goes hand in hand with political freedom, in a peaceful relationship with the West.

The false piety of the parents and the provocative sincerity of their children

The rupture between private and public life, the growing chasm between the rich and the poor, the lack of basic freedoms to access leisure activities, and nepotism and lack of meritocracy are causes of frustration and humiliation among young people and they feel no respect for mandatory Islamic standards. Under the Pahlavis, the Iranian middle classes internalized many secular values.[7]

On the eve of the Islamic Revolution in 1979, almost half a century after Reza Shah's secularization of the state in the 1930s, a large proportion of Iranian middle-class families had adopted secular mores. They were averse to mandatory religious prohibitions, but they naively believed that the so-called "Islamic Republic" would not be a hardline theocracy but a softened religious government.

More than four decades later, despite the Shi'i theocracy's attempts to Islamize society, young, ordinary people, and even the children of the ruling elite, expressed their opposition through the Mahsa Movement. In everyday life, young people behave in a secular manner in public and reject the dualistic behavior of their parents, who pretend to be pious Muslims in the street while they behave in quite opposite ways at home. What their parents experience as double-dealing with the government, they experience as hypocrisy at best and schizoid at worst, and, in either case, as demeaning.

Through the Mahsa Movement, young protesters rejected duplicity and hypocritical Islamic behavior in public, asserting the dignity of the citizens over a coerced religiosity imposed from above by the government.

The older generations have begrudgingly accepted the harsh reality of a disingenuous society and the disconnect between private and public life under government repression. Within families, including those of the lower middle classes and working classes, a huge gap exists between their attitude in private and in public regarding Islamic prohibitions. Besides the pious, conservative Muslim families (probably a minority of 10–15 percent of the population), fathers consume, at least occasionally, alcohol (rich people drink whiskey, the poor, low quality brandy, *araq*), they do not perform daily prayers, and young people especially watch the forbidden channels through satellite dishes and mentally exile themselves from a gloomy daily life by consuming drugs or by adhering to new religions (Evangelism in Iran is thriving in spite of harsh repression). In the street, they are compelled to pretend to be decent Muslims. The list of restrictions is extensive: no breaking of the Ramadan fast, no woman without a veil, no consumption of alcoholic beverages, no sign of collective joy, no mixing of men and women, no outward sign of bodily contact (kissing, hugging), and so on. On top of that, young women must, often in the stifling heat of hot summers, be tightly covered. They feel more intensely than men the injustice of a system that their subjectivity rejects, which seems senseless. Subjectivity among the youth clashes with the simulacrum of Islamic behavior among their parents; it constantly challenges religious standards that young people dismiss as alien to their worldview. The Islamic Republic has become the epitome of an arbitrary and unjustifiable domination, at odds with the youth, estranged from their emotions. The heavier the ban, the more unquenchable the thirst for forbidden pleasures among young people; they feel an unending desire for transgression, on top of their urge to behave according to their secular mindset. Unlike their parents who play the double game with little or no contrition, the youth feel it is a humiliation to pretend to be what they are not, to live an insincere life of duplicity, epitomizing an unbearable submission to an illegitimate authority. Where the parents keep up the appearances of Islamic behavior in the street, the young people, driven by a new spirit, seek to accentuate their rupture with the Regime by taking their revolt to its limits, adding provocation to the desire to be oneself in a secular manner.

The older generations, the fathers and grandfathers, because duplicity, or hypocrisy, as far as the State is concerned is a fact of life, are not deeply affected by the dichotomy between the public and the private spheres. They are more willing to play cat-and-mouse with the government than the youth are. They also believe in this way that they are duping the Islamic State and that their make-believe is some sort of revenge on its strictures. But unlike their parents, young people feel it is demeaning to play this duplicitous game with the Regime. For them, it represents an unjustifiable denial of recognition by the Islamic State and they think it is an undeniable right to be outside without a veil, in the case of young women, or for a young man to go out with his hair greased back and chest bare. Imposed duality is repugnant to them and they experience it as a humiliation.

The cultural difference with their parents is immense. They want to be accepted for who they are, not who the powers that be demand. They sense in this duality in public life an attack on their dignity and a perverse game through which the Islamic State tries to stifle them individually before oppressing them socially. They denounce the religious restrictions imposed by the Islamic regime as a denial of their existential freedom to dispose of their bodies and their social relations. To refuse theocratic Islam is to reject repression and a state which is the very antithesis of their vision not only of politics, but of life itself. In that respect they are profoundly different from their parents and grandparents, whose self-esteem is not as affected by the diktats of the Theocratic State concerning Islamic posturing in the public sphere. The cat-and-mouse game goes against their feeling of authenticity, whereas for their parents it is a nasty game that they play spontaneously, without a feeling of alienation. For their children, playing this game is total alienation.

It is no coincidence that the Mahsa Movement, whose leitmotif was the "joie de vivre," mobilized young people, but not the older generations. They live in two different worlds and communication between them is awkward.

What distinguished the revolt of the youth is that, on the one hand, they were not as fearful as their parents: they had not experienced the repression their parents had during the movements of 2016–19, in which they were too young to have taken part. But there is another reason: this government does not promise its young citizens a credible future. The Chinese government denies its citizens political freedom, but not the innocent joy of living (existential freedom they can moderately enjoy privately and in public, be what they are individually). Above all, it promises them an economic future that is brighter than the present, and this seems credible to many young people. But this is not the case in Iran where the Islamic Regime, at war with the West, prepares a future bleaker than the present, which is already darker than the past, as Iranian musicians remind us in their songs.

The new generations and the dismissal of the "Islamic patriarchal pact"

In Iran, from the 1930s under the Pahlavi monarchy up to 1979 when it was overthrown by a revolution spearheaded by Ayatollah Khomeini, women enjoyed a new legal status that was significantly superior to the Islamic tradition that prevailed before. Reza Shah's Iran followed in the footsteps of Atatürk's Turkey by involving women in the authoritarian modernization process from above. It forcibly removed their veil in 1936. Subsequently, after many decades, a large part of women in urban areas had internalized the unveiled identity and took off the veil, not anymore under constraint but by their own consent.

During the great demonstrations of the 1979 Revolution against the Shah, many modernized women temporarily wore headscarves to express their rejection of Mohammad Reza Shah's authoritarian regime, as a sign of unity with the revolutionary movement, which they, like the men, saw as bringing freedom and social justice and not Islamic restrictions.

After the 1979 Revolution, the regression of women's judicial status began in Tehran with a return to Islamic laws that denied women many rights and imposed the compulsory veil. Only two demonstrations by a few thousand women in protest against it took place, but they were not followed up, and the Islamic government applied the mandatory veil policy a few weeks after the Revolution, even before it was legally promulgated, denying unveiled women access to work in the public sector and then, forbidding women to appear without a veil in public.

This radical change was possible because many modernized and unveiled women lacked leadership and organization. In addition, left-wing female intellectuals like Homa Nategh believed that the veil had to be sacrificed to the petty-bourgeois revolution of 1979, which would be followed by a communist revolution in which women would regain their rights on an equal footing with men.

The modernized middle classes were devoid of organization because the Shah's authoritarianism had decapitated all political parties and organizations, and few men, while accustomed to unveiled women in private and in public, reacted against the compulsory veil. The only way of protesting was to leave the country (several hundred thousand – estimated between 3 and 5 million – Iranians left Iran and settled in the USA, Canada, Australia, Europe, and Turkey).

Revolutionary effervescence in turn contributed to this: everything seemed unassailable under the charismatic leadership of Ayatollah Khomeini, who was a saint, a prodigy, a wizard (he had achieved the impossible, by dethroning the Shah). For a large part of the population, his position was regarded as sacrosanct and could not be called into question, on pain of betraying the revolutionary ideal of a total rebirth of society under his aegis. Even some secular men who might have doubted the validity of his words seemed to believe in his thaumaturgic ability to put an end to social ills. His stance was attributed to his sacred sagacity. Had it not been for the revolutionary effervescence of a seething society, he would have met with far more resistance than the scattered demonstrations of a few thousand women in Tehran. After all, unveiled women had been actively present in the public arena for almost half a century.

An Islamic patriarchal pact was implicitly struck between the Theocratic Regime and a large part of the society, notably the clergy, the traditional bazaaris (the Iranian merchant class), the fundamentalists, the lower middle classes from small towns, and particularly the so-called "oppressed" (*mostaz'afeen*), the poor people. They believed that Ayatollah Khomeini's restoration of Islamic tradition would not only ensure their upward social mobility, but also, and above all, help them overcome the cultural traumas of authoritarian modernization under the Shah. In their eyes, the latter had destroyed tradition, without granting legitimacy to the new modernist culture. As for the modernized middle classes, while not supporting this patriarchal pact, they submitted to it because they had no organization to support them. The war launched by Iraq against Iran, which lasted over eight years (1980–8) and left several hundred thousand dead on both sides (over 500,000, including some 300,000 in Iran), made it difficult to protest against the religious constraints, because any effort in that direction was regarded as unpatriotic and the fight against the Iraqi enemy took precedence over all other considerations.

The patriarchal pact concluded with the Islamic State did not include the entire Iranian society. It was not, as in traditional societies, an all-encompassing social phenomenon with a deep-rooted cultural base, which would have imposed itself on society because patriarchy would have been the fundamental form of global identity.

I use the term "Islamic patriarchal pact" to distinguish my argument from that of Deniz Kandioty, who coined the term "Patriarchal bargain,"[8] particularly in reference to traditional societies undergoing modernization, notably those in sub-Saharan Africa and the Middle East. Her study is about women's strategies in the face of patriarchal attitudes rooted in culture: they suffer domination but also develop forms of resistance in the face of oppression. Her thesis is rooted in a global sociocultural framework in which the state is, at best, an adjunct to the cultural norms that dominate and oppress women. In Iran, on the contrary, under the Islamic Regime, the patriarchal pact was drawn up between the Theocratic State and large groups of men after the overthrow of the Pahlavi regime. The Islamic Regime that took power in 1979 challenged the status of women and removed many of their rights established since the 1930s. It was the clergy, the traditional strata, the urban poor (the "oppressed"), and the fundamentalists (reacting against the Shah's modernization) who forged an alliance with the Theocratic Regime to impose on women a subaltern status. Therefore, it was not a "traditional" patriarchy, but a resentful one, in reaction to the modernization of Iranian society for almost half a century, initiated by a theocratic state.

In short, the main force behind women's institutional inferiorization through the implementation of Islamic laws was the Theocratic State headed by the charismatic Ayatollah Khomeini, rather than the patriarchal culture of society, which had undergone a fundamental change under the Pahlavi regime. The long war with Iraq and the lack of capacity for action on the part of the modernized strata made possible this edict that hit several million people head-on, many of whom chose to go into exile and live abroad. This scenario was repeated several times under the Islamic Regime, with waves of migrants swelling the ranks of those who had already left, whether after the Green Movement of 2009 and its repression, then the movements of 2016–19 and finally, in the wake of the Mahsa Movement of 2022.

Therefore, the Islamic patriarchal pact is different in nature from Deniz Kandioty's patriarchal bargain: firstly, it is the state playing the essential role in the repression of women, and secondly, it was not Iran's global social culture at its roots, but the domination of the Shi'ite clergy within a theocratic state in the wake of a revolution that left the modernized middle classes bereft of leadership, with no ability for collective action.

The Islamic patriarchal pact had initially been embraced by a large part of a society in revolutionary fervor, except for the modernized middle classes who were a disempowered minority and whose youth had in part embraced the revolutionary ideals of the Marxist far left. While the poor (the "oppressed," *mostaz'afeen*) pushed for Islamization as a means of their empowerment, the modernized middle classes became a submissive social group which, while disagreeing with the religious fundamentalists, was unable to oppose them. With the help of his entourage and the revolutionary youth, Khomeini set up the Islamic Revolutionary Guards Corps (IRGC), which later became the main repressive force against urban protest, along with Basij, a youth volunteer organization that was quickly brought under the aegis of the IRGC. The Islamic patriarchal pact was built in opposition to the secular culture of the modernized middle classes. Ayatollah Khomeini, backed by the clergy, was seeking revenge for the decades-long suppression of the veil (*kashf hejab*) under the Pahlavis. He imposed it at a time when a veil-free identity had become commonplace among modern middle-class women and a significant proportion of Iran's female educated youth.

The paradox is that four decades later, the patriarchal pact was challenged by a new generation of women that included children of the new Islamic elites. Women gradually became aware of the impossible gender equality under Islamic rule. As for the young men, they also subscribed to this challenge. They rejected the Theocratic Regime's religious mores, which were at odds with their youthful identity. They had evolved towards a secularization that was opposed to the worldview championed by the patriarchal pact. The latter had been emptied of its meaning and had lost legitimacy after more than four decades. At the start of the 1979 Revolution, the "oppressed" strata (*mostaz'afeen*) believed that the Islamic project was synonymous with the restoration of a mythologized tradition and their social and economic ascent. The economic regression of the bulk of society and the conscientization of increasingly educated women in the following decades resulted in a growing section of society questioning the patriarchal pact. As for the growing number of the "oppressed," they no longer believed in the restoration of Islamic tradition, which would protect them from the woes of modernization, while ensuring their economic and social progress. With the Mahsa Movement, many decades after the 1979 Revolution, a large part of society was questioning the patriarchal pact against a theocratic state whose policies had shown that the so-called restoration of

Islamic tradition was synonymous with social, economic, and cultural regression for the vast majority.

The patriarchal pact was particularly discredited by the new generation of women, because it confined them to an increasingly unbearable inferiority in a society that did not believe anymore in the bright Islamic future promised by the Revolution, and by young men, because in their eyes, religious tradition increasingly meant calling into question their culture of "joie de vivre" so alien to the morbid religiosity of the Islamic Regime. Men and women alike rejected head-on a state that was driving society backwards, while denying them the freedom of mores they cherished by virtue of their secularization.

The main driving force behind the Mahsa Movement has been Iran's youth. According to the statistics of people arrested during the demonstrations, 80 percent of them were aged between fifteen and twenty-four, and 20 percent between twenty-five and forty-five. The share of those aged between fifteen and twenty-four years in the overall population of the country was about 13 percent, and those aged between twenty-five and forty-five, about 40 percent.[9] Without doubt, the Mahsa Movement has been a youth movement (more than six times their proportion in the overall population of fifteen to twenty-four year olds were arrested). This does not mean that the older generation, known in Iran as the "grey-haired generation" (*nasle khakestari*), were against the movement. Quite the contrary, they supported its demands, but they did not actively participate in the street demonstrations, for various reasons (lack of an alternative government, fear of the repressive Islamic Republic, concern for the family, fear of embarking on a new revolution having seen how the old revolution ended in deadlock and created a situation worse than the Shah's regime before).

The new youthful mindset presents a resourcefulness among women who are subject to far greater legal restrictions. The change in their mentality began in the 1980s in their attitude towards the number of children in the family. On the eve of the 1979 Revolution, women gave birth to seven children on average. Fertility dropped to two children in 2000. Over the next decade it dropped even further and in 2009 it reached 1.9 children.

The level of education of women rose continuously during those years. In 1976 only 8.7 percent of women had reached secondary school level, a figure which stood at 37.6 percent in 2016. In 1976 only 1.5 percent of women studied at university, whereas in 2016 nearly one-third of women (28.9 percent) attended university.[10]

It should be noted that the new female subjectivity appeared in Iran at the end of the twentieth century, especially with the expansion of education to women and their entry into university, where half of the students since the year 2000 are female. The universities, where more than 3 million students are enrolled, are the major breeding ground for this new awareness. The paradox is that the more women's cultural status is brought closer to men's through school, university, and the web, the more the Iranian Theocratic Regime hardens its stance towards them, especially under the populist President Ahmadinejad in 2005, and in 2021, the hardliner Raissi. Women have faced more extensive legal and social restrictions since then. Although they make up over 50 percent of university graduates, their participation in the workforce is only 15 percent according to the latest official statistical data.[11] The 2016 Global Gender Gap report, produced by the World Economic Forum, ranked Iran in the bottom five countries (141 out of 145) for gender equality, including equality in economic participation (a 2017 report by the Iranian Center for Statistics indicates that women make up 18.2 percent of the workforce). Moreover, these disparities exist at all levels of the economic hierarchy: women are severely underrepresented in high-level public positions and in private sector leadership positions. This significant gap in participation in the Iranian labor market has occurred against a backdrop of widespread violations of women's economic and social rights by the authorities. In 2012, under the presidency of Ahmadinejad, who fraudulently won the election by many accounts,[12] at least seventy-seven faculties in thirty-six different universities refused female students. The last years of his administration also coincided with the government's stated goal of population growth. During this period, several pieces of legislation were introduced in parliament that further marginalized women in the labor market.[13]

Many men in the new generations share the feeling of quasi-equality with women in everyday life, whether within the nuclear family or in social relations within the community. The Mahsa Movement has forged a tight alliance between young men and women against the Islamic Republic. They chanted in unison the slogan "Woman, life, freedom."

Inherent in this slogan are two complementary freedoms: an existential one, namely freedom of the individual to lead a life according to the secular "joie de vivre" opposed to the Shi'i view of life, which is perceived by them as carrying an infinite sadness, and an obsessive mourning in an endless succession of religious ceremonies; and second, a political one (democratic freedom).

The existential freedom has been especially claimed by women, the main targets of bodily coercion in the Islamic Republic. By allying itself with the most conservative segments of the high clergy (the ayatollahs) and population (from the bazaaris and traditionalist families), the theocratic government has attempted to acquire absolute Islamic legitimacy, notably by imposing a restrictive veil on women and by qualifying those loosely veiled as "badly veiled" (*bad hejab*), subject to legal penalties. Within this worldview, men have legal sovereignty over women, and this is supposed to console them for being deprived of their political sovereignty within the Islamic theocracy. Women's servitude has an all-round function: by imposing "modesty" upon them, the submission of women induces the men to submit in their turn to the government by finding a satisfaction in the supremacy that the system lavishes on them in regard to women. Repressed by the patriarchal regime, men can focus their anger on women and repress them in turn to avenge their own powerlessness in the face of a predatory state.

But the system no longer works among the country's youth like it used to among past generations. Young men and women question the Islamic patriarchal pact. Like all social phenomena, there is no single cause for this. The Regime's abysmal failure to ensure society's economic prosperity has reinforced the patriarchal pact. The more the Islamic Republic has failed to redress a drifting economy, the more it has been willing to repress women and their aspirations to modernity, to secure the consent of men. Therefore, restrictions on women are as much motivated by conservative theocracy as by the deficiencies of the government. Women are the scapegoats and their repression conceals the government's failure to promote social well-being.

The Islamization of women is represented by the theocratic government as one of its rare "successes" in the changes that the Revolution has sought to imprint on society since 1979. All other revolutionary ideals have failed: the "oppressed" (*mostaz'afeen*) who wanted to escape economic distress are now poorer, the middle classes are in economic and social decline, and Iran has turned into one of the most repressive regimes in the world, imprisoning, torturing, and executing[14] without the slightest concern for human rights. No social group is spared by this regime, that finds legitimacy not only in the repression of its citizens in general, but above all of the women, who are supposed to represent, through their submission to the governmental model, the Regime's success in promoting an Islamic society.

The Islamic Republic constantly pits the fundamentalist minority on its side against the rest of society to find accomplices to support it in the face of a society that is increasingly opposed to it. The coercion of women, their compulsory veiling, gender segregation, and the strict application of traditional Islamic law that imposes a legally inferior status on women are all part of this pact, in this case made with a specific social group, namely the traditionalists, against the great majority.

Another rationale for the "patriarchal pact" based on the submission of women is that if they are subjected to restraints, men will also be easier to restrain in their demand for freedom. The fear that the patriarchal order is supposed to inspire in women spreads to men. Like women, men will refrain from seeking political freedom, for fear of being repressed.

Islamic theocracy operated according to the "patriarchal pact" model until the current generation. Young men are refusing to play this fool's game, to give up their citizens' rights by accepting the double servitude of women, first to them, and then to the Islamic State. As for women, previous generations played along because they thought they would escape servitude through the reforms within the Islamic government launched by the Reformists (the election of Khatami in 1997 inaugurated a cycle of shaky reforms). The disappointment and abandonment of the dream of reforming the Regime from within and the new self-perception of young women, which is different from that of previous generations, has led to a forthright refusal, firstly, of bodily servitude (the repudiation of the imposed veil), secondly, of family servitude (the shrinking of the family to fewer than two children), and thirdly, of their servitude to men imposed by the state-sponsored patriarchal pact, which the new generation's male youth also refuse to respect.

The Mahsa Movement highlights the young men's refusal to give up their own political freedom in exchange for the patriarchal servitude of women within the Islamic State.

The opposition to the Theocratic State

The intolerable feeling of disempowerment

The new generations, young adults and teenagers between the ages of twelve and twenty-five, are characteristically different from the older generations. In particular, the revolt of young women against the veil over the last decade reveals a complicity with their male counterparts, who approve their dissent rather than regarding it as an attack on their Islamic honor. Young women feel infantilized by a government that denies them the sovereign right to dress as they please. Their rationale is aptly analyzed by the Iranian feminist Noushin Ahmadi Khorasani. She describes the emergence of a new subjectivity, much more rebellious towards the Islamic Regime than the generation before, due to the "selfie" phenomenon, the rise of the "self-image" among young people who care much more than the generation before about their appearance, and a new social relationship among them based on this shared view of the Self and the Others.[15] According to her the growth of individualism makes what one wears much more important than for their parents' generation, and what was a characteristic of movie and TV stars has spread to the larger society. These aspirations of the younger generation, even among the traditional groups, have become common and young girls do not accept the restrictions imposed on them in the name of Islam, not even daughters of families belonging to the Islamic power elites who, it would be supposed, would strictly respect Islamic standards.

She concludes:

> The mandatory hijab for our generation . . . was really an attack on our collective identity as a social group. For the girls of today's generation, for the reasons discussed above, the revolt against the compulsory hijab as an assault on their right to dress has gone beyond the level of an abstract right and has become an assault on their personal identity.[16]

The veil, which was perceived by the previous feminist generation as a marginal issue, has acquired a pivotal role in the identity claims of the new female generation, for whom the appropriation of their bodies is an essential part of their dignity. Within this reappropriated body, the right to be oneself is combined with the right to appear as they wish – a minor matter for their mothers' generation, a major one for the young.

In the youthful feminine culture (but even, to some extent, in the masculine one as well), the concern of the aesthetic self has taken on an importance that it did not assume in the previous generation. For them makeup was a "bourgeois" phenomenon. It was to be banned in the name of a stern vision of self – an alienating beauty which objectified women and made them the prey to male sexual consumption (the alienating consumerism analyzed by Western intellectuals influenced female and male intellectuals of the 1970s generation that took part in the 1979 Iranian Revolution). The underlying Islamic culture accentuated the distrust vis-à-vis the unveiled beauty. As for Muslim mothers, even the most modernized, on the eve of the Islamic Revolution the veil was part of their self-image. They believed that Islam would be tolerant and would not impose the veil on those who did not want to wear it; and furthermore, unlike the Shah's regime, which increasingly embodied antinomy to Islam, they believed that Islamic legitimacy would add to the freedom of men and women through tolerance and open-mindedness. It was this combination of open-mindedness and reconciliation with the religion of Allah that Ayatollah Khomeini seemed to promise – without fundamentally infringing the achievements of modernity that the Shah had granted them.

Four decades later, the "selfie culture" points to a new identity among young Iranian women. The clothing of the female body has become a new issue in women's assertiveness, an imperative part of their female identity. Defending one's beauty as a woman and one's rights as an individual go hand in hand for this generation. Caring about their physical appearance to assert their new feminine identity makes them much more rebellious towards the Theocratic Regime than the older women. The veil, earlier perceived as a side issue (legal gender equality was the main concern of the Iranian feminists, even a decade ago), has become a central issue for the new generation. For them their bodily freedom, to be beautiful and decide for themselves to veil or unveil, is an integral part of their liberty. The centrality of the body is not only restricted to young women. Young men share the "selfie culture" to a large extent, their appearance also being part of their "self-care." This new culture is devoid of the feelings of guilt of the older male generations, with their Islamic superego.[17] Nowadays, the advances of "joie de vivre" secular culture have loosened the hold of the Islamic superego among the youth. The exposure of their respective bodies and beauty to each other, free of guilt, creates an emotional bond among them.

In her analysis of the youth "selfie culture," Khorasani attributes too great an importance to technology (the smartphone) and not enough to other factors such as the influence of the diaspora, social media, and above all the secularization of the youth, which has led them to be much less respectful of Islamic values than their parents. At the same time, she overemphasizes the narcissistic side of feminine beauty without seeing this as a character trait also shared by young men, and the new complicity between men and women that goes beyond mere narcissism. It is a shared vision in which the relationship between the sexes takes on a meaning that opposes Islamic restrictions and asserts itself as autonomous from religious standards. What Khorasani perceives as narcissism is in fact an aesthetic expression of the individual, woman and man, freeing themselves from the religious ties that prevent them from asserting their sovereignty.

By repressing their quest for bodily freedom, the Islamic Regime unifies young men and women against itself, in the name of their earthly "joie de vivre."

It is worth noting that the Western intellectuals of the 1960s–1980s like Herbert Marcuse, Guy Debord, and Jean Baudrillard perceived as an alienation the consumerism, the narcissism induced by the society of the spectacle and simulacrum, and the various expressions of modern "frivolity" like the embellishment of the body by grooming. They denounced these new fake expressions of identity in the name of a revolutionary authenticity. However, in today's Iran, a complicit narcissism between young men and women, an exhibitionist beauty and the consumption of the image of oneself and the other leads to the political challenging of the Islamic Theocracy. The Mahsa Movement denounced the tyranny of puritanism and religious fundamentalism by resorting to an ostentatious narcissism turned into revolt. Through a powerful reversal, these topics were integrated into a claim for democracy, by starting from the concern of bodily self, and extending it to the whole political spectrum. In short, what was perceived by the European intellectuals as a false consciousness has become a principle of emancipation.

To combat the perfidy of women who constantly defy the mandatory veil laws, over the years the Regime has introduced notions such as "poorly veiled" (*bad hejab*) or "thinly veiled" (*kam hejab*), the extreme limit being unveiled (*bi hejab*). In his later speeches, the Supreme Leader introduced the neologism "loosely veiled" (*shol hejab*).

The poorly veiled are those who do not wear their veils properly, leave strands of their hair uncovered and sometimes use transparent fabrics that let their features be seen, thus accentuating their attractiveness. Or they are seen as women who distort the meaning of the veil, the function of which is to obscure woman's sexual attractiveness, so men are not sexually aroused by her beauty. Young women subvert the very purpose of the veil, they cut it or choose a brightly colored fabric, or often let it fall down around their neck. In the West, women are allowed to play out their sexual attraction without worrying about men's sexual drives, the latter being expected to control their sexuality in public. In the Muslim world, women must avoid men's indecent look, they must take precautions by veiling themselves and by avoiding the natural greed of the male gaze.

But the Muslim world is no longer what it used to be, and many Iranians, Turks, or Arabs think that the autonomy of women also depends on their ability to show off their beauty while relying on the ability of the opposite sex to control their sexual desire. This is part of the process of secularization that a significant part of Muslim societies has internalized for more than a century but that the oppressive governments repress in the name of orthodox Islam. They do so to exert their hold on society by counting on the feelings of guilt of some and the fear of modernity of others, especially the traditionalists. In the 1960s–1970s, unveiled women had become quite common: middle-class women did not wear the veil as a rule, but the government's intolerance towards those who did wear it had faded. Reza Shah, the founder of the Pahlavi dynasty, had banned the veil through coercion in 1936: the police would violently tear it from women's heads in the street, if necessary. Under Mohammad Reza Shah, there was latterly a move towards peaceful coexistence between veiled and unveiled women. However, the former were regarded as inferior to the latter, and were not admitted to official ceremonies.

The dialectics of cat-and-mouse: everyday schizophrenia

Throughout the Islamic Republic, women and especially young girls have learned to play a game of cat-and-mouse with the Vice Squad – at school, in hospitals, at the train station, in the airport, in brief anywhere in public. Young girls and teenagers often apply excessive makeup that exaggerates their features.

For them, the headscarf becomes part of a cosmetic ensemble – their lipstick is applied in thick layers and eye shadow used excessively to emphasize their facial beauty in spite of the veil; they distort its meaning, turning it into an accoutrement. They ridicule the veil and through it they over-exhibit the beauty it is meant to conceal. Islamic prohibitions are thus perverted into sexual incitement for young men whose admiration and company they encourage. In addition, their scarf leaves a large part of their hair uncovered. This makes them more mysterious. This part exposure of hair excites eager young men to leer at them. The headscarf is thus subverted into a beauty accessory that over-sexualizes the young women's faces rather than hiding their charm. Their veil perverts Islamic clothing restrictions by turning it into an additional incitement to the gaze of the young males. They try to approach them furtively, first by staring at them insistently, and then, by slipping their cell phone number into their pocket. Apart from the purpose of sexual attraction, young women over-apply their makeup in reaction to the forced veil, partly out of a desire to transgress Islamic standards: the face covered with a thick layer of foundation and powder makes the scarf ridiculously inoperative insofar as it does not divert the gaze of the young men from the face of the women, but on the contrary, attracts it by provocation. In the same way, during the summer, young girls let their legs and toes, often painted in hot colors, be seen by eager young men, which excites their sexual ardor. Even the offspring of the Islamic elites, the so-called *agha-zadegan*, whose parents are supposed to be paragons of Islamic piety, ironically live a "debauched" lifestyle in the upmarket areas of Tehran or in the US or Canada; sometimes furtively, other times without worrying about the reputation of their parents or grandparents.

Before the Mahsa Movement, when the morality brigades intervened to remind young women of the Islamic norms, they were often ignored. The women recklessly turned a deaf ear and sometimes answered back brazenly; other times they pretended to listen to them, but as soon as they left, they resumed their transgressive behavior. In short, those who enforced Islamic norms knew that they were constantly fooled by the smug attitude of these young women and adolescents who did as they pleased. Their refusal to comply was a consistent feature of their character.

The government had gradually come to impose increasingly harsher punishments on those recalcitrant and "badly veiled" girls who were deaf to the police injunctions, or even to their admonitions. Their attitude did not fundamentally change despite law enforcement's warnings, intimidation, and the heavy fines that their parents had to pay if they were arrested. The government considered physical repression as the only adequate solution to the arrogant attitude of the female youth. "Badly veiled" women were taken to the prison cells of the Vice Squad and beaten by violent female agents to coerce them into veiling themselves. The dramatic events that broke out on September 16, 2022, at the death of Mahsa Amini at the hands of Tehran's Vice Brigade (*gasht-e ershad*), were the result of the use of violence on young women by a government that no longer understands their mentality.

During the summer especially, the desire to remove the veil among young women who were suffocating in the stifling heat (it can reach over 45 degrees Celsius) becomes irresistible. Before the Mahsa Movement, the Vice Squad's female agents tried to repress them but often the "ill-veiled" (*bad hejab*) knew where the agents would gather (like Vanak Square, one of the central squares of Tehran, or the busy avenues). To protect themselves against the people's insults, the agents came in several cars, accompanied by male officers, to avoid being assaulted by the crowd, who hated them as a symbol of a repressive regime.

Families sometimes party at home and if the music is too loud or neighbors complain, the morality police show up at their apartment and arrest people or demand a hefty bribe. This supplements their income but holds families to ransom, unfairly penalized for innocent gatherings. Society thus plays hide-and-seek with the Islamic Regime over individual freedoms in increasingly antagonistic ways, as mutual mistrust grows. The dialogue of the deaf has become the dominant relationship between an abhorred government and an abused, sometime violently, society.

Since the establishment of the Islamic Republic in 1979, the daily life of large segments of the urban population has been based on hypocrisy and forced compliance with a repressive regime. The latter tolerates to a certain extent transgressive attitude in the private sphere – drinking alcohol, though not without trepidation, watching foreign TV via one's satellite dish while worrying that it might be confiscated, meeting with friends without a veil on fear of arrest, playing cards while running the risk of being arrested in the middle of a prohibited act. In return for this unacknowledged concession of freedom under surveillance in the private sphere, albeit without guarantee, the authorities demand conformity to Islamic norms in public. Adults follow these repressive standards because they are worried about their families and their standard of living (they might be put in jail and heavily fined). Young people over the last decade are refusing to submit because a subjective revolution has taken place in their minds that questions the legitimacy of the Islamic Regime. They fully assume a secular worldview in which Islamic prohibitions are repudiated in the name of their individual autonomy. In addition, they reject Islamic standards because they abhor the social hypocrisy and spineless attitude of their parents who will not refuse the predatory state.

The youth, by their demeanor, belie the timidity of their parents, their submission to the Islamic government, and reluctance to shake off its yoke and challenge its legitimacy. They show the immense generation gap and denounce the "folly" of their grandparents who took part in the Islamic Revolution and left power in the hands of Khomeini and his followers. Speaking for their grandparents, in the 2022 demonstrations, the young people shouted: "We were wrong/We offered the country without any second thought/To thieves!" (*ma echtebah kardim/do dasti mamlekat ra/taqdime dozda kardim*).

The adults, fathers and mothers, grandfathers, and grandmothers, have lived in the Islamic Republic for more than four decades and have internalized its repressive norms in fear and trepidation. They rose up and protested from 2016 to 2019, as a result of which more than a thousand of them died in confrontation with the predatory state. Since then, they have been reluctant to take to the streets. They have been unmoved by cultural motives since the failure of the Green Movement in 2009, such as the veil, sexual liberation, or expressions of public festivities, which they have learned to hide and only be enjoyed in small circles of family and friends. But young people are driven by diametrically opposed attitudes to the elders. They share the pleasures of the world on the web, they want to live a modernity which is denied to them in their daily life and which their access to the internet is pushing them to pursue, so much do they feel the oppressive weight of the reality that contradicts their desires.

The female body as a mediator between the existential and political freedom

In the Mahsa Movement, women and men united in their effort to show publicly their rejection of the mandatory veil. Women denounced the abusive domination of their bodies by the State. In contrast to their parents, who had submitted to the "Islamic patriarchal pact" with the Theocratic Regime, young men saw in women's servitude not only an attack against women, but also against themselves through the denial of close relationships with them, and more fundamentally, their own political freedom. In the movement, young women made their bodies the bulwark against the intrusion of the Islamic State. Female bodies became the emblem of their freedom. As for the young men, the denial of bodily autonomy to the women was the prohibition of free relationships with them in spite of their cultural complicity. The female body became the locus for a protest that extended to the political level, starting from female "corporality" (they called it by a neologism, *tanaanegi*, in the slogans chanted at Tehran University on April 16, 2023). In short, through the women's bodies the Islamic Regime denied them political freedom, but to men also.

This was the rationale behind the common revolt of young men and women against the Theocratic State. Existential bodily freedom went hand in hand with political freedom, to the point of becoming inseparable in the Mahsa Movement. For the first time in a Muslim society, women's bodies became not the site of male honor and his exclusive sexual desire (therefore, to be hidden from public) but the battlefield for political freedom for women, and for men too. A deep rupture thus occurred with the past by the transmutation of the sense of citizenship expressed through the body of female citizens moved by the will to be free. It embodied the political citizenship in a new gender relation. It was also the beginning of the recognition by men of women's equality. At this point, men and women were cooperating to restore their common political rights against the Theocratic Regime.

To summarize, in the Mahsa Movement, the freedom of the body turned into a political freedom, extending from the individual to the entire society. The female body was no longer just the body of a woman but the "political body" in the strict sense; it merged with other bodies and entered in communion with them, masculine and feminine. This body asked for freedom for all, i.e., political freedom, with no religious prohibition to hinder its claim, exhibiting itself in public without a cloak that withdrew it from the eyes of others. From a gendered body, it was transformed into a mediating body that bridged the gap with men in a communication that transcended sexuality and became political. The politicization of the female body took place in the effervescence of the festival, in the dancing, the spectacular setting the veil on fire, the twirling with the men, hand in hand, around the fire, or to the rhythm of rap songs where young women and men expressed in unison their desire for secular emancipation from the religious restrictions imposed by a theocracy, illegitimate in their eyes. This movement had the female body as its core, and around it revolved the revolutionary leitmotivs of overthrowing dictatorship and liberating women.

The Mahsa Movement has put the finishing touch to the transformation of the female body that began over a decade earlier, already visible in the 2009 Green Movement: from the body submitted to the Islamic prohibitions to that of the free citizen, by a secularization which had been in progress over several decades but whose awareness was accelerated by the protest movements. The Mahsa Movement operated as a catalyst of awareness, which made possible the deepened self-consciousness of women but also, their successful communication with men on this issue. The men followed the women and, as a sign of transgression, danced in circles with them, or took the women's hands and shouted slogans against the Islamic Regime. The body became the center of gravity of the movement, first among the young women, then among the young men in conjunction with the women, freed from religious constraints by rejecting the enforced veil. The feminine body made a leap forward by politicizing itself, but in doing so, it brought along also the men for whom the female body now played a different role from that of a sexual object forbidden to show itself in public so as not to tempt a man's sexual desire.

The feminine body became, in the demonstrations of the Mahsa Movement but also in its prolongation by the women who have strolled in the streets since February 2023 after the end of the demonstrations, the symbol of the new freedom. The Mahsa Movement closely associated political and bodily freedoms, the latter epitomized by women. This constitutes its major innovation, which has no equivalent in the Muslim world in which the two registers have been constantly separated. The social movements that appeared from the beginning of the nineteenth century in Egypt, the Ottoman Empire, Iran, among others, demanded political freedom. Women were associated with it not as figures in the vanguard but mostly as spouses, daughters, sisters, or mothers of men. Of course, groups of female intellectuals since the nineteenth century have acted, but they were a tiny minority and were not followed by women en masse.

In the Iranian 1979 Revolution, women had no proper slogan of their own, nor did they build a movement within it, although they participated massively in it. The first major feminist mobilization was in 2006 through the so-called Campaign for One Million Signatures, but it was a minority movement, with cultural undertones, spearheaded by female intellectuals and activists, within the framework of an idealized Islam, not in rupture with the Iranian Theocratic Regime.

Even in the Green Movement in 2009, women did not have a slogan of their own and did not denounce openly their subservience to Islamic norms.

Now, for the first time within a social movement (and not as individuals), women have risen to the status of full citizens and demanded the liberation of their bodies from the yoke of theocratic Islam. As for men, they not only did not oppose the women, but supported them. Women claimed freedom of the body and political freedom at the same time – the second being the consequence of the first one in their view.

Repudiating the Shi'i culture of grief and espousing the secular culture of "joie de vivre"

To understand the uniqueness of the new Iranian youth culture, which I have coined the "joie de vivre," it is necessary to contrast it with two cultures: traditional Shi'ism and its manifestation after the Revolution of 1979, theocratic Shi'ism.

Traditional Shi'ism: a culture of grief

In traditional Shi'ism, distinct from the majority Sunni Islam (around 10 percent of Muslims in the world are Shi'i, 90 percent Sunnis), the grief-stricken exhibitions of mourning in the celebrations of the Imams' martyrdom, particularly the third one, Hossein, play a key role. There are very few joyful festivals in traditional Shi'ism, except for the end of Ramadan, the birth of the Prophet, or the birth of the twelfth Imam, the Shi'i Messiah. The overwhelming majority of the ceremonies are in fact to do with mourning, lamenting the martyrdom of the Imams who died at the hands of the Umayyad or Abbasid caliphs (as the descendants of the Prophet the Imams had legitimate claim to the caliphate according to Shi'ism, and were killed to prevent this). In fact, Shi'ism denominates the Prophet's family as "the house of sorrow" (*beit ol azhan*). Tragic events such as the martyrdom of many members of the Prophet's family (the Imams) give rise to annual ceremonies and commemoration. The most important is the martyrdom of the third Imam, Hossein, grandson of the Prophet and son of Ali, the first Imam, who died in 680 in his struggle against the Umayyad Caliph Yazid in the desert of Karbala (present-day Iraq). For a whole month (Moharram) his tribulations and martyrdom are dramatized in public by processions of flagellants and religious standard bearers (*alam o kotal*).

Traditionally, the Shi'i experience the commemoration of Karbala as the unfolding of a tragedy that involves the dramatization of Hossein's and his seventy-two companions' martyrdom at the hands of the Caliph Yazid's army on October 10, 680. Hossein was defeated because the city of Kufa broke its promise to help him against Yazid. The ceremony is based on provoking feelings of guilt among the Shi'i faithful who dramatically recall this fateful event. During their mourning processions, Kufa's guilt falls on the shoulders of all believers, who must feel remorse for the failure to help the grandson of the Prophet. They try to redeem themselves by weeping, self-flagellation, and intense expressions of mourning during the processions reenacting Hossein's sufferings. Not only do the believers shoulder the blame for not having assisted Hossein, but they also remember that they endure injustice in this world, just as Hossein did, without losing hope in the divine justice. The ceremonies, which culminate in the fateful days of Tasu'a (the day before the martyrdom of Hossein) and Ashura (the day of his martyrdom), are experienced by the faithful taking part in processions and theatrical performances (*ta'zieh*) as a remorseful remembrance.

The processions have a double role: they express the guilt felt by the believers and, at the same time, its assuaging through tears, the affective forms of repentance expressed in the unending repetition of chants by the men, and the violence on the body to punish it (the self-flagellation). These acts atone for the fault and give a cathartic meaning to a renewed life by purifying it and reactivating the pact with the martyred Imam Hossein, broken by the betrayal of the city of Kufa many centuries ago. After a month of mourning, the horizon brightens, there is a catharsis and the community regains its original vigor despite all the hardships it endures in real life.

Hossein's martyrdom has a mainly symbolic value even though some of the flagellants whip themselves raw and some even use cutlasses to wound their own bodies. His death enhances the life of suffering believers in this world. The ceremonies of his martyrdom mitigate the misfortunes of those burdened by the hardships of earthly life. Hossein's passion is cathartic for the humble Shi'i, oppressed by the pains of life in an uncertain world. Historically, these ceremonies were a reminder of the suffering of Shi'ites under the domination of the Sunni majority, who repressed them due to their heterodox faith. The annual commemorations of Hossein's martyrdom play the role of a salvific suffering in Shi'ism, which can be compared to the Passion of Christ in Catholicism.[18]

Apart from this month of mourning and tribulation, most of the other Imams were supposed to have died as martyrs at the hands of the Umayyad and Abbasid caliphs. Historically, this was not always true, but Shi'i "grief culture" – a culture that relies mainly on a tragic vision of existence – mourns their supposed martyrdom in lamentation ceremonies that enhance the sense of life as a vale of tears.

In brief, Shi'ism is historically marked by a sorrowful, suffering religiosity, compared to Sunnism, which was until the Safavid era in the late fifteenth century, the religion of the political elites in most of the ruling dynasties in Iran. In part for historical reasons, but also to distinguish itself from Sunnism, Shi'ism locked itself into a cult of the Imams' death and more generally, into a conception of life as bereavement. This theological culture of grief was transformed into a *"modo"* or *"Gemüt,"* a kind of melancholy temperament, reflected, for example, in Iranian classical music. The world is a vale of tears, and to assume a woeful attitude towards it is the dominant feature of traditional Shi'ism; it espouses a "culture of this-worldly dolefulness." Its numerous mourning ceremonies, accentuated by the theocratic version promoted by the Islamic Republic, opposes the quest for joy and happiness in the eyes of the twenty-first-century Iranian youth.

The 1979 Revolution exacerbated the practice of lamentation. The major difference was that unlike traditional Shi'ism, which sought a catharsis in the ceremonies in spite of the inevitable misery and bereavement, Shi'i theocracy has become vengeful and its grief has given rise to an all-out war against the Others – that is all those who do not share its politicized attitude, in particular the evil West, which it anathematizes and against which a war to the death, on a symbolic and real level, has become a duty: the martyr is killed in the jihad against the "Great Satan" which is America and its acolytes, practically the entire West, in particular Israel.

Shi'i grief had a cathartic aspect insofar as the tribulations led to a reconciliation with life; collective mourning led to a peace of mind among the believers. Hossein's death was the occasion for a communal reconciliation, the believers vowing to live in peace among themselves and following the way of God leading to salvation through the twelfth Imam.

The dominant form of Shi'i religiosity was quietist, not vindictive. It was not so much a question of changing the world, but of inserting oneself into it by reenacting each year the events of Karbala and the covenant with Hossein, and experiencing the catharsis in a sorrowful world. As for politics, traditional Shi'ism turned away from it and postponed the revenge of the oppressed against the oppressors until the end of time (politics was illegitimate until the advent of the Shi'i Messiah, the twelfth Imam) acquiescing to the rule of evil. There were small minorities, however, that, in the name of the Coming Messiah (the twelfth Imam) brandished the banner of revolt against the political regimes and announced the end of time.[19]

Theocratic Shi'ism: a totalitarian ideology

Under the leadership of Ayatollah Khomeini, the 1979 Revolution made it impossible to reconcile with a world dominated by the forces of evil, embodied by the West. While traditional Shi'ism advocated reconciliation with the world through quietism and a mournful view of life, theocratic Shi'ism (the ideology of the Islamic Regime) propagates a culture of exacerbated antagonism towards the West. There is no longer any possible reconciliation, and death becomes the only horizon of possibility, either the sacred death as a martyr, or the inglorious death as a force of evil. Reaching a compromise within life as proposed by traditional Shi'ism becomes impossible. The vindictive nature of theocratic Shi'ism, which constantly seeks revenge on the West and the Westernized and identifies any insubordination to its rule as a sign of adherence to the damning Western worldview, is similar to that of Sunni jihadism, in this respect, as in many others.[20] This deep-seated resentment of the West as the irreconcilable enemy makes theocratic Shi'ism incapable of finding a compromise with it, especially with the United States, the embodiment of the evil West – other Western countries being less powerful and therefore less evil. At the same time, compromise in its most humiliating forms with China, which represses millions of Uighur Muslims, and servitude to Russia, which imposes unequal treatment on Iran, notably in the Caspian Sea area, becomes tolerable, even painless, because it is an alternative to the West, declared to be the mortal enemy of the Iranian Theocratic Regime. The "Satanic West" (especially the USA and Israel) and unveiled women who transgress Islamic standards become the mortal enemies of theocratic Islam.

In reviving the Shi'ism of mourning, the Islamic Regime added to the traditional martyrs many more: those who died in the last months of the 1979 Revolution, or in fighting against the Iraqi army (1980–8).

The secularization of large segments of the urban population in Iran under the Pahlavi dynasty put into question many aspects of traditional Shi'ism. The Islamic Republic's response to the Shah's modernism was to reinforce Islamic norms, undermined by the secular Pahlavi dynasty in the last half a century (1930s–1979). As the Islamic Republic failed to promote social and economic development to ensure a decent standard of living for the citizens and to justify its rule through effective achievements, it was at the symbolic level, by imposing a puritanical order, that it tried to legitimize its existence. Internally, its role consisted in putting on hold society's autonomy (in which public joy, transgressive of its ideology of perpetual mourning, was a major aspect), in banning alcohol and partying, and in repressing women, who became its real obsession. Externally, its denouncement of Israel and the United States served to detract from the successive failures of the Regime to promote economic and social development. Henceforth, the Regime's role was no longer to ensure social and economic progress but to maintain society in the straitjacket of a rigid Islamic identity – theocratic Shi'ism. The latter was the more inflexible as the symbolic order compensated for the government's inability to ensure the real progress of society. From then on, the repression of joy, particularly in public, and restrictions on gender relations became the main self-prescribed societal function of the Islamic Republic. Most Muslim societies have abandoned this model, except for the Taliban in Afghanistan and a few radical Islamist groups (even Saudi Arabia has relaxed the bans on the veil since 2019), but Iran now ranks, at least in legal terms, among the most repressive countries. The population often denounced the Regime during the Mahsa Movement by calling the government "Taliban" or "Daesh" (the jihadist state established in 2014 between Iraq and Syria and overthrown in 2017).

Theocratic Shi'ism radically changed the meaning of martyrdom in traditional Shi'ism. The 1979 Revolution inscribed it directly onto the bodies of youth aspiring to the sacred death. In the eight-year long war with Iraq, in which around 300,000 young Iranians died in the fighting, martyrdom took on a new meaning. The death of a superhuman and sacred being (Imam Hossein), which was experienced in a purely symbolic way by traditional believers, was secularized and transformed into something achievable by the young candidates for martyrdom, who provided cannon fodder in the long, murderous war against Iraq. In this way, the sacred death that once concerned only the members of a small elite (Hossein and his seventy-two companions) became a vast heroic movement, appealing to the young pretenders to the holy death (members of the voluntary organization, Basij). There was secularization to the extent that every young man could now imitate Hossein, the Prince of Martyrs. His image as an unattainable saint was transformed into that of a hero who could be imitated by any young man.

Ali Shariati was the major ideologue behind the new version of martyrdom and the youth's fascination with it. He distinguished between the death of the Prophet's followers (especially his uncle Hamza) and the conscious death of Hossein. Hamza died valiantly fighting the polytheists without wishing to die. Unlike him, Hossein desired to die for the cause of God in an unequal battle (himself and a few dozen of his disciples against the great army of the Umayyad Caliph Yazid). The martyr, according to Shariati, willingly goes towards death, and ardently desires to suffer martyrdom to realize the revolutionary ideal of Shi'i Islam, in the name of God.

The 1979 Revolution was the first modern revolution (earlier movements advocated salvific death but were not secularized) that inscribes death (and not life) as an essential theme, its leitmotif.[21] It quickly turned into a death-driven movement and transformed traditional martyrdom into totalitarian theocratic Shi'ism by politicizing the death of Hossein, which had a purely symbolic meaning, and secularizing what had been a transcendent martyrdom unattainable by mortals.

Shariati exalted the myth of martyrdom to make people believe that being a Shi'i was synonymous with being revolutionary (the ideology of the far left in the 1960s) and religious (the opposite of the pro-Western secularism of the Shah). Young people experienced the new martyrdom as a way of returning to the sources of their own Iranian and Islamic identity while being anti-imperialist and anti-traditionalist. This new religiosity exalting martyrdom as a conscious death at the service of lofty ideals claimed to be "authentic" in opposition to the nationalism advocated by the Shah, on the one hand, and the religious quietism defended by traditional Shi'ism, on the other. It was mainly the invention of intellectuals like Shariati – Shi'ism was for him the paragon of revolution – and Jalal Al-Ahmad, for whom Westernism was deemed a disease of cultural uprooting, or Westtoxification, *qarb-zadegi*.

In Shariati's view, to be a genuine Muslim meant to act for the sake of achieving the theological Oneness of God (the monotheistic uniqueness of God, *towhid*, the pillar of Islam) on earth, just as Marx intended to realize the ideal of philosophy into a concrete reality of a proletarian society (*towhid* as one God, proletarian society as the rule of one class). Shariati's martyrdom has a leftist streak: to be revolutionary is to merge the uniqueness of God and the uniqueness of the social class in the proletarian sense of the term; Islam is monotheistic in the same way that society must be made of a single class, against the duality of the oppressor versus the oppressed (*mostakbar/mostaz'af*, the Islamization of the Marxist bourgeois/proletarian). Class duality is a theological heresy with regard to Islamic monotheism.

The genuine Muslim is revolutionary to the point of wishing martyrdom to achieve his religious ideals of unity (achieving the unity of social classes is to spread the unity of God all over the world). The sacred death is put to the service of a politico-religious vision which advocates the godly revolution by blending Islam and Marxism, religion and politics. The strange fate of this notion is that it has been taken over by a theocratic order that detaches it from its leftist aspect to insist on a fundamentalist version of Shi'ism.

For more than forty years, the motif of martyrdom has been reiterated by the Islamic Regime while Iranian society has radically changed. Young people have now broken with the ideal of martyrdom that excited the revolutionary youth of the 1970s. Still, the Islamic Regime cherishes this culture of perpetual death, killing, and mourning, which is especially highlighted in the month of Moharram, when the death of Hossein is staged in grieving rituals and the processions of the flagellants (*ta'zieh*) are dramatized. In the late 1990s, young people sought to modernize these ceremonies by substituting traditional instruments with those of jazz and modern music (guitar, saxophone, trumpet, drums) and singing to blues rhythms. They were accused of desecrating religious rituals and transgressing Islamic standards under the pretext of updating them, innovating in the pejorative sense (*bid'ah*) by distorting its meaning and by imposing a secular content to it. They were arrested, beaten, and imprisoned.

The following charges were brought against the youngsters:[22]

- Using loudspeakers and loud and annoying audio equipment (especially synthesizers, for example).
- Designing and using images and icons that were attributed to the holy family of the Prophet; some of the images were viewed as sacrilege by traditional Shi'ism.
- Not wearing proper clothing and baring their chest during the flagellation processions.
- Extending the time of mourning sessions until after midnight.
- Mixing among male and female mourners.
- Using musical instruments such as organ, piano, etc. that are inappropriate for the mourning ceremonies.
- Not letting the preacher deliver his sermon or not paying attention to it.

In brief, young people gathered to change the mourning ceremonies into a "party," in which women and men sought to put an end to the segregation between them, used musical instruments to transform the themes of traditional religious music into modern ones, especially jazz instruments, and preferred to sing and dance, rather than listen to the boring sermons of the mullahs. In the meantime, they used flagellation to evade the ban on bare chests for men. In short, they intended to implicitly change the Shi'i tendency towards grief into a modern form of festivity. They thus sought to create an atmosphere of secular joyfulness instead of religious sorrow. The organizers of these gatherings were arrested, their attempts were repressed, the instruments confiscated, the songs forbidden. The modernization of the culture of martyrdom was thus nipped in the bud, as the Islamic State's repression made it impossible to update traditional Shi'i culture. The repression put an end to their attempts to breathe a new life into the ceremonies by breaking with perpetual mourning. Theocratic Shi'ism rejected it because the Islamic Regime founded its legitimacy in the inconsolable grief of those who refused to accommodate to the modern world under the pretext of its insurmountable adversity towards them (the West as an enemy forever).

Theocratic Shi'ism turns its version of martyrdom against the world, making it not an expression of faith but rather of antagonism towards the infidels. In traditional Shi'ism, martyrdom was a phenomenon linked to an unjust world, the valley of tears, which the faithful did not seek to reform, but to endure for the sake of bliss in the next world. In theocratic Shi'ism, the other world subordinates itself to this world in a devious way: we must not live, but die, not accept the world with its hazards, but refuse it in a fierce, eschatological struggle that substitutes death for life. Traditional Shi'ism made Hossein's death give meaning, above all, to the lives of the faithful here below. Theocratic Shi'ism makes Hossein's death the absolute role model for the faithful who must choose heroic death over down-to-earth life. A gulf separates theocratic Shi'ism from its traditional version, albeit under the guise of continuity between them.

Theocratic Shi'ism makes the intransigence of martyrdom absolute against the world through a disconsolate mourning, and tears testify to the illegitimacy of jubilation in this world. The cathartic dimension of martyrdom, fundamental in traditional Shi'ism, based on Hossein's death, which reconciles the community with life, totally disappears in its theocratic version. The mourning rituals whose aim was to symbolically renew life through the sacrifice of Hossein have been transformed into perpetual, inconsolable mourning. The Shi'i martyrdom that was the sacred death of a handful of elites has turned into the real death of thousands of young people in the service of a state that makes the death of its citizens a primary requirement for its legitimacy.

The secular culture of "joie de vivre" and the rejection of the culture of martyrdom

The Islamic Revolution of 1979 and the war against Iraq transformed martyrdom into the legitimizing ideology of the Islamic Republic in the new shape of theocratic Shi'ism. Today's youth, at odds with the latter, identify it as a killjoy and its gloomy vision as a pretext by which the Regime imprisons them to deny their right to the secular "joie de vivre." Expressing joy ostentatiously in the streets is therefore not just about showing innocent jubilation, as would happen in the West, but also about displaying opposition to a theocratic regime that makes mourning and grief the essence of life. The Islamic Regime has come, by its very ideology, to identify bereavement as a conventional attitude premised on the citizen's submission to its diktats, and merriment as an implicit revolt against its hegemony.

The notion of "joie de vivre" is implied in the slogan of the Mahsa Movement, namely "Woman, life, freedom"; most of all by the word "life" against a government who celebrates holy death (martyrdom) as its ideological motto. "Freedom" in the slogan expresses the existential dimension of being joyful against the backdrop of the Islamic Republic's gloomy worldview. It has two facets: on the one hand, political freedom, on the other, bodily freedom – the aspiration to live one's life outside of any religious or government restrictions.

Young people now oppose the earthly joy of life against the grim culture of theocratic Shi'ism. They no longer want to hear about death in any form. They advocate joyful life against a culture of perpetual grief, be it over the death of Imam Hossein or the leaders of the Islamic Regime (the latest being General Qassem Soleimani killed by American drones in Baghdad on January 3, 2020, now celebrated as a martyr by the Islamic Regime).

Women are more affected than men by theocratic Shi'ism because it imposes intolerable restrictions on their bodies in the name of Islamic decency by invoking the sacrifice of the martyrs (women should comply with the supposed wishes of the martyrs to defend Islamic mores). Their bodies must be desexualized and unattractive so as not to seduce men. In short, they must be covered with a veil, and not incite the sexual desire of men, which the Islamic Regime identifies with sin. In their view, the Regime denies them their individual right to lead their lives in accordance with their aspirations. Their individuality is based on their self-expression as a living body that seeks to be admired by others in a game of seduction and individual autonomy that no religious vision should prohibit.

The conception of life as "joie de vivre" has been highlighted in particular in the Iranian rap and blues music, which marks a decided break with the culture of melancholy in classical Iranian music and with the official music that celebrates martyrs. This music, promoted by young people, presents secularized themes that include social criticism, but also the exaltation of love and life in opposition to the morosity of everyday life under the Islamic Republic. It denounces the gloom that prevails under the Theocratic Regime and espouses the ideal of a world where young people could live without worrying about what is religiously forbidden, indulging in the carefree happiness to which they aspire. This music functions as a mental exile from an increasingly desperate daily life, gradually turned into a music of rupture not only with perpetual grief, but also with the Islamic Regime during the Mahsa Movement. Many singers became the organic intellectuals of the movement. The song *"Baraye"* (For) by Shervin Hajipour became its anthem.

Established intellectuals played a marginal role in the Mahsa Movement.[23] None of these singers is an intellectual in the traditional sense.

The cultural abyss between State and society

Aspiring to the secular culture of joyful life in which religion plays a marginal role, young men and women in twenty-first-century Iran have created an affective complicity. First, direct relations between men and women have been marked by rejecting the restrictions of Sharia in the name of licit and illicit patterns of behavior (*halal/haram*). Young men and women socialize spontaneously, especially where government forces are not visible, such as in the mountains north of Tehran, or in public gardens between the trees, or at private gatherings of friends and families. But the urge for transgressive joyful life is also expressed in a new kind of festivity through dancing and singing (both forbidden to women). The urge to break the barriers between men and women is at the heart of this aspiration for unbridled interaction, repressed by the Islamic State. The desire for closeness in love or friendship is all the more intense, because of the very prohibition that forbids it. Without this sword of Damocles threatening relations between young people of the opposite sex, some would have exercised restraint. Given the ogre-like role of the Islamic State, the desire among them to get closer to each other has become even more enticing as a forbidden fruit, and any feeling of unease due to the Islamic superego is swept away. The excess of repression makes the transgression somehow legitimate, even attractive. In a more neutral environment, without the constant threat of persecution, gender relations might have been more cautious, less iconoclastic. Antagonism towards the predatory government brings the youth, male and female, together to affirm their aspiration to live together, in open contempt of the prohibitions, in a joyful contestation.

The new generation is less fearful and by far more daring than the previous one in the face of the Islamic Regime. They are not afraid to confront its agents. The Regime's failure in social and economic fields gives an additional legitimacy to the young people for whom the government, unlike its Chinese counterpart, represents social decline and the lack of future prospects.

The Mahsa Movement represents an exacerbation of the desire to desecrate Islamic theocracy not only by removing the compulsory veil, but also by setting fire to it, dancing together, men and women in a circle, and trampling collectively over the religious interdictions in an ostentatious manner. It is more than a transgression, it is denial of the Regime's legitimacy, pure and simple, by a large part of the Iranian youth.

The case of the pre-Islamic festival of Sizdah bedar

The pre-Islamic festival of *Sizdah bedar* was originally meant to expel evil on the thirteenth day of the first month of spring for the entire year through purifying fire, by jumping over the fire, and throwing into moving water green sprouts that people had grown at home. Nowadays, this secular holiday is joyfully celebrated every year in such a way as to flout the prohibitions of the Theocratic State.

An example of the deep cultural rupture between the government and society is how the authorities reacted on this day in 2023 (April 2), as people sought to celebrate the festival in the parks and green spaces, as every year. However, mainly for fear of hostile demonstrations following the Mahsa Movement, the government used the fasting of Ramadan as a pretext for banning access to parks. Hence there was tension and a confrontation between the people and the police ensued. Here is a summary account of the attacks against the people who were feasting:

> While every year on the 13th day of Farvardin (April 2 this year), people go to parks, and green areas to hold the pre-Islamic festivities known as "expulsing the 13th (day)" (*sizdah bedar*), this year the Islamic Republic imposed a ban on entering the parks under the pretext of Ramadan.
> The official news agency of the Islamic Republic (IRNA) announced on the 13th of Farvardin, that the presence of people in the parks was forbidden that day, from morning to evening.
> The videos sent by the people from Masuleh Road [northern Iran] showed that while people gathered to celebrate that day by dancing, the officers fired tear gas to disperse them and attacked them with guns in their hands ... IRNA has announced the reason for this ban as protecting the sanctity of Ramadan.[24]

This illustrates once again the rupture between the culture of joyful life of the overwhelming majority, and the ideology of mourning and prohibition of the Islamic State that banishes the secular festivities in the name of religion.

The divorce between the State and society is not only political or economic, but more fundamentally, cultural, even ontological: two antagonistic ways of conceiving social life, one promoting the autonomy of a secular individual who has freed her- or himself from the tutelage of the theocratic religion, the other imposing subjugation in the name of religious prohibition.

The cultural prominence of the secular middle classes after decades of Islamic theocracy

The Islamic Revolution seemed to have succeeded in uprooting the secularized middle classes' political and cultural self-assertion.[25] After the Islamic Revolution, the secular middle classes were despondent. They had been denied political participation under the Shah: they expanded and did well economically, but politically, they were repressed and no autonomous voice on their part was tolerated by the Pahlavi regime. Anyone, even for expressing themselves moderately, was politically persecuted and had no right to autonomous organization. Economically thriving, politically dwarfed, collective political action was not within their reach after a long period of repression by the Shah that left only tiny extremist groups capable of acting. The imperial regime had made them politically subservient or radically transgressive, no moderate attitude being tolerated. Either radicalized (the small groups of leftist middle-class youth like the Fedayeen of the People, Peykar, the People's Mojahedin, etc.) or quietist with a nonpolitical stance, the secular middle classes were in a political vacuum once the Revolution began.

Given the division between the leftist revolutionaries and the core of the middle classes, and in the absence of any political structure, the secular middle classes became the victims of the 1979 Revolution, once Ayatollah Khomeini took the helm as its uncontested charismatic leader. The Pahlavi regime had shaped the core of the secular middle classes in a manner that gave them economic assets in exchange for political allegiance or at least, silence. Politically repressed by the Shah, the secular middle classes failed to assert themselves in the political arena. They were subdued and part of the youth among them was alienated, resentful, with far-left Marxist leanings.

What contributed to the uprising against the Shah was the almost unanimous acrimony of the middle classes. In the last years of his regime, he had succeeded in antagonizing almost every stratum of the middle classes. Still, the modernized middle classes had been able to achieve a major goal under the late Shah: a secular culture in which the definition of the Self and its activities were defined in a non-religious fashion.

After the overthrow of the Shah in 1979, Ayatollah Khomeini eliminated one by one the representatives of the modern middle classes from the political stage. This was followed by the ousting of the liberal Islamic middle classes headed by Mehdi Bazargan, the prime minister of the provisional government, who resigned nine months after his nomination, after the invasion and occupation of the US embassy by a group of radicalized Islamic youth, the Muslim Student Followers of the Imam's Path, on November 4, 1979. The next group to be eliminated were those who sided with the first President of the Republic, Banisadr, who resisted Khomeini's absolute rule and was ousted on June 21, 1981. The war with Iraq and the hegemony of the fundamentalist Islamic groups under the aegis of Ayatollah Khomeini made any prospect for an open political system impossible. The middle classes were reduced to silence and the new regime became involved in the physical elimination of its opponents, ending up in summer 1988 with the massacre in prison of many thousands of Islamic radicals who were mainly members of the Marxist-Islamic People's Mojahedin.

Up to the end of the war in 1988, and even the death of Ayatollah Khomeini in 1989, a period during which the Islamic Regime consolidated into a firmly entrenched theocracy under the rule of the Supreme Leader, there was no vocal opposition among the middle classes. The only way they expressed their discontent was by leaving the country, choosing migration to the West or Turkey. It is after Khomeini's death that a new trend set in through which the middle classes came to express their aspirations publicly. Those who epitomized these aspirations were first and foremost the so-called "new reformist intellectuals" (*now-andishmandane-dini*). They expressed their ideas in an Islamic idiom but distanced themselves from those who had justified revolutionary Islam (Shariati) or Islamic government (Khomeini). They sponsored a new type of ideology, close to democracy. They contested the legitimacy of the Islamic government and defended the idea of a spiritual Islam that would not extend its realm to politics: Abdolkarim Soroush and Mohammad Mojtahed Shabestari were the major protagonists of this Islamic spiritualism.

All in all, secularization occurred in the Islamic Regime under a new guise, against the government's policies, in an implicit rather than blatant manner. In spite of its attempts at countering the secularization of society, the Islamic Regime failed to achieve its goal. On the contrary, the new generations gradually espoused the cultural features of the secular middle classes. In this process, the role of the reformist intellectuals was paramount. They questioned the legitimacy of the Islamic theocracy (*Velayat faqih*) and proposed the separation of the social and political realms from religion in the name of Islam. They were deeply influenced by the secular Iranian intellectuals who spread the notion of civil society and its autonomy to emphasize the role of democracy within genuine Islam.[26]

After the 1979 Revolution the middle classes locked themselves away in the private sphere to preserve their values and protect their families. More than four decades later, the secularized youth are not afraid to display in public their non-religious stance and often collide with the repressive forces of the Islamic Regime. Instead of fading away, secular values have become paramount through the new generations, many the offspring of the traditional groups that had supported the Islamic Revolution. Politically impotent, the secular middle classes culturally flourished from the 1990s and the youth, in their majority, identify with them rather than with the Islamic Regime. Islamic theocracy has preserved its political hegemony through the oil revenues and its military and paramilitary repressive groups, but in the cultural arena, it has lost the battle to win the hearts of the people. As for the middle classes, with their secularized values, they got the upper hand. These values extended to many young people, even within the Islamic elite, and have given the youth a buoyancy that cannot be repressed through state violence or police intimidation. Politically, the Theocratic Regime maintains its hold on society, but culturally, it has lost the battle, and secular middle-class values have acquired an indisputable legitimacy. A rupture between a deeply secularized society and its youth, and the Islamic Republic characterizes today's Iran, in which those who politically dominate are devoid of legitimacy and those who promote legitimate cultural values lack political clout.

The everyday life of the impoverished middle classes

The Iranian middle class has been drawn into poverty since the beginning of the twenty-first century and more significantly, since 2018. One case of a small middle-class family known to the author deserves a brief analysis.

Mariam was a fifteen-year-old teenager, and her sister Mahine was eighteen in 2022. Both went to the Mahsa demonstrations to protest the wearing of the veil. They disobeyed their parents, who feared for their safety and vainly tried to stop them. Their mother has naturally worn the headscarf since her youth, not out of allegiance to the Islamic Republic, but out of devotion to her family's religious tradition. The father is not religious. He even drinks low quality licor (*araq*), so as not to spend too much, given the modest income of the family. Until 2018, the father managed to earn enough to meet the family's needs and even set some aside for birthdays or other family celebrations. With the slump in the Iranian economy and US President Trump's restrictive measures against the country in May 2018, the value of the dollar increased more than six times against the Iranian currency over a year, and inflation rate rose to more than 50 percent, which severely affected Iranian household incomes and made the daily life of this family increasingly difficult. The young girls, Mahine and Mariam, continuously participated in the protests by lifting up their veils and removing them ostentatiously in the street, creating a crisis within the family, not for religious reasons (the mother does not seek to impose the veil on her daughters for religion) but for fear of their arrest, or even death in the street by the Regime's henchmen, as was the case for several young women and teenagers. The parents, who are close to their children, are unable to make them listen to reason and find themselves powerless vis-à-vis their daughters, who have become rebellious on this subject.

The dissension also reflects the divide in many Iranian families, whose older members did not participate in the Mahsa Movement, unlike their offspring eager to take part in the street protests. The generation gap, especially between young women and their parents, is even more apparent, although not openly acknowledged. Indeed, the family remains the only pillar for protection in a society in which the government, instead of protecting, is an essential source of aggression and domination. Dependence on the family is coupled with a sense of guilt in the case of explicit dissent. Young girls, whether teenagers (twelve to sixteen years old) or adults (seventeen to twenty-five years old), are largely dependent on the family economically, but also emotionally. This did not prevent them from taking part in the street demonstrations that shook the government for several weeks (up to February 2023).

Families have witnessed the death of their young girls and boys in the street demonstrations or in prison. The experiences of the various movements between 2016 and 2019 revealed to them the futility of revolt because of the government's merciless repression, which resulted in several hundred deaths (up to

1,500 in the November 2019 demonstrations, which came to be known as "Bloody November" [*aban khuneen*]),[27] and the end of the protests. But the new generation does not accept this version of reality. Certainly, they had not directly endured the repressions of the past (they were too young), but nevertheless they associate freedom with a concern for the body and the will to no longer suffer a divide between their appearance in public and their private life.

Impoverishment has transformed the lives of the lower middle classes. Mariam and Mahine's parents used to take them to the neighborhood restaurants from time to time; they used to go on small pleasure trips to the north of Iran near the Caspian Sea; they used to buy them small gifts from Tehran's Geisha Square. In short, they used to let them participate in the secular culture of "joie de vivre" under the strict surveillance of the Islamic State in cafés and small restaurants (while those in the north of Tehran were reserved for the rich people). Since 2018, restaurants, trips to other parts of Iran, and treats (buying clothes, going out with girlfriends, or going to their homes with a small gift) have become too expensive, even inaccessible to these middle-class people facing poverty. The father feels ashamed in front of his children, but the harsh reality eventually sets in.

In the meantime, the girls have grown up and seen more and more the duality that governs the life of Iranians and especially Iranian women, and in particular the rupture between private and public life. In private, a large number of Iranian families lead a secular life. Many people no longer perform their daily prayers but pretend to, and alcohol is commonplace at home. Foreign TV channels broadcast via satellite dishes give the opportunity to live an imaginary life based on secular norms and attitudes. However, since the establishment of the Islamic Republic in 1979, public life has followed a different path. It is a place of cultural breakdown, especially for women. They have been the main targets of the morality brigades that monitor their wearing of the veil; they have to show "modesty," adhere to arbitrary rules about how much lipstick or makeup is or is not acceptable, cover their ankles, their face. Likewise, young men should not grease back their hair, nor bare their arms, nor wear ties or Bermuda shorts, nor publicly break the Ramadan fast. But still, the real victims have been the women who must, often in the stifling heat of increasingly torrid summers, closely envelop their body and particularly, their hair. Mariam and Mahine have tangible experience of this discomfort, and the opportunity to take off their headscarves in demonstrations during the Mahsa Movement gave them not only the joy of transgression, but also the comfort of freeing themselves from a trying confinement of their bodies in the veil against which their souls rebel.

For the youth, the Mahsa Movement has been almost like rejecting a split personality. Through it, they have expressed the will to end a pernicious double game, to assert their sovereignty over their own bodies and against a repressive government that enforces a hypocrisy on them. They do not believe in the Islamic veil and are much more secular than the Islamic State would have us believe. Removing the veil for the two young sisters was to experience a surge of sincerity and showed a determination to put an end to a servitude that masqueraded as piety. Through the demonstrations they gathered courage to end the pretense of embodying Islamic norms in public which they did not believe in. They were driven by the fervent desire to put an end to this hypocrisy which is theocratic Shi'ism. It destroys their secular identity by shackling them to a duality that undermines their spontaneity.

In short, through the Mahsa Movement, they showed that they were not the simulacrum of devout Muslims, but secular women. The secular attitude towards life united men and women in the demonstrations. Both were in search of sincerity, seeking to recover their dignity by refusing to pretend to be what they were not.

The "would-be middle-class" individual

Many Iranian sociologists, both male[28] and female,[29] rightly point to the impoverishment of the middle classes as one of the major causes of the protest movements, including the latest, the Mahsa Movement. This observation begs two remarks. The first is that in the major slogans of this movement, the economy is not explicitly mentioned. Whether it is "Woman, life, freedom" or "Down with the dictator," these two main slogans refer to women's freedom and general life on the one hand, and to the overthrow of the dictatorial government embodied by the Supreme Leader on the other. More generally, in the Mahsa Movement one rarely finds slogans in reference to the economy. Does this mean its absence? No, but in the hierarchy of demands it occupies a subordinate place. From the point of view of the protesters, middle-class impoverishment is due to the Islamic State and its anti-Western policies, to its corruption, and to the suffocation of the economy by the IRGC and Revolutionary Foundations under the aegis of the Supreme Leader. The Regime is named as the main culprit.

But the essential point is that the subjective meaning of the middle classes has changed in recent decades in Iran, and in much of the Arab world, within a new, secular culture. Being "middle class" usually refers to an economic situation where one enjoys a "decent" standard of living, not too high and not too low; where one can lead a life free of need and protected from poverty. The subjectivity of the middle classes is usually oriented around this understanding. Still, in Iran as in much of the Muslim world, major parts of the cultural middle classes are "middle class poor."[30]

The profound change in a large part of the Muslim world and especially Iran is the advent of a new group that has a middle-class culture, with an educational level that should guarantee them, in their eyes, a middle-class standard of living. Yet they are not able to lead a decent middle-class life due to the politics of the Islamic Regime. In Iran and in many Middle Eastern societies, the cultural level of the new generations is significantly higher than preceding ones. In Iran, both young men and women now enjoy a level of higher education that reaches many millions (there are around 4 million students in university). From their point of view, they are entitled to a middle-class standard of living, without having access to it. According to them, they are being denied a middle-class status due to the Islamic Regime's shortcomings. I call this stratum the "would-be middle class."[31] Mentally, they are middle class, but objectively they are poor, sometimes even destitute.

It is their subjectivity that classifies them as middle class. In Iran, they have either become impoverished during the last decade, or are young people from the working classes who have had access to higher education, have a university degree, and are convinced that under a meritocratic government they would have had access to a decent standard of living. This feeling had already been expressed in the demonstrations of 2009 in terms of dignity (*karamat*) and now, over a decade later, the indignity of an unbearable economic and political situation is the reason for their revolt.

If the would-be middle class does not enjoy a decent standard of living this is due, in their eyes, to the Islamic State's global policy, which unduly favors its own elites, but also has decimated the rise of the middle classes through its international and anti-Western policy. They reject the Islamic State not only for economic and political reasons but also for its cultural orientation (its compulsory religious norms).

Their subjective feeling is corroborated by the economic data available and above all by the speed of the economic decline of all strata in society in Iran between 2022 and 2023. According to Hanke's Misery Index,[32] Iran ranks 19th among the world's most miserable countries. This contrasts with a much more prosperous economic class a decade earlier.

Another indication of the rapid impoverishment of the population and particularly the middle classes is provided by the Iranian parliament itself. Following the report of the Majlis Research Center on the increase in poverty in the country over the past decade, the Eco-Iran website announced an additional 11 million people had fallen below the poverty line in the country. According to this report a third of the population is now below the poverty line and the middle class is not far away from poverty either. Meanwhile, the Central Bank's price index table has reported an increase in the inflation rate in April 2023 to 69 percent.[33]

It is not only the economic situation, but its articulation with the existential and political situation of the middle classes that is at the core of the youth protests. However, the middle classes per se did not take part in the Mahsa Movement. It was the youth of the would-be middle-class who rebelled against the Theocratic Regime. These were young people who had not yet had the experience of stable employment, either because they were unable to find employment in the crisis-ridden Iranian economy, or because they were still studying at university and sometimes even still at school. The youthful dimension is fundamental: they felt that the future was blocked under the Islamic Republic, and that their present was devoid of meaning due to the government's senseless restrictions, which denied them the secular life in addition to economic deprivation. This cultural assertion of self as secular and antagonistic to the killjoy religiosity of the Islamic theocracy has been central to the revolt of the young would-be middle classes. Because they had confidence in themselves and their ability to act, they did not give in to fear and believed that action could be taken by confronting the repressive government apparatus. This youth's capacity for action contrasted with the inaction of the middle-class parents and grandparents, who did not dare to take to the streets to support them. The young demonstrators were left to protest on their own despite the sympathy of the older generations, who preferred to protest symbolically, but not on the streets alongside their children. Young women were at the forefront of the revolt by their refusal to wear the veil, brandishing their hair as testimony to their secular tenets in denial of the Islamic government.

The new would-be middle-class youth are characterized by their secularization, which played a key role in the triggering and unfolding of the Mahsa Movement. In addition to the disastrous economic conditions of the working and middle classes, an increasingly untenable ecological destruction, and harsh political repression, theocratic Shi'ism imposes puritanical religious norms on young men and women, pushing them increasingly to the secular life. They are antagonistic to the prohibitive religious standards, whether it be the mandatory headscarf, the segregation of men and women, or the ban on parties and joyful festivities, in brief a secular down to earth joyful life. The religious restrictions are in direct opposition to a secular culture that gives a new definition of self-esteem to the new generations. They do not care about Islamic strictures; they just want to live their lives freely in their relationships with each other and the empowerment of their bodies.

This middle-class culture, which includes the aspiring middle classes, is strongly influenced by the web and the Iranian diaspora abroad. They are aware of their right to a decent life because of their cultural and scientific educational achievements (the acquisition of a university degree).

The women, culturally members of the middle classes (they share with men the higher educational level) and economically downtrodden (they represent a tiny 15 percent of the workforce), are a large proportion of the would-be middle classes. They are in opposition to the Islamic State, which denies them both individual freedom and economic access to a middle-class status due to its repudiation of meritocracy and its cultural and political closure as well as its antagonism towards the West, which entails its exclusion from the world economy.

The Islamic State is perceived by these would-be middle classes as the enemy, particularly with the economic decline of so many in Iran in the twenty-first century. The numerous protests from 2016 to 2019 and the Mahsa Movement in 2022–3 have an economic but also a cultural component: the Theocratic State opposes the secular aspirations of these social strata, which now include the impoverished middle classes and a large part of the educated lower classes. The Islamic Regime is regarded as the major obstacle to their access to a decent standard of living.

Shunning of the Mahsa Movement by the working classes

I have described the Mahsa Movement as the first global feminist movement in Iran, marked by two essential characteristics: women are the protagonists of the movement, and men followed them in protest.

At the same time, it is a type of movement which, in Iran and in many societies with authoritarian states, share the following characteristics. First is the protagonists' claim to a middle-class status, or the "would-be middle class," namely those who are convinced that they rightfully belong to the middle classes yet lack the means of material subsistence in line with their aspirations. The notion of middle class is defined for these strata as a way of life enjoying economic and political dignity, freedom from want, and freedom of expression. They do not have access to it because, in their eyes, the government does not give them the means and, through its autocracy and corruption, denies them the opportunity to enjoy the benefits of their knowledge and level of education. Second is the democratic will: they demand political freedom for all citizens, political equality between believers and non-believers, between members of ethnic and religious groups, between women and men.

The Mahsa Movement belongs to this type of would-be middle class movement insofar as many Iranian women are educated yet excluded from economic and political activity by patriarchy and theocratic rule in Iran, and many young men and women are convinced they have no future and must languish in Iran.

There have been two types of movement in Iran since the establishment of the Islamic Republic in 1979. First have been those with a precise and limited objective, such as the demand for higher wages and better working conditions among workers, high school teachers, bus and truck drivers, or ecological movements who protest against climate change and pollution without calling into question the political structure and the Islamic Regime. Second are the protests with explicitly political aims; these seek to denounce the Theocratic Regime while proposing an alternative, namely either far-reaching reform of political structures (the Green Movement of 2009) or the overthrow of the dictatorial regime (the Mahsa Movement).

The second type of movement – the "would-be middle class" movement – is mainly driven by members of the middle classes and all those who want to join the middle classes and enjoy a decent standard of living. This type of movement includes the Students' Movement (1999), the Campaign for One Million Signatures (2006), the Green Movement (2009), and the Mahsa Movement (2022–3). They are fundamentally based on demands for political freedom and social justice, with the emphasis on political emancipation and democracy among the middle classes and those who culturally identify with them, even if they are economically relegated to the lower strata.

These movements contest the legitimacy of the government to varying degrees: the Students' Movement in 1999, under the presidency of the reformist Khatami, called for the opening up of the political sphere and an end to repression in the name of theocratic Islam, starting with a protest against the closure of the newspaper *Salaam* by the Iranian judiciary, under the sway of the Supreme Leader. The Green Movement of 2009 demanded freedom for citizens and recognition of their dignity (*karamat*), as well as an end to the state violence that repressed citizens and manipulated the ballot to give the populist Ahmadinejad the presidency.

The majority of these movements did not question the legitimacy of the Islamic State, but demanded essential political reforms within it. They reflected the hopes of Iranian reformists who were trying to bring about political reform within the Islamic Regime, without calling for its overthrow.

The Mahsa Movement was based on the end of reformist hope and the realization that the Islamic State was unreformable. The demand for political freedom went hand in hand with rejection of the Regime; hence the slogan: "Down with the dictator."

Would-be middle-class movements challenge the Marxist paradigm of workers' head-on confrontation with capitalism. They call for democracy, and are not concerned with the class divide, but with the legitimate aspiration of access to a decent life as members of the middle classes, or as aspirants to the middle classes on account of their cultural and social level (the would-be middle class).

A major feature of these movements too is their secularization. They are not anti-religious, but areligious. For them, religion must not intervene directly in political relations, and it is the notion of the citizen, irrespective of his or her religious affiliation, that lies at the heart of their demands.

Another characteristic of these movements is the low or non-participation of the working class. Workers (in the oil industry, in large industrial units such as sugar production, etc.) played no significant role in either the Green Movement in 2009, for example, or the Mahsa Movement. They instrumentalized middle-class movements to put pressure on the government in order to satisfy their demands for better salaries: the government did not want to have both middle-class and working-class movements coming together and therefore were less intransigent towards the latter when the "global movements" that demanded democracy like the Mahsa Movement crashed. In other words, the workers' protest movements have so far not aimed at overthrowing the Islamic Regime, but at improving working conditions within it. Their demands have not been political in character, but economic, even corporatist (each sector demands an increase in its purchasing power).

The working class in Iran has become much more fragmented since the 2000s as a result of the Islamic State's privatization policies, which denationalized state property and handed it over to the private sector. This private sector comprises members of the IRGC elite, part of the high clergy (some ayatollahs), and a few large bazaari merchants affiliated to the Islamic Regime. Laws on minimum wages and workers' contracts were relaxed, and the unity among workers was fragmented. In the oil sector, for example, fewer than a third of workers are still under the management of the National Oil Company, while the remainder are contracted through intermediaries. The former, a small minority, are paid between three and five times more than the contract workers, who are also subject to job insecurity and have to regularly renew their contracts. The state workers benefit from open-term contracts with social security and health and safety protection. This sows division between the two groups, and the split between them makes industrial action difficult. Nevertheless, the strikes launched in July 2021 encompassed different types of workers, given the galloping inflation that was wiping out everyone's livelihoods. In the end, the strikes failed because of the multilayered employment structure made up of various subcontracting companies with different governing bodies and management policies.[34]

During the Mahsa Movement, the number of workers' strikes fell in comparison with the period preceding it. The number of strikes recorded by Enqelab.info, which collected data on the

Mahsa Movement, was ninety-two between October 1, 2022 and January 17, 2023 – a weekly average of 6.1; whereas there had been an average of fifteen strikes weekly between May 1, 2021 and April 17, 2022. As these figures show, the average weekly number of strikes during the Mahsa Movement was lower than in the previous year.[35]

Why did workers not use the political crisis that shook Iran in the final months of 2022 as an opportunity to organize more strikes?[36]

One can note that the Mahsa Movement did not address workers' socioeconomic grievances. On the other hand, strikes require resources such as job security, long-term employment, free unions that facilitate networks among workers from different locations, and financial reserves that help compensate for loss of income during strikes. By undermining the workers' meager resources, Iran's deteriorating socioeconomic conditions would have impeded strikes.[37]

Of course, many workers did take part in movements like Mahsa, but not as workers per se, but as would-be middle-class individuals, frustrated in their aspirations for a decent life, and not as part of the labor movement. It is not class struggle, but the struggle to acquire middle-class status within society, not in reference to work, but to the dignity of the citizen, that characterizes those who take part in the would-be middle-class movements such as Mahsa. When they took industrial action, the workers confined themselves above all to contesting their working conditions, their wages, the precariousness of their status, and the forms of exploitation from which they suffered. They did not seek to challenge the political order.

This feature is not confined to Iran and can be observed in many autocratic Middle Eastern and North African societies. Here too the protagonists of political protest movements aimed at democratizing society comprise the middle classes. Notably absent from these movements are members of the working class. Its members may join them as individuals, but they do not launch strikes or collective actions as a social class.

The new ethnicity

The ethnic movements in Iran are similar to those of the would-be middle class insofar as they demand the dignity of the citizen and, with it, the recognition of their specific cultures and religions. These movements are different from the past, when many ethnic movements demanded independence and separation from Iran, and which justified repression by the central government. Now, within the Mahsa Movement, the ethnic movements were not asking for secession but for inclusion in a citizens' movement to demand the recognition of their linguistic and more generally cultural and religious particularities.

Two Iranian provinces were particularly prominent in the Mahsa protest movement: Sistan and Baluchistan in the southeast and the province of Kurdistan in western Iran (with protests initially amassing in the capital Sanandaj, and in Saqez, Mahsa Amini's birthplace), as well as the city of Orumieh (capital of western Azerbaijan) in northwestern Iran, where Kurds and Iranian Turks (Azeris) live together.

Kurdistan has long demanded autonomy, even independence. But what characterized the 2022–3 demonstrations was the absence of slogans demanding independence, and the desire to be at one with the other Iranian provinces to preserve the country's unity in the struggle against the dictatorship.

The media spokesperson (especially on the internet) for Sistan and Baluchistan was the Sunni cleric Mowlavi Abdolhamid, who remained open-minded throughout the protests. He denounced the central government's repression, its undemocratic rule, and the compulsory veil. He claimed that the province was not separatist – despite the central government's discrimination towards cultural and ethnic minorities – and that everyone felt fully Iranian.[38] His case as a Sunni cleric contrasts with the Shi'i ruling clergy, denounced by the youth for its oppressive rule.

Moreover, unlike other parts of Iran where it was mostly young people demonstrating, in these two provinces, the parents' generation too took to the streets and joined the young demonstrators because of the additional repression Sunnis suffer under theocratic Shi'ism, which does not fully recognize them and discriminates against Sunni culture, in particular their languages and ethnic dress.

The slogans hailed a new patriotism shared among the non-ethnic demonstrators and those protesting in the two regions: non-Kurdish Iranians chanted "Kurdistan is the apple of Iran's eye" (*kordestan, tchechm o tcheraghe iran*), while Kurds called out: "We struggle, we die, we will take back Iran [by ridding the country of this despotic regime]" (*mijangim, mimirim, irano passe migirim*); "Neither kingship, nor the rule of Rahbar [Islamic Republic], but democracy and equality" (*na saltanat na rahbari, demokraci, barabari*). In Tehran, they intoned: "Mahabad, Kurdistan, the model for all of Iran" (*mahabad, kordestan, olgouye kolle iran*); "If Tehran becomes [like] Kurdistan, Iran will become [like] a flower garden" (*tehran becheh kordestan, iran micheh golestan*); "Kurdistan, graveyard of fascists [the Islamic Republic]" (*kordestan, gurestane fachistan*).

The Iranian provinces were united in denouncing the repression that invariably befalls everyone and that is particularly aimed at women: "From Kurdistan to Tehran, oppression of women" (*az Kordestan ta Tehran, setam aleyhé zanan*).

This new feeling of belonging to the same nation, composed of different ethnicities, is found in the lyrics of a singer of Bakhtiari origin, Toomaj Salehi, who has long rapped about the multi-ethnic makeup of Iran. He encourages unity between Iranians of different ethnic origins, implicitly against the predatory regime that subjugates the entire population: *"Stay with us, we've stood by you for years,"* Salehi raps in his song "The Battlefield" (*meydoone jang*). He lists Iran's ethnic groups in all their diversity, underlining the unity of the nation, which, like a sea, has the waters of many different rivers flowing into it:

> *It is not enough to be rebellious, we have revolutionary roots. Arab, Assyrian, Armenian, Turkmen, Mazandari [from Mazandaran, a northern province of Iran], Sistani, Baluchi, Talesh, Tatar, Azeri [Turk from Iranian Azerbaijan], Kurdish, Gilaki [from Gilan, a northern province of Iran], Lur [from Lorestan], Farsi [Persian-speaking Iranian], and Qashqai [from the eponymous tribe], we are the unity of the rivers: we are the sea.*

To encourage Iranian nationalism against ethnic groups, the Islamic Regime scapegoated the Kurds and the Baluchi, among others, and therefore it cracked down more in regions such as Kurdistan and Sistan and Baluchistan than elsewhere. One notorious example is "Black Friday" in Zahedan (in Sistan and Baluchistan) on September 30, 2022.[39] According to Iran International, the protests in Zahedan were sparked by accusations that a police chief in the port city of Chabahar (another city in the province) had raped a fifteen-year-old Baluchi girl. Iranian security forces fired on protesters, killing more than sixty people, including fifteen minors.

Ethnic discrimination and prejudice against Sunnis make this province, the poorest in Iran, the target of government crackdowns. According to Amnesty International in 2021, at least 19 percent of all those sentenced to death were members of the Baluchi ethnic minority, which makes up only 5 percent of Iran's population. As has happened in similar circumstances in Iran, fearing that the hospital was under the surveillance of the security forces who might arrest patients there, many people injured in the Zahedan protest did not go to the hospital; they tried to seek treatment at home, but some lost a lot of blood and succumbed to their injuries. Doctors helped the wounded at home and some of them were arrested and tortured, even sentenced to death (for instance, Dr. Hamid Ghare-Hassanlou was sentenced to death for treating patients at home, but his death sentence was overturned under international pressure). Many people were subsequently arrested after having been furtively filmed during the demonstrations.

According to Amnesty International, the security forces in Sistan and Baluchistan province used live ammunition to kill demonstrators, targeting their upper body, chest, and head.

On Wednesday, November 9, 2022, forty days after Zahedan's Black Friday, citizens from many parts of Iran came out in sympathy with the people of Sistan and Baluchistan by striking and demonstrating. During the day, people went on strike in Zahedan and many cities in Kurdistan as well as in Tehran. At nightfall, they gathered in many cities and chanted slogans against the Regime. In Mashhad, protesters chanted: "Sanandaj, Zahedan, the pupil of Iran's eye" (*sanandaj, Zahedan, cheshm o cheraq iran*) and in Sattar Khan Street in Tehran, protesters chanted: "Khodanur [young man killed in Sanandaj the day after the protests] was killed by the mercenaries [of the Regime]" (*kochteh shodeh khodanoor, beh daste chant ta mozdoor*).

In the demonstrations taking place in Tabriz in northwestern Iran (Turkish-speaking city) at the funeral of Azad Hossein-Pouri, a victim of the massacre in the city of Izeh on November 16, 2022, people chanted: "Kurdish, Baluchi and Iranian Turk/ Freedom and equality" (*Kordo, Balucho, Azari/ azadi o barabari*).

The demonstrations in Khash (a city in Sistan and Baluchistan) started after prayers on Friday, November 4, 2022, when protesters gathered in the streets and chanted slogans against the Islamic Republic. According to the Iranian authorities, who habitually give a distorted version of the reality, the protesters were aggressive and tried to occupy the city's sub-prefecture. Cleric Mowlavi Abdolhamid, the highest Sunni authority in Sistan and Baluchistan, announced in a statement that at least sixteen people had been killed and dozens injured in the incident, calling out as untruthful the government's reports of the incident.

In Mahabad, a city in Iranian Kurdistan, protesters chanted, "Kurd, Baluchi, Iranian Turk, freedom, equality" (*Kord, Baluch, Azari, azadi, barabari*).[40]

The new ethnicity is much more patriotic than in the past: it makes Iranian unity in the joint struggle against the predatory state the spearhead of civil society – which has no other weapon than its slogans and to protest with its bare hands.

The new ethnicity is not, however, in harmony with the cultural and political vision of a centralized Iran. The young generations prefer to silence their dissension and preserve national unity to secure the overthrow of the despotic regime, and then to put their demands for political autonomy, cultural recognition, and social justice on the table. In the Mahsa Movement, just like women, the ethnic populations played on the heartstrings of social unity against the tyrannical state. This did not mean, however, that there was no tension or dissension between women and men, or between Kurdish, Baluch, or Azeri Iranians and others. But the unity of society against the despotic state was respected by all.

2

Protest movements before the Mahsa Movement

A century of female presence and the lack of a feminist social movement in Iran

During and after the Constitutional Revolution (1906–11), women were active, founding underground magazines and women's societies, and pursuing three goals: women's education, changing the terms of marriage and divorce for women, and women and children's health and disease prevention. Being marginal citizens, they did not achieve all these aims.

During the Pahlavi reign, under Reza Shah, in his emulation of Atatürk, women on the whole gained a number of rights as a result of the modernization of the state apparatus (an autonomous judiciary, even if the influence of traditional Islam within it was not negligible) and the introduction of women into education and other sectors, not through social movements but from above, by the state. Women's education was carried out in schools, and gradually at university, without major obstacles. The women's movement in this period was virtually non-existent, although individual women did try to push for female emancipation. Nor was the despotic nature of the Pahlavi state conducive to the free expression of women's demands.

During the reign of Mohammad Reza Shah, the activities of independent women's groups were neglible.[1] Women's associations were forcibly integrated into state bodies, and there was no notable resistance on their part either. Admittedly, these associations comprised only a small number of women, often educated and from the upper or upper middle classes. Iran under the Pahlavis was a regime that granted benefits to women rather than women demanding them through protest movements, from below. The secular nature of the Pahlavi regime and the desire to follow the Western model meant that the introduction of women into the public sphere and the state was welcome as long as they did not question the authoritarian nature of the regime. Some women were active in far-left organizations opposed to Reza Shah, within movements such as the People's Mojahedin, Peykar, Fedayeen, or the Iranian Communist Party, the Tudeh, in the 1970s. But their presence did not call into question the masculinity of these organizations, with the possible exception of the Ashraf Dehghani's Fedayeen Minority group or the People's Mojahedin, in which power passed into the hands of Maryam Rajavi after the mysterious disappearance of her husband Mas'oud Rajavi.

However, individual women had their sights set on female emancipation, and someone like Mehrangiz Manouchehrian, Iran's first female jurist and senator, was subsequently celebrated after the 1979 Revolution by the work of two renowned Iranian feminists.[2]

The role of women in the demonstrations in the 1979 Revolution was significant, but no feminist demands, particularly with regard to Islam, which was becoming one of the major rallying points of the movement, were raised by female participants. Many female intellectuals (such as Homa Nategh), like many men, felt that women's demands had to be sacrificed to support the anti-imperialist movement launched by

Ayatollah Khomeini and a faction of the clergy, representatives of the petty-bourgeoisie. Once the revolution had succeeded, the flag of proletarian revolution could be raised, and women would be granted equal rights with men. Secular women wore headscarves to demonstrate their opposition to the Shah and their support of the protest movement, which few men and women imagined would turn into a dictatorial theocracy.

Two weeks after victory, Khomeini's office decided to rescind the family support law enacted under the Shah and make the Islamic hijab mandatory. In addition, one day before March 8, International Women's Day, Ayatollah Khomeini announced in a speech at the Refah Religious School that female government officials should observe the Islamic hijab to protect their dignity. The next day, unveiled women were refused entry to their workplaces. Many of them rejected the veil and those from the Ministry of Foreign Affairs demonstrated outside the building. Between 5,000 and 8,000 women gathered at Tehran University and chanted against the compulsory veil. In addition, female students joined the protest in Tehran. They were thwarted by the new government. Left-wing political groups ignored them and considered their demands inappropriate because the main enemy was capitalism and the struggle against the veil weakened the petty-bourgeois revolution which was considered by the intellectuals as anti-capitalist and a step towards the proletarian revolution.

The mobilization of a small group of Iranian feminists and their male supporters began on June 12, 2006 in Tehran, after the election of Ahmadinejad in 2005, a populist and conservative candidate who opposed reformist aims and women's demands. The movement was suppressed by the police. Three months later, the Campaign for One Million Signatures was launched, calling for signatures to a petition for equal rights for women in public spaces. The activists were arrested on March 4, 2007, four days before International Women's Day on March 8. It was a movement that did not develop into a social movement and was nipped in the bud by the authorities. It did contribute to women's awareness of the need for large-scale collective action, but this did not manifest itself in June 2009, when women demonstrated alongside men to denounce Ahmadinejad's fraudulent re-election against Mir Hossein Moussavi.[3] Even then, there was no specific feminine dimension to the movement. True, the dream of reformist social and political change from within was still alive, and a large part of Iranian society believed that reforms towards democracy could be achieved within the Islamic theocracy. The Green Movement of 2009 and its repression by the Islamic Regime put an end to this hope. Many women realized the impossibility of action within the Islamic Regime, and a large part of civil society became aware that the Iranian Regime was radically opposed to political reforms towards democracy. The slogan "Where is my vote?" marked the emergence of a deep-rooted civic and democratic subjectivity in Iranian society.

Historical reminder of the veil

The foundation of the Islamic Republic after the 1979 Revolution was for its leaders (including Ayatollah Khomeini) a revenge on the Pahlavi regime and its secularization of Iran. The clerical regime retaliated against the forced unveiling of women under Reza Shah in 1936 by intimidating women to re-veil in 1979. The imperial regime had created a judicial system independent of the clergy and Islam, inspired by European (Belgian) law; in reaction, the clerics forcefully reimposed the Islamization of justice by reintroducing Sharia as the linchpin of the judiciary system and by reintroducing flogging, more exceptionally stoning and cutting off the hand as punishment, re-establishing the talion law, or "an eye for an eye" (*qisas*), which had been abolished by the Pahlavi regime. A historical memory has thus been at work in the Islamic Republic since its beginning, driven by resentment and the desire to undo secularization and to reassert the role of the clergy as the protagonist and interpreter of Islamic law. In doing so, the clerical regime did violence to a large segment of Iranian society that had embraced secular customs and practices and no longer identified with Islamic laws and traditional gender relations after half a century of intense modernization from above.

Before 1979, a significant proportion of middle-class women had internalized the non-veiled identity, and unveiled women in public had become commonplace in the cities. What the imperial regime had violently imposed almost half a century before, unveiling, was not transformed into a psychological repression but into a new identity, freed from the constraints that had caused unveiling in the earlier era. On the eve of the 1979 Revolution, many urban Iranian women were unveiled, because that was their way of life, and it was no longer a question of duress. The Western origin of the unveiled woman was not a problem, and they did not experience the unveiling as alien; it was taken for granted just like the use of electricity or the car.

Some Iranian Third Worldist intellectuals, however, among others, played a reactionary role by attributing this new habitus among women but also men (the modernization of their conduct, their individualism, etc.) to a Western travesty, or even a "Western disease" (*qarb-zadegi*), as Marxist and Third Worldist intellectual Jalal Al-Ahmad put it. He believed that a proletarian revolution could be achieved through Islam, and that the Westernization of the country was a cultural and social catastrophe. This idea, which characterized the malaise of Iranian intellectuals, was far removed from the experience of unveiled women, who embodied their way of life without being perturbed by its Western origin, and identified with a modernity that was properly Iranian and would gradually ensure a better and freer future for them. In fact, in the 1960s and 1970s, the unveiled woman had become under Mohammad Reza Shah paradigmatic among middle-class women, and many pious women would alternately wear the veil during prayers and remove it in public without feeling pressured by the government. In short, the model of the unveiled woman among the Iranian middle classes, especially in large urban areas and among young people, was gaining ground in 1970s Iran, through cultural habit, independent of state coercion.

The 1979 Revolution was motivated by the growing discontent of the modernized middle classes due to the increasing arbitrariness of the Shah, who, as time went on, closed rather than opened the political system, so that the last years of his reign saw the exclusion of all political parties but one, subservient to him. In the demonstrations against the Shah that led to his overthrow in 1979, secular middle-class men and women demonstrated against the regime, which was modernizing society from above and at the same time, arbitrarily suppressing the political and social consequences of his modernization by closing, rather than opening, the political arena.

Still, Iranian society was far from highly educated (there were fewer than 300,000 students in 1978) and among the newly modernized lower middle classes, self-awareness was accompanied by an ambiguous sense of guilt. They felt modernization from above by the Shah as a betrayal of Islam.

During the demonstrations that led to the Revolution, many secular middle-class women sided with Khomeini. They believed that once the Shah was gone, they would return to their former daily lives and modern mores would not be forfeited under Khomeini. As for the Marxist intellectuals, their major enemy was capitalism, embodied by the Shah, and fundamentalist Islam represented by Khomeini was transient: after Ayatollah Khomeini seized power, they could carry out the proletarian revolution and get rid of the petty-bourgeoisie he represented. Women would recover their full freedom through an egalitarian social justice.

The Marxist intellectuals like Jalal Al-Ahmad and Iranian leftists like the poet Khosro Gole-Sorkhi (he was sentenced to death under the Shah in 1973 for having led a violent Marxist group) considered the Islamic Revolution as the first step towards the proletarian revolution.

In short, the Iranian Revolution was an unprecedented movement of the masses (hundreds of thousands in the streets of Tehran in the last week of the Pahlavi regime) based on collective credulity about a mythical Islamic state, supposedly devoid of the shortcomings of the Shah's regime. The latter's despotism had made it impossible for the Iranian intelligentsia to take a critical view of politics. As for democracy, it was regarded as a ploy by global capitalism to enslave the Third World. Society fell victim to the Revolution's effervescence and blind trust in the person of Ayatollah Khomeini.

In short, the ideology among leftists and many female intellectuals at the time was that the Revolution was the main goal and women's specific problems had to be subordinated to it for a short while, before Khomeini's government would be toppled by a genuine communist revolution. Exceptions to this view did exist, like the famous public letter written by Mostafa Rahimi to Ayatollah Khomeini a month before the overthrow of the Shah in January 1979, in which he explained why he was opposed to the Islamic Republic, which he, presciently, feared would be a religious dictatorship in the wake of the secular dictatorship of the Shah.[4]

But those who questioned the Islamic Revolution were virtually inaudible, and all too often the voices of the millions of demonstrators who led to the overthrow of the imperial regime stifled any hint of resistance to an Islamic utopia that would establish paradise on earth.

Ayatollah Khomeini concurred with the demonstrators, that once the revolution was over, he would retire to the holy city of Qom and leave the leadership to the people and their elected representatives. Later, he claimed that he had lied for the sake of Islam, in the name of *taqiyeh* or *ketman*, which was permissible because the ultimate goal, Islamic theocracy, justified the means, even if the arguments were based on a fallacy.

The 1979 revolutionary slogan "Independence, freedom, Islamic republic" left the status of Islam totally undetermined, and each social group interpreted Islam according to their own dreams and ideals. The ambiguity of Islam, which could range from theocracy to democracy, was encouraged by Ayatollah Khomeini, who sought to impose himself by concealing the theocratic nature of the regime he wanted to establish with the help of a section of the clergy and fundamentalists who rejected modernity in the name of a return to Islamic values. Khomeini's charisma worked like a charm, opening all the doors in an effervescent society where reality dissipated in the spectacle of collective madness.

He founded a theocratic republic, first by relying on his charisma, then by a repressive apparatus that proved to be far more brutal than that of the Shah. One of the consequences of the establishment of the Theocratic Regime was the exodus of more than 3 million educated and middle-class Iranians to the West or to neighboring countries for the decades to come. The Islamic Revolution has resulted in a painful social, economic, ecological, and political regression for Iran. Khomeini was creating an Islamic Regime, in which society was subservient, dominated in the name of God (a theme addressed in his book *Velayat Faqih*).

The struggle against the compulsory veil under the Islamic Republic

Iranian women's struggle against religious and social constraints can be traced back to the nineteenth century. But the focus here is on the period covering the Pahlavi dynasty and the Islamic Republic.[5]

The situation of women has been subject to profound legal regression since the 1979 Revolution. Now all women, even non-Muslims, are required to wear the hijab in public. The Theocratic State, founded in 1979, imposed on women a wide range of legal restrictions, placing them in a legally inferior status to men. In 2016, the World Economic Forum ranked Iran 141st out of 145 for gender equality. According to available data from the United Nations released in December 2019, in 2016, 184 out of 194 countries granted at least formal equality to women in their constitutions. Iran was not among them.[6] Iran is among the 29 countries out of 187 in which the man is the head of the family and can alone decide on major issues.[7]

Saudi Arabia has in effect reversed the law on the compulsory veil since 2019. Iran's Islamic Republic and the Taliban in Afghanistan are the only two states that impose the compulsory veil on pain of legal punishment, in addition to jihadist groups such as al-Qaeda, ISIS, and Boko Haram. The penalty for violating the law can be up to seventy-two lashes and two months in prison as well as heavy fines. Since the Mahsa Movement, the Islamic Regime is toughening the law against unveiled women, with up to ten years' imprisonment.

Although until 1983, there was no specific law on wearing the Islamic veil, as mentioned women were forbidden to work in the administration without a veil and all those who appeared unveiled were barred from their office. The Hezbollahi (a derogatory term referring to the violent militias of the Islamic Regime) intimidated and assaulted women if they were not veiled, sometimes even attacking them with razors or throwing acid in their faces.

On March 7, 1979, shortly after the revolution that brought him to power, Ayatollah Khomeini announced to the theology students in Qom:

> Islamic women must wear the Islamic hijab. Not for pride. Women are still working in offices with the previous status

[of the Shah's time]. Women should change their status ... I was told that women are "naked" [which means for traditionalists, unveiled] in our ministries, and this is against the Sharia. Women can participate in social work, but with an Islamic hijab.

The first law concerning women's clothing was Article 102 of the Penal Code, legislated much later in 1996.[8] According to the law "whoever actually pretends to commit an illicit (*haram*) act in public, in public places and on (public) thoroughfares, shall be sentenced to a fine of ten days to two months in prison or 72 lashes in addition to the punishment of the act." And it states more specifically in a note: "Women who appear without religious hijab in the streets and in public will be sentenced to a prison term of ten days to two months or a fine of 50,000 to 500,000 rials."

Since the 1979 Revolution, any questioning of the veil has been considered a sign of immorality and indecency (*bi effati*) by the Islamic Republic.

After the 1979 Revolution, women's activities were put on the back burner for over a decade, and it was only after the end of the war with Iraq and the death of Ayatollah Khomeini that women emerged not within social movements, but in the press, in public speaking, in forms of self-expression in literature – in activities that were previously almost exclusively male. Where women began to assert themselves, such as in journalism, their breakthrough, especially during and after Khatami's presidency (1997–2005), was striking. Under the editorship of Shahla Sherkat, the magazine *Zanan* (Women), for example, published articles on the situation of women in Iran, and *Salam*, the reformist newspaper, gave a voice to women in the 1990s.

A prominent case of individual protest against the compulsory veil: Homa Darabi

The story of Homa Darabi, a feminist and social activist, is an inspiring one in the struggle against the mandatory veil at the individual level. Born in 1940 in Tehran into a middle-class family, she was a pediatrician and psychiatrist who, from her youth, showed an unyielding will to act for political freedom and women's emancipation. In 1960, she became an early member of the National Front, a democratic political party founded by Mossadegh, and on successfully passing the entrance exam was enrolled into the medical school at Tehran University. She was an activist in the student movement and was imprisoned for a time under the Shah for her political militancy. She took part in the protests that led to the 1979 Revolution.

Homa Darabi earned her degree in psychiatry in the United States and practiced medicine there before returning to Iran in 1974. She became a professor at Tehran University Medical School, and also opened her own private clinic. After the Revolution, she refused to wear the veil. In 1990, she was dismissed as a university professor for refusing to wear the hijab on the charge of "disrespecting Islamic mores." Her clinic was also closed down by the authorities.

As a social and political activist, Homa Darabi cherished high hopes for the 1979 Revolution and initially expected it to lead to the improvement of women's situation, but she was deeply disappointed by the regression in their status. She set herself on fire in Tajrish Square, northern Tehran on February 21, 1994, in protest against the compulsory veil.

The Campaign for One Million Signatures

After the protest demonstrations against the compulsory veil following the 1979 Revolution, the long war launched by Iraq against Iran in 1980 had the effect of stifling any attempt by women at speaking out publicly. After the war (1988) and the death of Ayatollah Khomeini in 1989, a new chapter seemed to open in which certain freedoms could be gained through negotiation, or at least through the attempt by the "new religious intellectuals" (*now-andishmandane-dini*) to interpret Islam along pluralist lines. They argued for a non-theocratic and democratic version of Islam. They entered into a confrontational dialogue with the authorities without putting the Islamic Regime in question.

The election of the reformist Mohammad Khatami as President of the Republic in 1997 opened new vistas. Feminist activists thought they could launch, with the help of Islamic feminists, a campaign to restore women's rights. The Iranian jurist, judge, and human rights lawyer Shirin Ebadi, who in 2003 won the Nobel Peace Prize, was among those who supported Khatami's election. Also, during several years, she affirmed, like the Iranian reformist intellectuals, that equal gender rights as well as democracy are in conformity with genuine Islam[9] and could be implemented by the Islamic Regime without betraying the principles of Allah's religion.

In this period a new generation of Iranian woman activist appeared. After the Islamic Revolution, women were pushed back to a situation of legal inferiority. For example, Shirin Ebadi had been promoted in 1975 to be the first female judge in Iran. After the Revolution, she lost her position as a magistrate and was relegated to the status of a court clerk.

The struggle for equal rights continued over the following decades, culminating in the launch of the Campaign for One Million Signatures in 2006, after the failure of the reformist president Khatami to change the situation of women. Over the previous three years, Iranian women's rights activists had become increasingly visible internationally. After Shirin Ebadi received the Nobel Peace Prize in 2003, Iranian feminists organized a series of seminars on women's rights that culminated in a demonstration against gender inequality in front of Tehran University on June 12, 2005. This event brought together several hundred activists, men and women, and the following year they held another demonstration on August 28, 2006, in Hafte-Tir Square in Tehran, which was supported by national and international human rights groups such as Amnesty International. The demonstrators called for the reform of the laws, especially family laws, that discriminate against women. They also distributed a pamphlet on "The Effects of Islamic Laws on Women's Lives" throughout Tehran. The protest was quashed by the security forces who beat and pepper sprayed the protesters, and arrested seventy people. Several of them were sentenced to prison terms and flogging.

In March 2007, thirty-three women were arrested, most of them outside a Tehran court where they had gathered to peacefully protest the trial of five women – Fariba Davoudi Mohajer, Shahla Entesari, Noushin Ahmadi Khorasani, Parvin Ardalan, and Sussan Tahmasebi – who were accused of propaganda against the Islamic Republic, undermining national security, and participating in illegal demonstrations.

Bahareh Hedayat, one of the founding members of the Campaign for One Million Signatures, was arrested on July 9, 2007, and on August 9, 2007, but released on bail. She was again arrested and released in 2008 and in 2010 and then sentenced to nine and a half years' imprisonment for anti-state propaganda.[10]

On November 4, 2007, Ronak Safazadeh was arrested, the day after she collected signatures at a Children's Day celebration for the Campaign for One Million Signatures, organized in support of gender equality.

On June 12, 2008, Nasrin Sotoudeh and eight other women were arrested by security forces as they were about to attend a conference commemorating the National Solidarity Day of Iranian Women.

The journalist and activist Parvin Ardalan was scheduled to be in Stockholm on March 6, 2008, to receive the 2007 Olof

Palme Prize in recognition of her leading role in the Campaign for One Million Signatures for gender equality. However, on March 3, airport security officers prevented her from leaving, seized her passport and handed her a summons to appear in court.

Subsequently, the Islamic Regime's judiciary sentenced four female leaders of the movement, Maryam Hosseinkhah, Nahid Keshavarz, Jelveh Javaheri, and Parvin Ardalan, to prison terms for contributing to banned websites.

This campaign, launched after the failure of the reformist President Khatami to open up the political system and under the presidency of the populist Ahmadinejad, was the last major feminist movement on reform of the legal framework of the Islamic Regime, which repressed it, often with heavy prison terms and exorbitant bail, the threat of confiscation of their property, and pressure on the activists' families. This movement was driven by a new generation of women activists and intellectuals who often combined writing and public activism in defense of gender equality. It was also the first generation whose leaders routinely went to prison, endured psychological and physical torture, sometimes flogging, and other mental and material pressures. The movement did not gather momentum and the number of women and men involved in it was limited. It was rather a cultural movement that did not mobilize women in the same way as the Mahsa Movement would do in 2022, in which a generation of young women, accompanied by men, launched a nationwide protest against the Islamic Regime, with women at its helm.

Women's protest against the compulsory veil in 2017–2018

The Campaign for One Million Signatures was fundamentally about women's rights and did not focus on the veil. In December 2017, another limited movement began, rejecting the compulsory veil as a symbol of the subjugation of women and their inferiority as citizens. On December 27, 2017, thirty-one-year-old Vida Movahed removed her headscarf in Enqelab Avenue, a central thoroughfare in Tehran. She stood on an electrical distribution box and for nearly an hour silently held her scarf at the end of a stick before being arrested. This movement was coincidental with another one that mobilized people in many towns to denounce government corruption and the growing poverty of the population. More than 4,000 arrests took place in many cities and cast a shadow over the rejection of the veil by a limited number of young women. Movahed's lawyer, Nasrin Sotoudeh, herself a famous feminist, took up her defense and she was released on January 28 on the condition that she stopped protesting. Until October 2018, she complied, but she reappeared again in public unveiled, standing on the dome built at the center of Enqelab Square from which she waved white and red balloons.

Another woman, Narges Hosseini, thirty-three, went to the same platform as Vida Movahed and lifted her white headscarf in January 2018. In the days that followed, many other women removed their veils and repeated the same action. Narges Hosseini was arrested and put in jail. Nasrin Sotoudeh assumed her legal representation. In the following days, women and men protested against the compulsory veil. These young women became known as the "Girls of Enqelab Avenue" (*dokhtaran khiaban enqelab*) and gained prominence on social media. Hosseini was sentenced to three months in prison for "inciting prostitution" and not wearing the hijab.

This movement, which did not become widespread, was the prelude to the Mahsa Movement, more than four years later in September 2022.

3

The Mahsa Movement: the first sweeping feminist movement in Iran

The Mahsa Movement has had its precedents in the history of women in Iran. Since the nineteenth century, many women had expressed their rejection of the patriarchal order in the country. Female intellectuals and artists in particular voiced their demand for emancipation, notably through their creations, songs, lifestyle, and symbolic acts (for instance, taking off the veil in public).

In the nineteenth century, exceptional women like Tahereh Ghorrat ol-Eyn (1817–52) pioneered feminism in Iran. In a public appearance in 1848, she spoke out in favor of gender equality and unveiled herself. A poet and follower of the recent religion of Babiism, she asserted herself so freely that the Qajar authorities put her to death. The Constitutional Revolution saw a small group of women from high social backgrounds (as in the rest of the Muslim world) attempt to promote the cause of women. It was above all at the cultural level, through the opening of girls' schools, that they attempted to step into the social arena.

Qamar ol-Moluk Vaziri's famous song "The Daughters of Cyrus" (*dokhtaran sirus*) was performed by her in 1924 on the stage of the Grand Hotel in Tehran. She appeared unveiled onstage several years before the law banning the veil (*kashf hejab*) in Iran, promulgated by Reza Shah in 1936:

> O *Daughters of Cyrus* [the great Achaemenid king, one of the world's first empire founders],
> Until when in anguish?
> Oppressed by men,
> Until when in chains?
> O *Daughters of Sassan* [the ancestor of the founder of the pre-Islamic Sasanian dynasty],
> Until when will you be silenced?
> No one notices that
> No one cares what's right or wrong [about the major issues]
> O you political elites of Iran,
> Is woman not a human being?

Women's legal condition improved under the Pahlavi dynasty, with the founder, Reza Shah, granting them new rights in imitation of Atatürk, the founder of the Turkish Republic, notably through the legalization of education for girls and certain professions (e.g., teacher, nurse), in which a minority of them were able to acquire financial autonomy.

Under Mohammad Reza Shah, they gained access to parliament and even ministerial posts, as well as to university. However, their promotion was not due to a women's movements, but to the Shah's regime itself, in its attempts to modernize society in an authoritarian, top-down, and secular fashion.

In the 1979 Revolution, a large number of women took to the streets (up to a third of the demonstrators, according to some estimates). But it was not a women's movement: there was no women's slogan at its heart. The protests against the compulsory veil decreed by Ayatollah Khomeini in the wake of the Shah's overthrow brought together a few thousand women, but this was a group against the compulsory veil rather than a women's movement with a social project (they rejected the veil, but they had no alternative project to the patriarchal Islamic order).

The first women's movement with explicit aims for women's emancipation (equal rights with men) was the Campaign for One Million Signatures in 2006. But this was a cultural movement mobilizing dozens of women and men; again not a social movement as such. This movement had a major impact on the awareness of many women thereafter. The protest by women who lifted their veils in 2018 following Vida Movahed's removal of her veil in Enqelab Avenue (the so-called "Girls of Enqelab Avenue" movement) still did not mobilize a large number of women. It was not until September 2022, following the tragic death of Mahsa Amini at the hands of Tehran's Vice Squad, that the first women's movement, in the strict sense of the term, mobilizing thousands of women, as well as men, under the slogan "Woman, life, freedom," was launched in Iran. This can be understood as the first massive feminist movement in Iran, whose main protagonists were women, with a rallying cry that focused on women, with men joining them in protest against the Islamic Regime.

Long before the Mahsa Movement of September 2022, the Islamic Regime was aware of the problem of the veil. Various classified investigations were carried out, which indisputably revealed the resistance of women and more broadly, the population, to the compulsory veil. In 2018, Parvaneh Salahshuri, a parliamentarian of the Islamic Republic, announced the failure of the Regime regarding the compulsory veil and suffered the hostile reactions of male officials. Among her findings she commented:

> Not only young women are not convinced about the hijab, but they are being driven away . . . We are only working on Islamic appearance, with hypocrisy . . . The hijab has been treated as

a political issue, not a cultural one, from the beginning. This politicization has ruined its effectiveness . . . Aren't the morals of not lying, being non-hypocritical, and dozens of other traits in Islamic morality [also] important? Why is lying so prevalent in our country [implicitly: lying by the authorities]?

With regard to the twenty-six government agencies and over 300 cultural bodies dedicated to promoting women's hijab, the question is according to her:

Why have these organizations failed to educate young Muslim women in this vein? Why has the Qom Religious School with a budget of several billions [tens of millions of Euros] not succeeded in this task? Why have the veil promotion organizations with their huge budgets been ineffective on the hijab issue?

A special report by Iran's parliament conceded that:

The traditional hijab (*chador*) is accepted only by about 35% of Iranian women, and nearly 70% of them either do not believe in the hijab or are among those who are described as "ill-veiled" who protest against the mandatory hijab in Iran.[1]

According to statistics published by the Gamaan Institute in 2020, 72 percent of Iranians, both men and women, are against the mandatory hijab. Only 15 percent are in favor of it. Individually, 58 percent do not believe in the hijab, while 26.6 percent believe in it. More than 50,000 people participated in the survey and about 90 percent of them resided in Iran.[2] Also in September 2019, Mehdi Nassiri, the former editor-in-chief of the hardliner *Keyhan* newspaper (unofficial spokesman for the Supreme Leader, Ayatollah Khamenei), announced on the official TV Channel Four that: "According to a survey conducted by the Ministry of Culture and Islamic Guidance, 70 percent of Iranian people are against the mandatory hijab." He also added that the number of those who wear it decreased every year by about 5 percent and the results of the latest survey conducted by the ministry showed that even in religious cities like Qom, most people were against the mandatory veil. Nassiri also announced that the authorities had banned the release of the survey because they considered its results unfavorable to the image of the Islamic Republic.[3]

The Fars News Agency is under the direction of the Revolutionary Guards (IRGC) and much of its information is secret and exclusively intended for the leadership. In its bulletin of August 3, 2022, the Black Rewards hackers revealed the following information: a poll was conducted on the veil issue among a significant sample of the population by asking the question: If you had a daughter, at what age would you like her to wear the veil: beginning in childhood, puberty, or the age of marriage? The answer by 60 percent of the sample was: "Never!" This underlined the fact that it was not only women, but also men who rejected the veil by a large majority.

The Mahsa Movement was launched following the death of the twenty-two-year-old Kurdish woman Mahsa Amini (Jina by her Kurdish first name) in the Tehran headquarters of the Vice Squad after she had been arrested for wearing an ill-fitting veil (*bad hejab*, "mal-veiled").

Demonstrations began on September 16, 2022, following the arrest of Mahsa Amini on September 13, her falling into a coma in the premises of Tehran's Vice Squad, and then her death on September 16. The young woman was buried on September 17 in Saqez, which was the scene of major protests that day. Another demonstration took place in Sanandaj, the capital of the Kurdistan province. These protests went on to take place in other cities of Kurdistan but also throughout Iran. They were coordinated on social networks, using the hashtag #mahsa_amini in Roman text and Persian. On September 18 in Sanandaj, several women removed their veils in protest, as well as in the capital where students from Tehran University marched, chanting the slogan "Woman! Life! Freedom!" inspired by the Kurdish *"Jin, Jiyan,'azadi."*

On September 19, internet access was cut off in central Tehran. Demonstrations took place in many Iranian city centers, where the chant for "Death to the dictator" was increasingly heard. On the same day, three protesters were killed by the security forces during a demonstration in Kurdistan province and a twenty-three-year-old man, Farjad Darvishi, was also killed in the town of Valiasr in Urmia in northwestern Iran, which is inhabited mostly by Iranian Kurds and Turks.

On September 20, anti-government protests broke out in at least sixteen provinces out of a total of thirty-one. Women removed their veils and cut off their ponytails during the demonstrations as a token of grief and protest at the death of Mahsa Amini. The rallies would quickly gather and then dissipate to make it difficult for the security forces to crack down.

By the evening of September 21, Iran's internet connection to the rest of the world was severely disrupted, preventing the use of sites like WhatsApp and Instagram through which protesters attempted to coordinate their action. That day, at least eight protesters were killed. One of the victims, sixteen-year-old Nika Shahkarami, became the second symbol of the Islamic Regime's murderous brutality towards women.

On September 22, the demonstrations continued, especially in Tehran, but also in many medium-sized cities in most of Iran's provinces. That day, the death toll among the demonstrators reached twenty-two.

On September 23, protests continued throughout the country. According to various sources, at least thirty people were killed among the demonstrators, and the police fired live ammunition. Counterdemonstrations were also organized by the government, with little success.

On September 24, large demonstrations took place in many Iranian cities, including in front of Tehran University. The same day, in the province of Gilan in northern Iran, the security forces arrested 739 people, including at least sixty women. They opened fire on the crowd in several cities. A dozen journalists were arrested, including the journalist Niloofar Hamidi and on September 28, Elaheh Mohammadi. Both had covered the story of Mahsa Amini. The poet Mona Boroui was also arrested for publishing a poem on her death. The two journalists were awarded in May 2023 the UNESCO's World Press Freedom Prize, while in prison.

On September 26, the death toll rose to nearly seventy-six people according to the NGO Iran Human Rights Watch. At the same time, protests continued in thirty of the country's thirty-one provinces, and the movement spread to several universities.

On September 27, clashes between the security forces and demonstrators continued in several cities.

On September 29, footballer Hossein Mahini, a former member of the national team, was arrested for posting the hashtag Mahsa Amini on his Twitter account. Several players, in solidarity with the protesters, wore a black hoodie during the national anthem at their match against Senegal, played behind closed doors in Austria on September 27.

On September 30, a new wave of arrests was unleashed by the government. In the city of Zahedan, the military fired on residents before the end of the Friday collective prayer, killing several people. The Iranian singer Shervin Hajipour, who had posted on Instagram the song *"Baraye"* (For) that went viral with more than 40 million hits in a few days, was arrested on October 2, then released on bail on October 4.

The protests continued on Saturday, October 1.

The count of the protesters killed in Iran, carried out by the association Iran Human Rights Watch, reached at least ninety-two people between September 16 and October 2, 2022, while the government forces violently confronted the students at Sharif University in Tehran.[4] Many other universities took part in the movement. More than twenty-five reporters and journalists were arrested in the first two weeks of the protest, according to Iran Human Rights Watch.

The Supreme Leader Ayatollah Khamenei spoke on October 3 and claimed that the movement was being masterminded by the United States and Israel to destabilize Iran, assisted by Iranian traitors abroad.

On October 4, in Mashhad, students chanted the slogan "A referendum [on the current regime] is what we want."

The next day, October 5, Iranian security forces moved into universities in several cities, intensifying their efforts to suppress more than two weeks of demonstrations. From the universities the movement spread to high schools, and videos shared on social networks showed high school girls in Tehran removing their headscarves and chanting "Death to Khamenei."

On October 9, a strike among staff was launched in the large petrochemical complex of Asalouyeh in southern Iran, as well as in other cities. In Rasht in the north of Iran, Lakan prison was set on fire. During this incident, ten prisoners were shot dead.

In the north of Tehran, during the night of October 15–16, part of Evin prison was also set on fire. The previous day, slogans against the Supreme Leader Khamenei had been chanted by prisoners. During the night of October 15, tear gas was shot at the prisoners by the special forces.

On October 16, 2022, Elnaz Rekabi, an Iranian climber, took part in the Asian championships without wearing the veil and finished in fourth place. Two days later, on October 18, under heavy pressure from the security services, she posted a message on her Instagram account stating that her "headscarf had inadvertently fallen off." However, she was under house arrest and on December 2, the authorities proceeded to demolish the house where she resided with her family.[5] Her brother, another national champion, was fined and the entire family was threatened by the authorities.

The protests entered their third month, with a death toll approaching five hundred, including about fifty minors. Alongside the demonstrations in which the crowds shouted slogans against the Regime, there were other silent demonstrations, such as in Tehran and Isfahan on December 19, 2022.[6] They were repressed. But the crackdown could not stop the demonstrations that took place in 160 cities in 544 rallies as of December 8, 2022.[7]

Under massive repression (19,400 arrests, often followed by torture, and 522 deaths up to January 14, 2023[8]), the movement began to show signs of weakening and by March, apart from the two provinces of Kurdistan and Baluchistan, the demonstrations had stopped. Occasional protests over the fortieth day of the death of some demonstrators or on International Women's Day (March 8) occurred but were not sustained. Young women refused to wear the veil on the street, tags appeared on the walls during the night, and the symbolic acts of Iranian celebrities in Iran and internationally continued to denounce the Islamic Regime.

The movement failed politically and did not succeed in overthrowing the Islamic Regime. But it succeeded culturally, revealing the Regime's deep crisis and its illegitimacy. Women continued to challenge it by not wearing the veil.

The peculiar features of the Mahsa Movement

The Islamic Regime, by following the theocratic version of Shi'ism, imposes ways of life that are totally out of step with the mores of the youth, eager to live a secular life. Religion is used by the Islamic Regime to deny not only political, but also existential freedom to the citizen. In the Mahsa Movement young people demanded not just political freedom, but also the freedom to lead a "joyful" life in opposition to the Regime's ideology of grief and bereavement. Any autonomous manifestation of joyful life is at variance with its morose worldview and is condemned as heretical.

The Mahsa Movement as a feminist movement

The feminist dimension of the Mahsa Movement is undeniable: the refusal to wear the imposed veil, and the demonstrations in the streets where the young women stayed out for long periods and exposed their uninhibited bodies in opposition to the customary Islamic traditions, which take a dim view of women's presence in the public space and prefer them to pass through quickly so as not to expose themselves to the male gaze. Young women stayed in the street by protesting and occupying the center stage. Young men joined them. There was an alliance of bodies and hearts against the predatory state. Young people, male and female, shared the same concern for freedom: bodily and political freedom were mixed within the "joie de vivre," and the exhibition of it on the streets, to the great annoyance of the Theocratic State, was an essential feature of the Mahsa Movement. But the unanimity against the Islamic Republic and its repression obscured the feminism of young women. They muted their demands against male domination out of a desire to unite with men against the killjoy regime.

As long as the theocracy remains, feminist demands will be expressed in consensus with men who share an ideal of freedom with them. One day, when the dictatorial regime is gone, feminist demands based on reclaiming women's dignity in distinction to men and in confrontation with them, will surface. There are male prejudices against women that are not limited to those of the Theocratic Regime but exist beyond it. For the time being, many of the feminist demands are being muted by women, to fight against the oppressive Islamic Regime, in close collaboration with men. Women have prioritized unity with men over their feminist demands to gain effectiveness in the fight against the Islamic theocracy. But there is nevertheless a consensus between young men and women on the need to restore women's fundamental rights, even if the consensus on this point does not erase all male prejudices against women's equality.

Another aspect of the Mahsa Movement is a sense of sacrifice that animates young women, who do not hesitate to defy a repressive state by putting their lives at grave risk for freedom, bodily and political. They lend meaning to a new brand of feminism in the Muslim world; they constitute a milestone in the liberation of women, but also of men, in this part of the world. Their example will be a landmark in other Muslim countries and beyond.

The new subjectivity: joy as a promoter of social protest

In most social protest movements joyfulness is a common feature. Fire crackers, dancing, singing, and more generally a festive atmosphere ridicule the rulers, targeting those responsible for social domination. However, not all social movements are joyful. The 1979 Revolution, apart from the final joy at the imperial regime's overthrow, was rather sorrowful. The martyrdom that was at the core of the Islamic Revolution did not leave much room for joy, which was viewed with suspicion by the demonstrators as an arrogant, Westernized attitude. The revolutionary feelings were impregnated with sacrifice and anti-secular emotions. In its revolutionary version, Shi'ism was used to denounce the Shah's Westernized secularism. Revolutionary grief was adorned with the virtues of questioning a selfish joy, the one that Ali Shariati denounced by promoting revolutionary death through the slogan: "Die or put [the other] to death" (*bemir ya bemiran*).[9]

The sad view of the revolutionary Self at the dawn of the 1979 Islamic Revolution is the opposite to the Mahsa Movement's in which earthly joy is blessed and the Islamic Regime's ideology is denounced as morbid and macabre. The major change is the new generation's culture and worldview, diametrically opposed to the Islamic Regime's. They no longer accept the Regime's global fiasco, unable to ensure a decent life for the people within a convivial society.

Indeed, the Mahsa Movement is the very antithesis to the Islamic Revolution in their appreciation of a happy life and individual freedom. It is marked by a contentious, secular joyfulness. It is not the simple joy of rejoicing or ridiculing the authorities, but the festive joy of protest that goes far beyond the mocking of the government and targets the ideology of the Islamic Regime based on the mourning for the martyrs and the stern ideology of the powerholders towards earthly life. For the younger generations, daily life under the Islamic Republic means exclusion of joy and a morose atmosphere of gloom, an enemy of life. Joy becomes the vector of secular liberation from the yoke of a theocratic religion, at the service of a predatory state.

The subjectivity within the Mahsa Movement is many-sided and among researchers, Nayereh Tohidi[10] sees as its main feature an attempt at achieving a dignified normal life against the Islamic Regime; for Asef Bayat, it expresses itself in a movement to give meaning to a free and dignified existence, in direct opposition to the Islamic State,[11] against which the new generations bear a feeling of "internal colonization"; for Kamran Talattof,[12] the sexual dimension and the profound changes in Iranian popular culture are highlighted by a "paradigm shift" in Iranian society, directed against the Islamic Regime.

The demand for "joie de vivre" is most visible among the women, as they are the ones most affected by repression, according to the traditional view of them as the vectors of temptation and promoters of vice. The Islamic Regime, in its quest for symbolic legitimacy, has used these religious and social prejudices, reinforcing them through its repressive forces such as the Vice Squad. The more the Regime fails in the real world, with its economy adrift and society on the brink of impoverishment, the more it falls back on the symbolic realm, trying to polarize men against women, notably by reinforcing their machismo, which it exploits to redeem its legitimacy. Failing to achieve economic prosperity and political freedom, Islamic theocracy champions the preservation of patriarchy against women, who become its sacrificial victims.

Through the Mahsa Movement, men and women alike refused to play the perverse game of "Islamic honor" brandished by the Regime, making patriarchy the principle of its political legitimacy. They considered it profoundly illegitimate due to its multiple failures, whether in the economic sphere (the impoverishment of the majority), the political sphere (a dictatorship that has turned into a totalitarianism), the cultural sphere (an ideology of martyrdom that stands in stark contrast to young people's desire for a joyful life), or the international sphere (the Islamic Regime's antagonism towards the Western world is rejected by the vast majority).

By brandishing joy defiantly, the Mahsa Movement has challenged the patriarchal bargain between the Islamic State and men that has endured for four decades. The shared joy between men and women has become the major human component in the revolt against the grim rule of the Iranian theocracy. During the demonstrations, alongside expressions of anger, secular joy became the mortal enemy of the Islamic Republic. Numerous manifestations of joy could be witnessed among young women in their jubilantly burning their veils and dancing around them. They danced unveiled, sometimes accompanied by men (even in the so-called traditionalist province of Baluchistan, for instance in the town of Minab), in public, in blatant opposition to the Islamic Regime.[13] Men and women also displayed their joy in their ironic tags and caricatures, both on the web and clandestinely graffitied in the streets, ridiculing the haggard and woeful ideology of the Islamic Republic and its dreary rituals of mourning – a cloak for despotism.

This shared joy is testimony to the agreement forged between men and women against the Theocratic State in a rediscovered harmony by contesting the "patriarchal bargain" imposed by the latter for more than four decades. The joy is, of course, the joy of living without religious restrictions, rejoicing in the reclaimed freedom of the body, a feeling experienced by each of the individuals taking part in the collective demonstrations. But it is also the joy of the reciprocal understanding between men and women on this issue, an intersubjectivity finally harmonious that makes them rejoice in a provocative and transgressive relationship against the Theocratic State. This joy assumes a plurality of social and anthropological meanings and is irreducible to a simple fact of individual euphoria. It manifests itself in particular in the dancing of women and men, alone or together, where the body expresses its exultation in the eyes of a public encompassing the whole of society and even the whole world via the internet. It has been seen in Iran on many occasions, before, during, and after the Mahsa Movement. The individual jubilant dimension, the intersubjectivity in unison between men and women, and the transgressive and provocative stance towards the killjoy state are omnipresent in these dances, where the gesticulations of the body speak louder than a thousand words.

In the Mahsa Movement, there are also two other dimensions to this joy: it is conjugated in the future; it is the collective hope of seeing the end of the Theocratic State, which has brought about the impoverishment of society and the decline of the country. The joy is also mixed with anger: by shouting "Down with the dictator" the demonstrators emphasized their hope of the end of the dictatorship by a jubilant act mixed with outrage, denouncing and disparaging it in the eyes of the entire world.

Dancing, singing, and the joyful body

One of the recurrent manifestations in the Mahsa Movement is the dancing of unveiled women, sometimes with men, to the rhythm of modern music (Western or Iranian) in public. They express the freedom of their body to participate in the modern world, and show their transgression towards the Theocratic State, manifesting their global rupture with the government: they do not only denounce it, but they also stage their emancipation in a creative manner, in moving their body in opposition to the constraints of the Islamic State. By dancing with men, they also contest, in consonance with them, Islamic gender segregation.

Dancing reveals the "joie de vivre" of the young people, moving their bodies to the sound of both traditional and modern music. A case in point was a park in Tehran,[14] where young men and women were dancing to the music of a traditional Iranian wind instrument, each taking a video of the other and posting it on the web. It is often in the spontaneity of the moment, as gatherings must be ad hoc to catch the Regime's repressive forces unawares. Often, before the police arrive, the crowd disperses. The forbidden event goes unpunished, revealing the powerlessness of the prohibiting state to impose its diktats in the face of people's spontaneous and unpredictable festive mindset.

Dancing, and more generally expressing the joy of living are in line with the history of Iranian secularization over the past century. The Islamic constraints that force the female body to hide from the gaze of others through the veil and the segregation of men and women are experienced by the Iranian youth as contrary to their worldview. Secularization has rendered the segregation that was taken for granted in traditional Islamic society (at least in urban areas) no longer self-evident and is experienced as unnatural and artificial, especially among the new generations, imbued with a cosmopolitan culture through the internet.

Dancing in public is more than infringement of the Islamic laws; it is also the revelation of the new bodily freedom, of its emancipation from the rigid religious codes that force it to renounce its spontaneity and submit to the hegemony of the Theocratic State. The latter coerces the individual not only on the political level (as the Syrian, Egyptian, or Algerian regimes do), but also on the existential level, specific to theocratic Iran and the Taliban's Afghanistan.

Singing is also a bodily expression, banned by the Islamic Regime for women whose voice could incite the sexual desire of men. The protest dimension of women's songs is, above all, the self-affirmation of a new individual whose body refuses to bow to theocratic Shi'ism's prohibition of their voices in public, showing their creativity and their art as well as their unveiled body. Singing is sometimes accompanied by collective dancing, whereby the voice and the body's movement are in unison to deny the authorities their ability to repress the body's freedom. Emancipation goes beyond protest insofar as it expresses the initiative of an individual to affirm her existence as a free being, leading her own life and showing herself in direct opposition to any religious commandment that would thwart her will to assert herself.

Dancing has a political meaning in Islamic Iran: it is in contradiction to the policy of the Islamic Regime, which forbids any "lascivious" movement of the body and makes it an offense, subject to harsh legal punishment. Dancing is not only about denouncing the government's repressive policy towards women's bodies, not only about performing an act of transgression by removing the veil, but also about expressing an active spontaneity, revealing one's deep nature – in short, showing, beyond the acts of denunciation, what a free woman is in her secular "joie de vivre." At the same time, she would like to be recognized not only in Iran, but by the whole world for her action and her jovial spirit in removal of the veil, by publishing it on the web. They call on a global civil society to be witness to their emancipation and to condemn the repressive action of the Islamic government which will be prompt to punish them for their iconoclastic act in public which flouts religious prohibitions. The female body that removes the veil and the male body that mingles with women and who dance and sing become the mirrors of citizenship: the public refusal to submit to the standards of the Islamic State in the name of the inalienable rights of citizens, while proposing an alternative to its norms of behavior.

Existential freedom is expressed through its festive character (I take off the veil and I dance, I smile, I sing, and I expose myself), which contrasts with the killjoy view of the Islamic theocracy that proclaims it is illicit (*haram*) for a woman to show her uncovered hair, to dance or sing. This is combined with the denunciation of the dictatorship (the slogan "Death to the dictator") and the demand for a secular and democratic political regime. The existential and social dimension of freedom are articulated in two transgressive actions: removing the veil by women, joining the unveiled women by men.

With the Mahsa Movement, dancing has taken on a political meaning that goes far beyond the one it had before, repressed by the Islamic Regime, but viewed as a relatively minor transgression.

From now on, the veil takes on a subversive political meaning, insofar as many young women refuse to submit to it, even after the end of the collective protest movement in February 2023. The single acts of resistance by women transform the meaning of their unveiling into an explicit contestation of the Regime's omnipotence on the streets at an individual level. The authorities thought they had recovered the public space by putting an end to the demonstrations. The scattered resistance of women reminds them of their refusal to submit.

They believe that they can overcome women's resistance by repression. Legal punishments have therefore become more severe and can extend to several years' imprisonment, as in the following case. A young woman, Astiaj Haqiqi, danced unveiled with her husband Amir Mohammad Ahmadi in Azadi Square in Tehran at the end of October 2022. They filmed their dance and put it on the web. On November 1, 2022, security forces arrested them ruthlessly at their home in Tehran. They were sentenced each to ten and a half years' imprisonment and flogging, for "promotion of impurity and indecency, assembly and collusion against national security, and propaganda against the Regime." They have also been banned from social activities on the internet and leaving the country for two years. They were denied access to a lawyer during the legal proceedings. The Islamic Regime manipulated the facts and falsely claimed that the sentences were reduced to five years' imprisonment each.[15] Other sources confirm the ten-year sentence for each of them.[16]

This young couple knew full well that they risked heavy sentences not only for dancing in Azadi Square but also for publishing it on the web, to communicate their "joie de vivre" to the world. In this new culture there is a transgressive dimension in relation to the killjoy Islamic laws. The young couple wanted to exhibit their way of life, in defiance of the Islamic government. The degrading and repressive treatment they were subjected to after their arrest testifies to the lack of understanding of the authorities towards the youth and the new civil society in Iran. They believe only in outright repression to subdue the youth: the couple were harshly beaten, forced to undress in front of their torturers, and to suffer the insults of the clerical judge at the hearing as well as the inhuman sentence of more than ten years' imprisonment.[17]

Another notable case is a video of five young girls, not wearing veils, released on the web on March 8, 2023, on International Women's Day. They danced to the tune of Rema and Szelena Gomez's "Calm Down," in front of Block 13 of the Ekbatan residential district in Tehran, one of the centers of anti-government protests since the beginning of the Mahsa Movement. The release of their dance video on social networks was enthusiastically welcomed in Iran and was shared and viewed thousands of times.

The next day security forces were looking for CCTV footage of Block 13 in Ekbatan to identify the girls. They checked the cameras and questioned the caretakers of the building.[18] The girls were arrested and had to make a public confession by veiling themselves and apologizing on video to escape the punishment of the Theocratic State.

The body that aims to live the "joie de vivre" also has an urgent need to bring the genders together. It seeks other bodies, those of other women and men, to mingle publicly and to end the segregation that has lasted for more than four decades and seems even more intolerable since the Mahsa Movement. The unveiled female body and the male body in communion inevitably come into conflict with the Theocratic Regime. Their act entails the demand for political freedom as well, its direct consequence: freedom to associate, men and women, to come together by rejecting the religious constraints. In short, bodily and political freedom are closely intertwined in the Mahsa Movement.

This feature distinguishes it from the 2009 Green Movement in which only political freedom was targeted, or from the protests of 2016–19 in which economic demands were paramount. In the Mahsa Movement, the demand for gender and political freedom go hand in hand. The daily life of the individual with their simple joys is associated with their aspiration to political freedom. In this respect, young people, male and female, shared the same desire: to live freely, side by side, without being constrained by repressive norms based on theocratic Islam, and to be free to choose a secular regime that suits them. Secularization has made obsolete the enforcement of sacred norms by a theocracy that claims to represent God and, in fact, tramples the dignity of its secular citizens.

The conjunction between the demands of women and men does not stop there. The minimalist demands of women to which men subscribe are in perfect convergence with men as long as the repressive government lasts. In the case it is overthrown, women will be able to express their feminist demands in a freer political environment. But before that, women are content with a demand for civic freedom that does not conflict with men.

Prior to the Mahsa Movement, women and men often sought to live the "joie de vivre" despite the risks involved, namely financial (heavy fines) but also sometimes prison and physical punishment (flogging), or humiliation by brutal agents. The mental escape of society from the clutches of a killjoy state has never been risk-free since 1979. People often pay a heavy price for rejecting Islamic strictures that forbid promiscuity between men and women and manifestations of their collective joy, especially in dancing and consuming alcohol.

A common example is the arrest of men and women seeking freedom to dance in a party atmosphere, which can be clearly seen in the following case, reported by the media:

> According to Harana news agency, citing [the news site] Tabnak, Mohammad Sadegh Akbari, the head of justice of Mazandaran province [northern Iran] announced in June 2022 the arrest by the security police of 120 tourists in Pirajah forest in the capital city of Neka. Mixed dancing and the removal of the veil by women [*kashfe hedjab*] are among the charges [levelled against them]. According to him, the members of this tour were arrested by the security police for putting up banners of Satanism and [committing] criminal acts such as drinking alcohol, illicit relations between men and women, mixed dancing, removal of the hijab, and other acts contrary to the sharia and the law. A lawsuit has been filed in this regard.[19]

"Illicit relations" often boil down to talking or holding hands or dancing or drinking together, in short, what seem innocuous basic rights in most countries around the world. As far as "Satanism" is concerned, it is often a way of conferring pretext to unfounded accusations of deviance and only serves to justify the undue sentences meted out to the defendants.

The second phase of the Mahsa Movement

After the repression of the movement by government forces by March 2023, the essential dimension of the protest, namely collective street demonstrations, had disappeared in most Iranian provinces except Sistan and Baluchistan and Kurdistan, which had been the scene of the most sustained and deadly demonstrations during the Mahsa Movement. But in these two ethnic provinces too, from April 2023 onwards, collective protests were crushed by government forces. The only thing that remained was the veil, which young women refused to put back on in the street. The collective protest movement turned into a refusal to wear the veil by individual young women. The demonstrations that aimed to overthrow the Islamic State gave way to the individual stance of young women who would not yield to the intimidation of the female agents of the Islamic State to put the veil back on. Until then, there had been no antagonism between veiled women and those who removed the veil. What unified them in the demonstrations was the rejection of the predatory state and the will to put an end to its illegitimate hegemony over society.

The Islamic State has employed strictly veiled female agents to confront young veil-less youth to caution them, often aggressively, regarding their lack of hijab. But often the young women are not intimidated, and this leads to aggressive behavior on both sides and one woman died in the town of Mahan in the southern province of Kerman;[20] and other cases have been reported where, for example, women have been slapped by veiled women in the service of the Islamic Regime.

Another way of subduing the unveiled women has been to film them on the street and to close down stores, restaurants, banks, or other places they enter. This is called "plumbing" (*polomb kardan*) and restaurants and stores belonging to people who supported the Mahsa Movement have been made to cease business by the police, particularly those belonging to influential people. The fight against unveiled women launched by the Regime continues in this way, without their accepting the forced re-veiling.

The Mahsa Movement has had a major consequence: the loss of fear on the part of many young women who find themselves in the grip of the Islamic Regime and lead the struggle against it in the absence of collective demonstration, at the individual level. Often taken to task by the veiled female agents in the service of the Islamic State, they refuse to comply and passers-by often side with the non-veiled women, resulting in tension, and the failure of the Regime's agents to impose veiling on the resistant young women.

Some women now ride motorcycles, a new provocation against the Regime, and again, an expression of their bodily freedom.[21] Before the Mahsa Movement, they used to dress as men to avoid arousing suspicion, but now, unveiled, they wear women's clothing to express their new-found but threatened freedom.

The Mahsa Movement began collectively. Now women are acting individually. They are exposed to the abuses of the Regime's militias, but given their sheer numbers, the Islamic State has to mobilize its security forces to fight them, which stretches its resources.

Women as pioneering social activists

Feminist intellectuals in Iran: a major cultural movement

Two types of intellectuals have marked Iran since the Islamic Revolution. The first are the so-called reformist intellectuals (*eslah-talaban*) who challenged the legitimacy of the Shi'ite theocracy (*Velayat faqih*) within Islamic thought and proposed a pluralist conception of Islam. Their position originated in the dissociation between Islam and politics in the name of Islamic tenets. According to their view, genuine Islam would leave the political arena to civil society and would confine the faith to the spiritual world of the believers. Their influence heightened in the 1980s–1990s but since then, has progressively waned. In the twenty-first century, Islam has been questioned as a political framework by the new generations, who no longer raise the question of freedom within Islam but in a secular cultural context, outside the religious realm. It should be noted that Iranian secular intellectuals have silently developed, during the last decades, a non-religious conception of social and political life.

As for the feminist intellectuals, they first raised gender issues, insisting on their compatibility with Islam. They have been women who live in Iran or are part of the Iranian diaspora, especially in Europe, the USA, and Canada. Certainly, those who have lived in Iran for a long time have exerted a more direct influence insofar as they have expressed themselves in Persian within society. But those who lived in the West and often expressed themselves in English (more rarely in French or German) also influenced Iranian feminists, notably through translations and sometimes through direct work on Iran in association with Iranian women, as we shall see.

That the Mahsa Movement is the culmination of an increasingly acute feminist consciousness in Iran, especially since the establishment of the Islamic Republic in 1979, which instituted the legal inferiority of women in relation to men, is self-evident.

We can cite the rather timid beginnings of *Zanan* magazine under the direction of Shahla Sherkat; then the active participation of Iranian feminists such as Mahnaz Afkhami, and Islamic feminists like Faezeh Hashemi and Zahra Rahnavard among others in the reformist movement that elected Khatami as President of the Republic in 1997; then in 2006 the limited Campaign for One Million Signatures movement, which was in the end only able to gather a very limited number of signatures (probably around 10,000); and the participation of Iranian feminist intellectuals from the diaspora such as Nayereh Tohidi, Ziba Mir Hosseini, Valentine Moghadam, Farzaneh Milani, Shadi Mokhtari, Neda Nazmi, Arzoo Osanloo, Marie Ladier-Fouladi, Azadeh Kian, and Fariba Adelkhah, as well as feminist journalists like Masih Alinejad; their intellectual influence and critical contribution is unquestionable. But the Mahsa Movement is also at odds with some fundamental trends of Iranian intellectual feminism mainly within Iran, and that is its relationship to the body through the rejection of the veil and the self-affirmation of young men and women in the simple joy of living, on the one hand, and the radical rejection of the Islamic Regime, on the other. The Mahsa Movement was launched by young women and men who were first and foremost driven by the desire to live their lives in physical *and then*, political freedom, and by the quest for a non-religious, secularized vision of existence, in direct opposition to theocratic Islam and its stifling vision of life. Previous movements in Iran had not made an anthropological and ontological break with the Islamic Regime, nor did they dare to question its body-related puritanism head-on.

Another characteristic of the Mahsa Movement is that most of the movement's protagonists are young (in their twenties), sometimes teenagers, young girls and boys with a new culture, far removed from that of Iranian feminists who had a "tempered" attitude towards Shi'ite Islam and a neutral relationship to the body. In other words, the Mahsa Movement has certainly been influenced by the feminism of its mothers and grandmothers, but it is also at odds with it in fundamental respects, namely the existential relationship to the body and its joy of living, and to politics as an extension of bodily freedom rather than an abstract, exclusively legal vision of gender equality. In this new relationship, no compromise with the Islamic Regime was possible, and the latter no longer had any legitimacy, always on the basis of an existential experience of everyday life marked, as we shall see, by hypocrisy and even a schizoid personality.

It is a complete turnaround from a limited movement like the 2006 Campaign for One Million Signatures, which began with a demand for legal gender equality within the framework of democratic Islam. The Mahsa Movement starts at the bottom, i.e., women's bodies, and extends upwards, i.e., political freedom. Likewise, unlike the former Campaign's Islamic referent, the Mahsa Movement is part of a secular framework that banishes religion from the public sphere in the name of a culture of "joie de vivre," without reference to any conception of the transcendent or sacred. The difference is immeasurable: we are dealing with a radically different subjectivity, a generation that claims to be part of a secularized culture that leaves no room for compromise with the mortifying ideology of theocratic Islam. In these respects, the new generation is at odds with the old, and in particular with the dominant currents of feminism in Iran, established by the generation of mothers and grandmothers, as the brief biographies of these women in this book will reveal. In particular, the difference is perceptible in a new human existential joy, absent among the feminist intellectuals of the last two generations in Iran.

Since the early 2000s, young people's thinking has been detached from religion and has evolved in a secular intellectual context. More generally, since the Green Movement of 2009, Iranian society has been moving in the direction of secularization, not within Islam, but independently of it, in terms of secular modernity. There is thus a twofold process of secularization among intellectuals, which was expressed by religious reformist intellectuals within Islam until the beginning of the twenty-first century, and then progressively by artists and new thinkers, outside the religious realm, within a secular conception of society. This one ignores religion, does not speak about it; it certainly does not reject Islam, but marginalizes it by posing the question of politics in purely secular terms. Since the failure of the 2009 Green Movement to implement political reform within the Islamic Republic, social movements reflect this change of perspective: religious slogans have been extremely rare since that time and social issues have been expressed in a purely secular fashion.

Besides the religious reformists, the second type of intellectuals who have played a major role in Iranian cultural life after the 1979 Revolution are the feminists who have promoted female self-assertion by venturing massively into the field of literature, art in general (theater, cinema, painting), and professions that were previously almost entirely male such as journalism, scientific research, the law, medicine, and teaching.

Iranian female intellectuals have played a significant role in initiating an original self-awareness among women. Alongside the producers of ideas, there are also female social activists who have opened the contestation to new areas by challenging the veil, which has become the symbol of women's bodily expropriation. In doing so, they have entered in direct confrontation with the Islamic Regime. The bodily prohibitions (the veil, but also dancing, and gender fraternizing) have become the focus of the latest protest movement, the Mahsa Movement.

The body and its language as the focus of symbolic forms of protest

The bodily gestures and the modes of expression beyond words and speech are one of the distinctive features of this movement. It is, to begin with, a civil insubordination. On the part of women, it is not just a protest but rejecting violence against their body by engaging individually in the fight against the compulsory veil and then collectively with men, in protesting in the name of "women, freedom, life." The young women who removed the veil did so first and foremost alone, on the street, as early as 2018, before gathering in groups and waving their headscarves in the air in September 2022 to mark not only their rejection, but their ridicule of a constraint they repudiated. These gestures revolved, to begin with, around the veil: taking it off, twirling it in the air, sometimes setting it on fire, and other times tying it to the end of a pole to defy the illegitimate authority that imposed it. Hair too is a symbol of insubordination: not only is the veil removed, but hair is ostentatiously exhibited or chopped off and set alight to express a happiness in defiance of the authorities. Transgression and "joie de vivre" in cutting off one's hair go hand in hand. The "joie de vivre" collides with the culture of the Islamic Regime, which is experienced as not only mournful, but also a killjoy, artificially sacrificial (the disembodied cult of martyrdom). The "culture of joie de vivre" manifests itself in total dissonance with the "culture of death." The new generation, who above all want to live and express their joy with their peers, are challenging the Islamic State not only in its policies, but more fundamentally, in its ideology.

Women cutting their hair is another act of defiance and by extension, in a metaphorical way, some men have imitated this, such as the Iranian beach soccer player Said Piramoon, who mimicked the act of cutting his hair at the end of the regional competition in Dubai on November 6, 2022. Cutting one's hair was later staged by Iranian women in the diaspora and many female celebrities in the West in support of Iranian women.

Teenage girls played an important role in writing slogans against the Regime in the street. The practice of covering walls at night with graffiti that mocked theocratic rule became routine in the neighborhoods of many cities during those months.

The slogans chanted in demonstrations were another way of expressing rejection of the illegitimate rule embodied by the clerical Regime. There are also songs written, of which *"Baraye"* (For) has been the most eloquent symbol of protest; but also and in Lor (the idiom of Iranian Lorestan), the poignant song "Mother, Mother, it's Time for War" (*dayé, dayé, vaqte djangué*) sung decades ago by Reza Saqaï during regional demonstrations; or the Italian revolutionary song *"Bella ciao,"* sung in Persian on the web by an Iranian woman who, among other things, denounced the anti-Western bias of the Regime. It went viral.

The slogans of the Mahsa Movement are generally of two kinds: those calling for the freedom of women, of the body, of life in its daily expressions (living without the compulsory veil, the right of men and women to mix, dancing, singing), and those demanding the overthrow of the dictator, the Supreme Leader. More rarely, other considerations like poverty or ethnic and regional issues have become leitmotifs.

Sometimes the slogans are "vulgar," of a sexual nature and targeting the Regime's supporters in a crude way. They are chanted when the demonstrators are in a high state of excitement, or on hearing of the execution or killing of fellow protesters. Very few of them are seen on the web, but the media affiliated to the Islamic Republic have given coverage to this type of chanting, which they do not repeat verbatim but allude to as "vulgar slogans," to call into question the decency of the protesters. For example Fars News Agency, affiliated to the IRGC, commented: "The profane slogans of the Sharif University student demonstrators are a disgrace to the dignity of this university" (*shoar haye rakik daneshjuyan daneshgah sharif lakkeye nang saahat daneshgah*).[22] For the others it is the attitude of the authorities that pushed the demonstrators towards undignified expressions: as the newspaper *Ettelaat* noted: "When young people witness the harsh and violent literature of the authorities, they break the norms."[23]

For Djamileh Kadivar, a reformist female intellectual who published an article on the subject alongside her photo duly veiled (otherwise she would not have been published), and in words carefully chosen (not to be censored):

> There is no doubt that the design of obscene slogans should be examined in context. With the decrease in the influence of religion and religious and moral values and the weakened role of religious institutions and agents and in the absence of groups that were considered the intellectual authority of the society in the past and in the wake of the increased influence of sports and artistic celebrities with their own literature among the youth and teenagers, the slogans' dominant tone during the protests of recent years, and especially in the protests of this year [Mahsa Movement], has undergone a significant change.[24]

According to the reformist intellectual Abbas Abdi, "The new Fundamentalists introduced obscene and mocking words into political literature." He stressed the fact that before 2009, slogans and political exchanges were polite and people did not use obscene words in their speeches, or demonstrators in their slogans.[25] Already in the 2016–19 movements, swear words were used by the protesters for whom politeness was no longer an option against lawless rulers who not only had impoverished them and undermined their standard of living, but also crushed their self-respect by eliminating dialogue and any intermediary political group like the Reformists.

In the Mahsa Movement words like *"aldang"* (asshole, with derogatory sexual undertones), *"hiz"* (someone inclined to debauchery, with a wanton attitude to women), *"harzeh"* (women, but also men who are sexually promiscuous or deviant), and "fuck" (an English word, directly passed into Persian) were used in the slogans against the Islamic Regime. Some of these pointed to the perverse side of a Theocratic Regime that forced women into the compulsory veil, because its supporters were themselves debauched and bestial. Thus, in the town of Chahriar, on the outskirts of Tehran, in response to the Supreme Leader's comments that they were perverts, young high school girls chanted: "You are the pervert, you are the debauchee, I am a free woman" (*hiz to'ee, harzeh to'ee, zané azadeh manam*).

Contrary to the language that might be expected of well-bred young girls, they collectively raised their arms and pointed the middle finger in the air in the "fuck you" sign, borrowing the American gesture, which they chanted in a rhyming slogan: "It's you less than nothing, it's you worthy of this fuck!" (*khas o khachak to'ee, layeghe in fuck to'ee*).

The slogans denounced the state for being anti-woman: "An anti-woman state, we don't want it, we don't want it!" (*hokumate zedde zan, nemikhaym, nemikhaym*).

They referred to Mahsa Amini (whose death had initiated the protests) as a collective: "We are all Mahsa, you make war on us, we make war on you!" (*ma hamé mahsa hastim, bejang ta bejanguim*).

The repudiation of the Theocratic State by a secularized youth was chanted by the crowd: "The Islamic Republic, we don't want it, we don't want it" (*jomhuriye eslamee, nemikhaym, nemikhaym*).

Similarly, the compulsory veil was rejected as a sign of female servitude: "We don't want the veil imposed on us, we don't want it!" (*hejab zoor zoorakee nemikhaym, nemikhaym*).

The Supreme Leader has been blamed for the executions both in the streets and in prisons: "Khamenei is a murderer, his religious legitimacy is null and void" (*khamenei qatelle, velayatesh batele*). They were not afraid to name him directly on pain of heavy penalties, even death: "Our shame, our shame, our asshole leader!" (*nange ma, nange ma, rahbare aldange ma*).

In passing, the illegitimate power of Khamenei, who claims to be like Hossein (the third Imam) and who is in reality his antithesis, Yazid (the Omayyad caliph who ordered the killing of Hossein and represents in Shi'ism the epitome of evil), was emphasized: "Khamenei has become Yazid, Yazid is innocent in comparison to him" (*Khamenei yazid shodeh, yazid ru sefid shodeh*).

The Supreme Leader's illegitimacy as a cleric is extended to the clergy as a whole, accomplices of a bloodthirsty government: "As long as the mullah is not wrapped in a shroud, this country will not be a real country!" (*ta akhund kafan nashavad, in vatan vatan nashavad*). Or again: "We want neither sheikh nor mullah, damn the ayatollah!" (*na sheikh mikhaym na molla, la'nat be ayatollah*).

The false martyrdom and hypocritical reference to the third Shi'i Imam Hossein (the paragon of martyrdom) by the Islamic Regime is also denounced: "Hossein, Hossein is your slogan, killing the people, your vocation" (*Hossein, Hossein sho'aretun, koshtane melat karetun*).

A revolutionary spirit swept through the youth: "This is no longer a protest, this is the beginning of a revolution!" (*ine digeh e'teraz nist, shoru'e enghelabeh*).

The denunciation of the crimes committed by the Islamic Regime was also the target of the chants: "All these years of crimes, damn this Islamic Rule!" (*ine hameh sal jenayat, nang bar in velayat*).

The forces of repression were denounced in the demonstrations. One example is Basij, against which the demonstrators chanted: "O you dishonorable Basiji [member of Basij], you are our Daesh" (*Basijiy-e bi gheyrat, Daesh-e ma choma'ee*). (Daesh is the Islamic State of Syria and Iraq, established between 2014 and 2019, representing the model of absolute repression in the eyes of young Iranians.) Or: "Oh you member of the Basij, Oh you member of the Revolutionary Guard, you are our Daesh" (*Basiji, sepahi, daeshe ma choma'ee*).

In reference to the venality of Basij members: "Oh you Basiji mercenary, fill your belly [with the bounties of the Regime], it is well the end [of the Regime]!" (*Basiji-e jireh khor, akharesheh khub bokhor*).

The demonstrators chanted against the police: "Our shame, our shame, our police assholes!" (*nange ma, nange ma, policé aldange ma*).

Many Iranian celebrities have transgressed the repressive norms in force in Iran and given their support to the Mahsa Movement. This was the case of several Iranian film actresses and TV presenters who exhibited their unveiled face on social networks. Many were arrested and 150 fell victim to the judicial system (condemned to harsh prison terms or physically abused) up to early December 2022.[26]

Symbolic acts included changing street names: on October 25, 2022 in Mashhad, protesters changed the name of Hijab Boulevard to Mahsa Amini Boulevard.[27]

Similarly, students in many universities signified their rejection of gender segregation in university restaurants by eating lunch together outside the premises.

As protesters chanted "Death to the dictator," "Down with the Regime," cars began to honk their horns insistently in solidarity. Security forces shot and killed drivers at the wheel. Sometimes the bullet ricocheted and killed children (such as ten-year-old Kian Pirfalak, killed on November 16, 2022, in Izeh in northeastern Khuzestan). To intimidate the protesters, the police and its mounted brigade appeared in the east of Tehran, Falake Sadeghieh, on November 7, 2022, and rushed at them. Firing tear gas and stun grenades to shock the demonstrators, and firing rubber or live bullets or using a taser became increasingly common.

On April 16, 2023, students in Tehran, in at least two social science faculties in Allameh and Tehran universities, protested against the mandatory veil, and chanted slogans such as "Forward to life, femininity, bodiness [corporeity]" (*pish beh suye zendegi, zananegi, tananegi*).[28] They innovatively coined the neologism "*tananegi*," which means corporeity.

Despite Iran's abysmal economic situation, economic slogans were rare in the Mahsa Movement. Political slogans ("Down with the dictator") or existential ones ("Woman, life, freedom") prevailed. However, slogans such as "Poverty, corruption, high prices. We are going to overthrow [the Regime]" (*faqr, fesad, geruni, mirim ta sarneguni*) were heard in the city of Najaf-Abad in the province of Isfahan, for example.[29] From the protesters' viewpoint, the economic issues could only be solved by overthrowing the Theocratic Regime.

The symbolic innovations of the Mahsa Movement

The movement, which ran from September 2022 to February 2023 and continues with the refusal of young women to wear the veil at the time of writing these lines (June 2023), has made major innovations in the landscape of social movements in Iran and even in the Muslim world.

To begin with, women were in the vanguard of the movement, and they participated en masse as women and citizens and not as wives, sisters, daughters, or mothers as is often the case in the Muslim world. The massive nature of women's mobilization in the name of bodily and political freedom is one of the distinctive features of this movement (they were not a limited number of female intellectuals). It was launched by women and joined by men, who set aside their supposed Islamic pride (*gheyrat*) with regard to gender to fight against the Theocratic State. Later, assuming a democratic regime would be established, then women would explicitly formulate their feminist demands.

But the movement staged the liberation of women's bodies

by rejecting the compulsory veil and that of men by mingling with women in demonstrations. It was a movement that took note of secularization, women publicly taking off their veils and men joining them in demonstrations, dancing, partying, and denouncing the puritanical ideology of the regime.

This movement has given rise to a neo-ethnicity in which men and women of ethnic origin (particularly Kurds and Baluchis) have set aside their long-held dissent towards Iranian society, and demonstrated together with the majority of Persians to denounce the dictatorial nature of the Regime. Like the women, they would hold back on their demands until the fall of the Theocratic State. But like the women too, the vast majority of them acknowledged their full citizenship and celebrated their unanimity with civil society in recognizing their Iranian sense of belonging, in response to the slogans chanted in support of their dignity (see chapter 1).

This movement set the "joie de vivre" against the Regime's ideology of martyrdom and grief. It has done so without a tyrannical Islamic superego bearing down to inflict intense feelings of guilt among the protesters, as was the case in the past (there is no longer any trace of a desire to return to original Islam or of the denunciation of "the Western disease").

In this movement, the West is no longer diabolical but perceived with a benevolent neutrality, not least in view of the relative success of the Iranian diaspora, several million strong, scattered across Western countries. Following on from the Green Movement of 2009, this movement has cemented the close link between the Iranian diaspora and domestic society in their shared desire to establish a democratic regime in Iran.

It is a movement driven by young women and men, in which the generation of fathers and mothers did not actively participate. Alongside the lack of leadership and organization (due to the Regime's repression), the non-participation of the previous generations is one of its major weaknesses.

It is a movement that is not driven by Marxist or communist

ideology, but has been carried out in the context of the impoverished middle classes and what I have called the "would-be middle class," i.e., those who have the culture and level of education of the middle classes and who are denied access to a respective standard of living. This is where politics (the overthrow of the dictatorial regime) meets economics (access of the would-be middle class to a decent standard of living).

It is a movement where the intellectuals are mainly hip-hop and rap singers, football stars, TV and movie stars, quick to denounce the Islamic Regime in their songs, social media messages, and symbolic acts (appearing unveiled), and not the traditional intellectuals, whose role has been at best marginal.

Finally, it is a movement that failed politically to overthrow the Islamic Regime but succeeded culturally in revealing its deep crisis of legitimacy within Iranian society. Women continue to engage in civil disobedience by stepping out unveiled into the public space, despite the failure of the Mahsa Movement to overthrow the Theocratic Regime.

The global civil sphere (GCS)

The Mahsa Movement refers to a global civil sphere (GCS), which is in part imaginary like any social construct but also, in part real, or to be accomplished through social action. It refers to a reality in the making. There are differences between the civil sphere as developed classically within given societies and the global civil sphere. In the GCS, the imaginary dimension is much more important than in the classical civil sphere. Whereas in the civil sphere within a given society one can name tangible, real characteristics, and the areas in which it is exercised, in the GCS the actors assume the existence of a global moral order which cannot be proven directly and which, in their imaginary, assumes a capital importance, often disproportionate to its concrete reality.

Most prominently, this civil sphere refers to a world conceived as a universal civil sphere, distinct from states. At the same time, this world is called upon to be, to exist as a witness to the social drama unfolding in Iran, whose judgment will be moral before assuming any legal potency.

Jeffrey Alexander,[30] a major thinker on the civil sphere, refers to Us versus Them in a dichotomy reminiscent of that of social movements as theorized by Alain Touraine.[31] The particular feature of the GCS is that, over and above the confrontation between the Us and Them that we find in the Mahsa Movement (and which is the opposition of the vast majority of the people to the Theocratic State), we observe a third element, an imaginary universal judge representing the universal civil sphere who is called upon to rule on the moral validity of the demonstrators' claims calling for the overthrow of the tyrannical state. This ultimate authority is not purely imaginary, of course, and is to be found in international bodies, human rights organizations, and the various institutions that award prizes to those who suffer the injustice of states that abuse citizens' rights. Relevant examples can be found among Iranian feminists, who suffer from infringements of their rights, and fight for gender equality while enduring multiple forms of mistreatment, ranging from imprisonment to various forms of psychological and sometimes physical torture. They have found recognition in global institutions where they have won numerous international prizes, which testify to the support of "moral" authorities at the international level. Similarly, another instance of the GCS, international human rights organizations, is referred to by Iranian activists. Both men and women refer to it, not only as a legal body, but as a moral one that exists but to which activists attribute a much more tangible existence than in concrete reality (the imaginary side of the GCS). Finally, the sphere of human rights becomes part of a GCS, not only through organizations and associations, but as a human link that makes possible the constitution of a global, universal, world society in reference to international institutions, to human rights organizations within the United Nations, as an ideal sphere (a "would-be civil sphere" projected onto an indeterminate future). This GCS would promote a world free from illegitimate violence. Thus, in Iran, where the number of executions per capita is the highest in the world, we see individuals and groups calling for the abolition of the death penalty in the name of a human dignity superior to the laws in force, in reference to the GCS, where there is no place for capital punishment.

This new imaginary civil sphere is the defining feature of the Mahsa Movement as much as of the Green Movement in 2009 and most probably, many social movements with a democratic content. In the Green Movement, the reclamation of the citizen's dignity in reference to "Where is my vote?" pointed to an ideal world where the rights of the citizen would be respected, regardless of nationality and gender.

In the Mahsa Movement, the emergence of women as major social actors refers not only to the demand for their equal dignity as citizens, but also to gender-free ethical values. The fact that many women lawyers defend men and children in the name of human rights marks the quest for a GCS, distinct from governments: an imaginary world where distinctions of gender, age, and ethnicity will be subordinated to the recognition of their full humanity. This imaginary GCS does not resist, *in fine*, the rigors of reality, but by the very fact of its ideal nature, it refers to a humanity less violent than that of the Iranian society.

Who are the slogans addressed to? To the rest of society that has not yet joined the protesters, but also to the reviled Regime that can no longer pretend to ignore the demonstrators, and more generally, to the global Iranian society. But beyond that, they are addressed to the GCS that includes other societies, distinct from their states, in an idealized form. Here the universal civil sphere serves as a witness within an imaginary globalized court of law. The GCS assesses the actions of the Islamic Regime (which it is bound to condemn from the viewpoint of the demonstrators) and those of the protesters (which it will approve).

The GCS is thus doubly structured: on the one hand, it is an idealized world of justice and freedom, which the protesters refer to as their ultimate goal, a moral witness to their legitimacy; on the other, it is endowed with the task of judge: it judges the Iranian government's illegitimate violence towards the protesters. The GCS is at one and the same time, Judge and Witness, which might seem contradictory. But the function of the witness is explicit, that of the judge more implicit, based on the aspiration to a better world that does not yet exist, but for which the protesters hope and pray. The very display of the demonstrations and the slogans are calling on the verdict of this GCS.

This universal civil sphere is the one that the demonstrators hope can intervene via international legal bodies such as the United Nations or international courts or even national civil spheres to condemn the inhumane actions of the Iranian government. While it is constructed by the imaginary of the demonstrators, at the same time, its creation is accelerated by their invocations all over the world (there were large-scale demonstrations in many Western cities in support of the Mahsa Movement).

The GCS's subjective existence is reinforced by the intersubjectivity of the demonstrators who project their inflamed imaginations onto each other and unite them.

The GCS is not entirely a product of the demonstrators' imaginary. As noted above, that demonstrations for the Iranian women took place in many other countries is testimony to its factual existence. Similarly, symbolic acts by celebrities and famous women (publicly cutting their hair off in support of Iranian women, for example) around the world testified to this universal civil sphere in the making.

There are several concrete examples of GCS within this movement. After the death of Mahsa Amini in custody at the Vice Squad premises, Niloofar Hamedi, a reporter for the Iranian *Sharq* newspaper, announced the death and was arrested by the Iranian security forces a few days later. Elaheh Mohammadi, a journalist at the Iranian *Ham-Mihan* newspaper, published a report on Mahsa Amini's funeral ceremony, and was arrested and jailed.

These two journalists were jointly awarded the international Freedom of the Press award by Canadian Journalists Supporting Freedom of Expression and received the Lyons award from the Nieman Journalism Foundation at Harvard University. Niloofar Hamedi and Elaheh Mohammadi also made it to *Time* magazine's list of 100 influential figures in 2023. Along with Narges Mohammadi, a famous Iranian feminist, they were announced on May 13, 2023 as the winners of the year's UNESCO International Press Freedom Award, known as "Guillermo Cano."

These prizes and distinctions have been awarded by non-governmental organizations and are regarded by the Iranian demonstrators as emanating from and recognition by the GCS, supporting them in their struggle against a predatory state. Their international renown at least partially protects them from torture and ill-treatment by the Iranian government.

The case of Nasrin Sotoudeh and the intervention of the international institutions in support of her is also worth mentioning. Her frequent hunger strikes challenge the Regime but also are a testimony to the GCS bestowing legitimacy on her act against an illegitimate state. Her hunger strikes are non-violent acts that put her fragile health at risk as a token of her dedication to the cause of women, and are considered by her and a large part of Iranian society as testimony before this imaginary GCS court to the legitimacy of the cause she is defending (equal rights for men and women) and the illegitimacy of the brutal Islamic State.

This means that not only collectively, through a social movement, but also individually, in its relationship with individuals, the GCS acts as a half-imaginary, half-real interlocutor, witness and judge at one and the same time.

Another noteworthy case is Narges Mohammadi, who has been persecuted by the Iran authorities for several years, like many other feminists. She has received numerous international awards and honors, as will be discussed later. These awards refer to the GCS, imaginary and real all at once: the transnational body that recognizes her legitimacy and the validity of her non-violent fight for a just cause, that of women, but also human rights in general.

Journalists as promoters of the global civil sphere in the Mahsa Movement

Iranian journalists are forbidden to cover stories whose consequences could lead to revolt and disorder. They are thus seen as responsible for the consequences of their actions, which leads to self-censorship and the fear of being accused of fomenting unrest against the State. Nevertheless, many of them try to practice their profession, while accepting the risk of imprisonment and dismissal. The case of the two journalists who covered the death of Mahsa Amini is instructive.

Independent Iranian journalists try to expose social and political problems while evading censorship by rephrasing what they would like to say in seemingly innocent ways or expressing their ideas in a roundabout, metaphorical style that can be understood by citizens themselves exposed to government censorship and repression. The Islamic Regime has retaliated by creating official state press services that toe the line of the official interpretation: the Islamic Republic of Iran Broadcasting (IRIB), and the media under the direction of the IRGC (Fars News Agency, Tasnim News Agency), which have substantial financial resources at their disposal, and which spread their version of the facts.

The role of independent journalists is to implicitly deconstruct the official version of the powers that be and expose social reality – as though through the looking glass of an imaginary civil society with universal pretensions. The objectivity that journalists pursue is that which would be approved by that civil society. Respect for reality is in fact the denial of legitimacy to the Islamic State, which imposes its version of society and delegitimizes social autonomy. This reality is one based on universal intersubjectivity within a global civil sphere, to which the journalist conforms, breaking with the norms of the Islamic State.

Women journalists in particular have played an essential role in the Mahsa Movement. They tried to show how the movement was not a "plot" hatched by the West, but the actions of a section of society against the social and political deficiencies of the Islamic Regime and, in particular, the inferiorization of women by the Islamic State, which does not recognize them as having an autonomous subjectivity in relation to men.

I have already mentioned the two female journalists Niloofar Hamedi and Elaheh Mohammadi, who, for covering Mahsa's death and the protest movement that bears her name, were arrested and sentenced to several years in prison. Their imprisonment was denounced by the Committee to Protect Journalists (CPJ), which condemned their closed-door trials and their punishment.[32]

Iranian journalists Saeedeh Shafiei and Nasim Sultanbeigi were each sentenced to four years and three months in prison on charges of "assembly and collusion" and propaganda against the Islamic Republic. They were arrested in October 2022, along with a number of other journalists, in the wake of the widespread protests sparked by the death of Mahsa Amini. The CPJ's 2022 prison census ranked Iran as having the worst record in the world for the imprisonment of journalists, documenting those behind bars. The Islamic Republic detained at least ninety-five journalists during the nationwide protests. Some have been released on bail while awaiting trial, others given multi-year prison sentences.[33]

As of December 14, 2022 (some months before the end of the Mahsa Movement), according to the CPJ, the authorities had imprisoned a record number of female journalists – twenty-two out of the forty-nine arrested since the start of the protests were women.[34]

The role of the diaspora in the Mahsa Movement

The role of the Iranian diaspora residing in the West has been crucial throughout the Mahsa Movement. Since the decline of the protests in Iran in March 2023 due to massive repression, the mobilization in the diaspora has intensified. One of its tasks is to cast opprobrium on the Islamic State before international public opinion. The bond between the Iranian diaspora and the movement in Iran is profound: by organizing demonstrations and sit-ins in front of political institutions (national parliaments, the European Parliament, the American Congress) or international institutions (e.g., United Nations), Iranians outside Iran are trying not only to mobilize international public opinion, but also to instill new life into the protest movement in Iran itself. The protest in Iran is now carried out alone by individual women, by refusing to wear the veil. They risk being arrested, beaten, or having their social rights taken away. The diaspora is at one with them and supports them closely. To this end, the diaspora organizes conferences and via the web tries to involve known members of the Iranian opposition within the country itself (political prisoners, men and women) in the debate on the movement and its future, as well as on establishing democracy in Iran.

One can mention the "Dialogue to Save Iran" (*goftegu baraye nejate iran*), a two-session virtual conference held on April 21 and 22, 2023 by a group of opponents of the Islamic Republic of Iran on the Club House social network. Important figures from inside Iran and the diaspora took part in it in six different panels. Many Iranians residing in Iran were afterwards arrested.

Another conference on "The Future of Women and Minorities in the Revolution of 'Woman, Life, Freedom'" was held in Brussels on Wednesday, April 26, with the presence of representatives of Iran's ethnic and religious minorities, including Arabs, Kurds, Baloch, Turks, and Baha'is.

The diaspora thus fulfills three distinct functions in the service of the protest movement in this phase of it, in which women are left alone in the face of a repressive government: supporting them, denouncing the violence of the Islamic Republic, and preparing the future of democracy in Iran.

4

The new intellectuals

Three generations of feminist intellectuals since 1979[1]

Two major cultural movements marked Iranian society after the 1979 Revolution. The first was the reformist religious intellectuals who challenged the *Velayat faqih* (the Islamic theocracy embodied by the Supreme Leader) in the 1980s–2000s,[2] and then, the feminist intellectuals who challenged gender inequality in Iran in the 2000s.

The dozen or so feminist intellectuals who began their activities at the beginning of the twenty-first century laid the foundations of a groundbreaking cultural movement. While influenced by Western feminism, they were nonetheless sensitive to Iranian cultural features, especially under the Islamic theocracy. They focused on the role of women in society, in the government, in Islam, and in democracy. To begin with, they did not reject Islam but focused on the legal equality of men and women. They demanded gender equality as an essential condition for democracy. They behaved (and continue to do so) as activists and did not fear imprisonment and denial of rights by the Islamic Regime, and often sacrificed their family life, or even their very own life, in pursuit of gender equality. They gradually came to question the legitimacy of the Islamic State.

Since 2017, a new generation of feminists has become prominent in Iran. In contrast to the previous generation, they have begun to act not in a legalistic way, but by challenging the law imposing the veil. They have taken it off publicly.

The two types of action, formal (focusing on the legal rights) and existential (focusing on the body), created a new type of social action that culminated in the Mahsa Movement. The ground has been laid by three generations of feminist intellectuals and activists since 2006. The first generation almost entirely comprised intellectuals and professionals (lawyers, human rights activists, educated middle-class people) who launched the Campaign for One Million Signatures in 2006. The second included the young women from the middle and working classes who have been contesting the veil since 2017. The third is made up of young women, even teenagers, who dare to defy the repressive Regime. Not only have they thrown off the veil individually, but they have expressed their anger collectively in the streets by rejecting head-on the image of submissive women.

The third generation is not so well versed in the writings of feminists; they live in a culturally different world and their slogans have little to do with the feminists of the preceding generation. But while mostly unaware of their writings, the young female protesters were nonetheless influenced by their questioning of patriarchal Islam, which paved the way for their protest against the veil, seen as a constraint on women's bodies when imposed by the state.

The first generation was born in the 1940s–1950s. Mehrangiz Kar (b. 1944), Shirin Ebadi (b. 1947), and Shahla Sherkat (b. 1956), for example, spent their youth under the Shah and started to engage in feminist action after the 1979 Revolution, and particularly, after the death of Ayatollah Khomeini.

The second generation was born in the 1960s–1970s and came of age under the Islamic Regime, such as Mansoureh Shojaee (b. 1958), Nasrin Sotoudeh (b. 1963), Parvin Ardalan (b. 1967), Noushin Ahmadi Khorasani (b. 1969), and Narges Mohammadi (b. 1972). Finally, the third generation was born in the 1980s–1990s, such as Bahareh Hedayat (born 1981), Atena Daemi (b. 1988), and Nahid Keshavarz (born in the 1980s).[3] Most of both these generations belong to the educated middle classes, with a few from the lower middle class like Atena Daemi or Nasrin Sotoudeh.

The feminist generations fear neither prison nor psychological or physical torture: long-term incarceration, denial of medicines, lashing, rape, beating, threatening their children and parents. They have thrown themselves wholeheartedly into the feminist movement since the end of the twentieth century.

The third generation, between fifteen and twenty-five years of age, have been directly involved in the street protests and paid a heavy price in terms of death or torture at the hands of the government's henchmen. They are often too young to have an intellectual output or a global vision of the feminist movement. This does not prevent them from being consummate activists. Some of them have paid with their lives in the struggle against the Islamic Regime: killed in the demonstrations, arrested, tortured, and then died mysteriously (suicide or because of their physical and psychological torture). They started with a concrete action, namely the public rejection of the compulsory veil, combined with the denunciation of the Islamic Regime, which they denominated, in unison with the young men, as a dictatorship, chanting "Death to the dictator."

In the early 2000s some of the first and second generation feminists moved to the West because of the repression they faced. But they continued to fight for the cause of women, in collaboration with their counterparts residing in Iran. This group includes Shirin Ebadi, Parvin Ardalan, and Mansoureh Shojaee.

The biographies of some of the most eminent feminists give an idea of their diversity and the social and political issues they have shared for almost half a century.[4] They reveal the role of repression in the Islamic Regime's strategy to break their mental resistance: sentenced to exorbitant prison sentences on charges unacceptable under human rights law, unbearable conditions of incarceration such as solitary confinement or filthy cells, pressure on their families, psychological and sometimes physical torture, denial of access to health services in prison.

Shirin Ebadi

Shirin Ebadi, who I introduced earlier in the book, was born in 1947 and is an Iranian human rights activist, lawyer, and former judge. She was born in Hamadan, in western Iran. Her father, Mohammad Ali Ebadi, was the city's chief notary and professor of commercial law. Her family moved to Tehran in 1948. She was admitted to the Law Department of Tehran University in 1965 and in 1969, after graduation, she passed the qualifying exams to become a judge. After a six-month internship, she officially became a judge in March 1969. In the meantime, she continued her studies at the University of Tehran to complete a PhD in law in 1971. In 1975, she became the first female magistrate in Iran and served in this capacity until the 1979 Revolution. With the establishment of the Islamic Republic, she was no longer allowed to be a judge, which was a role exclusively reserved for men. Having the license to practice as a lawyer, she tried to obtain authorization, which was granted to her only in 1993, fourteen years after the revolution. During this period, she used her time of enforced idleness to write books and numerous articles in Iranian periodicals.

By 2004, Ebadi was teaching law at Tehran University while working as a lawyer. She advocated for the strengthening of the legal status of children and women and was committed to the reformist Mohammad Khatami in the May 1997 presidential election. This was followed by the eight-year period covering the two presidencies of Khatami (1997–2005), which raised hopes of a likely democratization of the Islamic Regime. This view, which subsequently proved illusory, nevertheless inspired many Iranian liberals who wanted to avoid a new revolution.

As a lawyer, Ebadi took on the pro bono cases of dissident figures who had fallen foul of the Islamic Republic's justice system. The judiciary consistently acted as a brake on Khatami's reformism and cracked down on those who fought for the opening up of the political system. Ebadi defended the family of Dariush Forouhar, a dissident intellectual and politician who was stabbed to death in his home. His wife, Parvaneh Eskandari, was also murdered at the same time. The couple were among several dissidents who died in a series of gruesome murders that terrorized the Iranian intellectual community. Suspicion centered on the Regime's hardliners, who were determined to put an end to the political liberalization advocated by Khatami. The murders were committed by a team of Interior Ministry officials whose leader, Saeed Emami, allegedly committed suicide in prison (or was put to death by the Regime's top hierarchy who feared being ousted by him).

Ebadi also represented the family of Ezzat Ebrahim-Nejad, who was killed during the student protests in July 1999. In 2000, she was accused of manipulating the videotaped confession of Amir Farshad Ebrahimi, a former member of Ansar-e Hezbollah, a violent militia group under the aegis of the authorities. Ebrahimi confessed his involvement in the attacks against the students on the orders of high-level conservative authorities. Ebadi claimed that she only videotaped Ebrahimi's confession to present it in court. Ebadi was sentenced to five years in prison and suspension of her law license for sending

Ebrahimi's video statement to President Khatami and the head of the judiciary. The sentences were later overturned by the Supreme Court of the judiciary.

Ebadi also defended various child abuse cases, including Ariane Golshani, a child who was abused for years and then beaten to death by her father and half-brother. Ebadi highlighted the flaws in the law, according to which custody of children in divorce cases is given to the father, even in Ariane's case, while her mother had told the court that the father was abusive and had begged the judge to give her custody of her daughter. Ebadi also dealt with the case of Leila, a teenage girl who was raped and murdered. She was not able to win the case, but she brought an international spotlight to a deeply unjust law. She also addressed cases involving media censorship. She launched two non-governmental organizations with Western funding, the Society for the Protection of Children's Rights (SPRC) in 1994 and the Defenders of Human Rights Center (DHRC) in 2001.

She helped draft a bill against physical abuse of children that was passed by the Iranian parliament in 2002. Female parliamentarians also asked Ebadi to draft a text explaining how a woman's right to divorce is in accordance with Sharia (Islamic law). She presented the bill to the government, but its male members rejected it.

In 2003, Ebadi was awarded the Nobel Peace Prize, for her pioneering efforts for democracy and human rights, especially the rights of women, children, and refugees, which gave her an international stature that worried the hard-liners of the Islamic Republic.

Like many Iranian feminists, before the 2009 Green Movement, she tried to express her ideas not against Islam but in accordance with a pluralist version of Islam, represented by the reformist religious intellectuals. In her book *Iran's Awakening* (*bidari iran*), she explained her politico-religious views on Islam, democracy, and gender equality:

> For the past 23 years, from the day I was removed from my position as a judge to the years I fought in Tehran's revolutionary courts, I have repeated a refrain: an interpretation of Islam that is in harmony with [gender] equality and democracy is an authentic expression of faith. It is not religion that binds women, but the selective dictates of those who wish them to be cloistered. This belief, along with the belief that change in Iran must come peacefully and from within, has underpinned my work.[5]

In April 2008, she told Reuters News Agency that Iran's human rights record had deteriorated over the past two years, and agreed to defend the Baha'is (members of a persecuted religious group in Iran) arrested in May 2008.

In April 2008, Ebadi also issued a statement noting threats against her and her family. In August 2008, the Islamic Republic News Agency (IRNA) published an article attacking Ebadi's ties to the Baha'i faith and accused her of seeking Western support. It also accused her of defending homosexuals, appearing unveiled abroad, questioning Islamic punishments, and "defending CIA agents." In December 2008, Iranian police closed the office of a human rights group she ran.

Since Hassan Rouhani's victory in the 2013 Iranian presidential election, Shirin Ebadi has repeatedly expressed concern about the growing human rights violations in her native country. In 2018, breaking with her previous statements, she concluded in an interview with Bloomberg her belief that the Islamic Republic had reached a point of no return and was irreformable. She called for a democratic referendum on the Islamic Republic.

Ebadi teamed up with Reza Pahlavi (son of the Shah), feminist Masih Alinejad, and five other opposition figures to the Islamic Republic, to unify the Iranian opposition outside Iran in January 2023. The group failed to resist rifts and dissolved a few weeks later.

Parvin Ardalan

Parvin Ardalan, who we met earlier in the book, born in 1967 in Tehran, is a feminist activist, writer, and journalist. She was awarded the Olof Palme Prize in 2007 for her struggle for equal rights for men and women in Iran.

In the 1990s, Ardalan with Noushin Ahmadi Khorasani and others founded the Women's Cultural Center (*Markaz Farhangi Zanan*). Since 2005, Ardalan has been editor and publisher of Iran's first online magazine on women's rights, *Zanestan*. Under Khatami's presidency, the magazine was repeatedly censored and closed down by the judiciary. With the complicity of the reformers in power, it was published under a new name, dealing with marriage, prostitution, education, AIDS, and violence against women. In the end, it did not survive the censorship.

Ardalan is one of the founding members of the Campaign for One Million Signatures for equal rights for women. As part of this campaign, she took part in demonstrations that were harshly repressed by the authorities. In 2007, she and Noushin Ahmadi Khorasani were sentenced to three years in prison for "threatening national security" for their commitment to women's rights. Four other women activists were later given the same sentence.

In 2012, the Swedish Migration Board granted Ardalan permanent residence in Sweden, where she had taken refuge three years earlier.

Mansoureh Shojaee

Mansoureh Shojaee, born in 1958 in Tehran, is an Iranian women's rights activist and writer.[6] For over twenty years, she has been one of the leading figures of the Iranian women's rights movement. She was a librarian at the National Library in Tehran for twenty-two years and worked as a journalist, freelance writer, and literary French translator. From 1994 to 2004, as part of the Children's Book Council of Iran (IBBYP – International Board on Books for Young People), she worked with blind children and enabled them to access literature by teaching them the use of audiobooks. For her efforts, she received the 2010 Testimonial Statute Honors Award from the IBBYP. She also worked with other organizations including UNICEF to develop mobile libraries geared towards Iranian women and children. A close confidant of Shirin Ebadi, Mansoureh Shojaee was committed to fulfilling Ebadi's idea of an Iranian women's museum. The project was scheduled to start in the Banu library in Ahvaz in southwest Iran but was banned in the early stages. In 2000, she co-founded (with the journalist, feminist, and political activist Noushin Ahmadi Khorasani and other like-minded women) the Women's Cultural Center (*Markaz Farhangi Zanan*), where she opened the Women's Library Sadige Dolatabadi in 2003. She is one of the initiators of the Campaign for One Million Signatures and co-founder of the website The Feminist School. Because of her dedicated efforts, she was imprisoned several times, most recently on December 27, 2009. After a month, she was released on bail and was free to leave Iran. Having already suffered a four-year travel ban, she promptly went into exile. She was initially accepted at the Heinrich Böll Foundation and was part of the Writers in Exile Program from 2011 until 2013. In 2013, her book *Shahrzade's Sisters* was published. She continues to work as a women's rights activist, writer, and journalist in exile.

In 2020, she founded the Iran Women's Movement Documentation Center (IranWomen.Center) as a platform in which the recent projects of Shojaee and her companions are publicized.

Noushin Ahmadi Khorasani

Noushin Ahmadi Khorasani was born in 1969 in Nezamabad, a working-class neighborhood in southern Tehran. She received her undergraduate degrees in public health and English translation from Tehran and Azad universities. She also holds a master's degree in Women's Studies from Tehran University. She is married to her fellow publisher and editor-in-chief, Javad Mousavi Khorasani. Bilingual in Persian and English, she has written and translated in both languages. She also works on short videos that highlight issues facing Iranian women, some of which can be accessed on her personal YouTube channel.[7] In a September 2003 interview, she described her motivations for championing women's rights, explaining that issues of gender discrimination played an important role in a society where she felt guilty for being a woman. She began writing and publishing to "connect and start a conversation with other women."[8]

Noushin Ahmadi is one of the founding members of the Campaign for One Million Signatures. She was also co-founder of the Women's Cultural Center (*Markaz Farhangi Zanan*). The latter focused on women's health, as well as on legal issues affecting women. She has also written several books on the women's movement in Iran. She was the 2004 recipient of the Latifeh Yarshater Award, given by the Persian Heritage Foundation, for a book she co-authored with Parvin Ardalan on the country's first female lawyer, Mehrangiz Manouchehrian, entitled *Senator: The Work of Senator Mehrangiz Manouchehrian in the Struggle for Women's Legal Rights*.

Up to the year 2007, like Shirin Ebadi, she maintained: "I am convinced that reform [of discriminatory laws] is possible within the framework of Islam."[9]

In 2007, she and Parvin Ardalan were sentenced to three years in prison for threatening national security. Noushin Ahmadi was released on September 22, 2010, after appearing before the Evin Prison Court. On September 23, she was charged with propaganda activities against the Islamic Regime by writing and publishing works against it on the website of The Feminist School and for participating in illegal rallies after the 2009 presidential election. On June 9, 2012, she was sentenced to a one-year suspended prison term and five years' probation.

Nasrin Sotoudeh

Nasrin Sotoudeh was born in 1963 into a middle-class religious family. Her father was a merchant with no university education. She studied law at Shahid Beheshti University in Tehran. After completing her studies in international law, Sotoudeh passed the bar exam in 1995, but due to her status as a woman, she had to wait eight years before she was allowed to practice law. Her work includes the defense of women as well as the protection of abused children to prevent their custody by a violent father (as noted earlier, in Iran, in the case of divorce, the custody of the child is given to the father).

After the arrest of the Million Signatures Campaign's founders in 2006, she defended them along with Shirin Ebadi and Leyla Ali-Karami. She also took on the defense of many activists and journalists, men and women, as well as the cases of child abuse.

As a result of her legal activities, the International Organization for Human Rights of Italy awarded her its prize in 2008. The award ceremony was held in the city of Milan on December 10, but she was unable to attend due to the travel ban imposed on her by an Islamic court.

During the 2009 presidential election, Sotoudeh tried to raise public awareness about women's rights. After the election, she campaigned for equal gender rights for citizens.

Ahmadinejad's election was challenged by the Green Movement, which the Islamic Regime subsequently suppressed.

Sotoudeh defended activists who were sentenced to death for taking part in the protests.

On September 4, 2010, Iranian authorities arrested her on charges of spreading propaganda and conspiracy to endanger national security, following her defense of Zahra Bahrami, a woman of dual nationality (Dutch Iranian), who was charged with national security offenses. She was held in Evin prison north of Tehran.

Amnesty International called for her release as a prisoner of conscience, saying she was at risk of torture and other ill treatment. She was held in solitary confinement.

On September 25, 2010, she began a hunger strike in protest of the ban on visits and phone calls from her family. She ended the hunger strike four weeks later, on October 23. In October 2010, international organizations joined Amnesty International in denouncing Sotoudeh's imprisonment and calling for her immediate release.

On October 31, according to the International Campaign for Human Rights in Iran, Sotoudeh protested her detention and mistreatment by going on a strict hunger strike (refusing not only food, but also water). On November 4, her two young children were allowed to visit her in prison for the first time. They found her in poor health. She began a third hunger strike on October 17, 2012, to have her daughter's rights restored, following a judicial ban on her leaving the country.

On January 9, 2011, Iranian authorities sentenced Sotoudeh to six years in prison on charges including participating in activities that jeopardize national security and propaganda against the Islamic Regime. The sentence was accompanied by a ban on practicing her profession and leaving the country for twenty years.

On September 18, 2013, she was pardoned and released. The election of the new Iranian President Hassan Rouhani, who sought to give a more open image of Iran, was a decisive factor in her release.

In 2016, she spoke out in the film *Taxi Tehran* directed by Jafar Panahi about the totalitarian methods used by the Islamic Regime to make life unbearable for human rights activists, and their deceptive freedom even outside prison:

> They make sure we know they are watching us. Their tactics are obvious. They create a political record for you. You become an agent of Mossad, CIA, MI6 ... Then they add a vice case. They make your life a prison. You're out [of prison], but the outside world has become a big prison. They make your best friends your worst enemies. You must flee the country or pray to go back to the slammer. So that's all there is to it: don't worry about it!

In 2017–18, she defended several young Iranian women who had unveiled in public.

She was arrested on June 13, 2018, by reason of a fabricated five-year prison sentence, of which neither she nor her husband had been aware. She was sentenced, on March 11, 2019, to an additional thirty-three years in prison and 148 lashes for collusion to harm national security, propaganda against the state, membership of an illegal group, spreading false information, disturbing public order, as well as appearing unveiled in public and promoting "depravity."

Sotoudeh has repeatedly managed to get letters out of prison through her husband Reza Khandan, who himself was sentenced in January 2019 to six years in prison but is still free. In them, she defends the cause of the women who refuse to wear the compulsory veil.

On August 11, 2020, after two years of imprisonment, she began a hunger strike for the release of political prisoners in Iran. She was granted a temporary leave of absence on November 7. After less than a month of provisional freedom, she was incarcerated again on December 2, 2020, despite her worrying health condition. From Evin she was sent to Qarchak prison where family visits are much more difficult.

Her husband announced that she was granted a temporary release again on January 8, 2021, due to cardiac complications. She was imprisoned again a few days later, on January 20, 2021.

On October 26, 2012, the European Parliament awarded her and Jafar Panahi its Sakharov Prize "for Freedom of Thought." On September 21, 2018, she was awarded the Ludovic Trarieux International Human Rights Prize, an annual award given to a lawyer. She is also the recipient of the 2020 Alternative Nobel Prize (Right Livelihood Award) "for her fearless activism, at great risk to her life, to promote political freedoms and human rights in Iran."

Narges Mohammadi

Narges Mohammadi is another example of the courage of Iranian feminists who do not back down in the face of relentless repression, but continue their struggle in an unequal battle where the Regime attempts to crush them mentally and physically. She was born in 1972 in Zandjan, a city in northeastern Iran. She attended university and graduated with a degree in applied physics, with the aim of become an engineer. As a student, she wrote articles in student newspapers in support of women's rights and was arrested twice in meetings of a student activist group, the Enlightened Student Group (*Tashakkol Daneshjuyi Roshangaran*). A member of the mountaineering group, she was denied participation in their activities because of her political activism. She later worked as a journalist with several reformist groups to improve women's rights. In 2003, Iranian feminist Shirin Ebadi won the Nobel Peace Prize and Mohammadi joined her in the organization she founded, the Defenders of Human Rights Center, and later became its vice-president. She married the journalist and activist Taqi Rahmani in 1999, who was arrested soon after and spent fourteen years in prison. In 2012, he left Iran to save the lives and future of their two children and moved to France. Narges Mohammadi remains in Iran to continue her struggle not only for women's rights, but also to support human rights activists, men and women alike.

Mohammadi's life has been punctuated by imprisonment, temporary release, re-imprisonment, increasingly severe sentences, and the attempts to crush her mind through physical and psychological torture, which she calls "white torture" (*chekandjeh sefid*): assault by common prisoners whom the authorities sometimes incite to abuse her, and various perverse forms of pressure. This made her life impossible. Suffering from an epilepsy-like illness that causes neural and muscular paralysis resulting in hemiplegia and major breathing difficulties, she has often been denied medical assistance in prison.

She has endured a succession of prison sentences from 1998 to the present, followed by intimidation of her relatives and assaults such as in 2019 when she was transferred from Evin to Zanjan prison after a sit-in in solidarity with the families of those killed in the November 2019 Iran protests. According to Amnesty International, government forces put to death between November 15 and 19, 321 people (more if we add those whose names could not be traced, as their families were intimidated by the security forces). During her transfer, she was forced into the vehicle extremely violently, causing bruising and mental shock to her fragile body. Showing exceptional courage, during her periods of freedom she defended the cause of women and men, victims of the abuses. At the end of July 2012, she was released from prison and on October 31, 2014, she gave an unambiguous speech blaming the Islamic State for the death of the activist Sattar Beheshti. Born in 1977, he died in November 2012 under torture in Evin prison. As a blogger he had dared to criticize the Iranian Regime on Facebook. The extreme violence meted to Sattar Beheshti leading to his death caused an international outcry in 2012, but his death is far from an isolated case in Evin and in many other Iranian prisons. The video of Narges Mohammadi's October 31 speech quickly went viral on social networks, leading to her being summoned to court. On May 5, 2016, she was arrested again on new charges.

Mohammadi furthermore denounces human rights violations regarding men, participating in an association for the abolition of the death penalty (Legam). Iran ranks second in the world for its use of capital punishment: in 2021, at least 333 people, including seventeen women, were sentenced to death. China is ranked first in number of executions per capita.[10]

She made her observations public in a book in which she interviewed several political prisoners who described the abuses they suffered in prison, both psychological torture (threats of death, violence against their relatives, violence, and rape for women), and physical violence (beatings, torture leading to irreversible after-effects or death). Here are the words of Atena Daemi, an activist for women's rights in prison, reproduced in Mohammadi's book:

> The prosecutor read the charges ... I think there were 18–20 written ones ... While he was reading the sheet, I was constantly threatened with death ... It was as if they wanted to cut me into pieces with their teeth ... I knew that no one would come to my rescue. They said my sisters had also been arrested ... They said I had to cooperate, maybe then I wouldn't be executed.[11]

In May 2016, Tehran's Revolutionary Court found Narges Mohammadi guilty of establishing and leading the illegal underground group Legam. She was sentenced to sixteen years in prison.

Overall, Mohammadi's life has been punctuated by increasingly longer stays in prison and periodic releases, probably because the Regime feared she would die in prison, which would create an international outcry. Suffering persecution in Iran, like many other feminists, Mohammadi has received numerous international awards and honors: the 2018 Andrei Sakharov Prize from the American Physical Society, the 2016 Human Rights Prize from the city of Weimar in Germany, the 2011 Per Anger Prize from the Swedish government for human rights, and the 2009 Alexander Langer Prize. On October 6, 2023, she was awarded the Nobel Peace Prize for her "fight against the oppression of women in Iran and her fight to promote human rights and freedom for all," in the words of the Nobel Committee.

Atena Daemi

Fateme Daemi Khoshknudhani, known as Atena Daemi, was born in 1988 in Foumane, Guilan county, northern Iran, to a family of three girls. Her parents both worked in the private sector. Daemi studied up to high school level and because of the family's economic problems, instead of going to university, she started working as a secretary at the Revolution Sports Club in Tehran. She also worked as a makeup artist with her mother. She met people of the same age with identical concerns on social networks. They had gathered around the songs of Shahin Najafi, an Iranian protest singer, for which she was later indicted in court, for violating Islamic laws. Daemi and her friends tried to take their protests to the streets. They contacted civic groups and helped hold and organize public rallies. Children's rights were one of her main concerns and she set up painting classes and exhibitions for working-class and street children. The group's activities also included the publication of an underground nightly newspaper, to protest against death sentences. She drew the attention of the Intelligence Services and was arrested in September 2014. She was transferred to Ward 2-A of Evin prison, directly managed by the Revolutionary Guards. The prison population of political and civic activists, journalists, and bloggers under their absolute control are subjected to extreme forms of pressure and torture.

She was placed in solitary confinement, denied access to a lawyer, and interrogated relentlessly for eighty-six days to break her psychologically. She spent the first twenty-eight days of her detention in an insect-infested cell with no access to a lavatory. On January 14, 2016, she was transferred to the women's wing of Evin prison where conditions are less inhumane. She was charged with gathering and colluding against national security, spreading propaganda against the system, concealing evidence, and insulting the founder of the Islamic Republic of Iran and the Supreme Leader. She was released on bail, after her family paid 5,500 million rials on February 15, 2016 (more than US$100,000, an exorbitant amount for a middle-class family). She was sentenced on May 21, 2016, to fourteen years in prison. Daemi's conviction came after a fifteen-minute trial. The peaceful activities for which she was tried and convicted were the distribution of leaflets against the death penalty and posts on Facebook and Twitter criticizing the high number of executions in Iran. She is considered a prisoner of conscience by Amnesty International.

She was arrested again at her parents' home in front of her sisters on November 26, 2016, and she was sent back to Evin prison. As a mark of her fighting spirit, she officially filed a complaint to the prosecutor's office from Evin prison against the actions of the IRGC's members who arrested her, with no illusion about the outcome.

On March 23, 2017, Daemi and her sisters were charged and convicted of contempt of public officials on duty. After an hour-long trial in criminal court, they were sentenced to three months and one day in prison. This jail sentence was added to Daemi's first sentence but was suspended for her sisters.

In April 2017, Daemi began a hunger strike to protest the new charges against her and her sisters. A letter sent by Amnesty International on May 17, 2017, requested that Daemi be transferred from prison to a hospital. According to Amnesty, Daemi, who had been on hunger strike for forty days at the time, was coughing up blood, vomiting regularly, had a blood pressure problem, kidney pain, and had lost a lot of weight. Doctors warned that she needed immediate hospitalization. However, the Evin prison authorities refused to allow her to be transferred to a hospital outside the prison.

Her strike ended on June 1, 2017, after the new charges against her and her sisters were dropped at a second Court of Appeal hearing.

On January 24, 2018, Daemi was transferred to Shahr-e Rey prison in Varamin, near Tehran. She was moved along with Golrokh Ebrahimi Iraee, who was imprisoned for writing a short story in which she criticized the practice of stoning women as a cruel death penalty. Their transfer to Shahr-e Rey, a prison for violent offenders, was denounced as illegal, because it violates Iranian regulations on the classification of prisoners.

Both women went on hunger strike on February 3, 2018, following their transfer. Amnesty International again called for their immediate and unconditional release on the grounds that they were imprisoned for the peaceful exercise of their human rights.

Atena Daemi continued her hunger strike until February 25, 2018, for twenty-two days. Golrokh Ebrahimi Iraee continued it for eighty-one days, until April 24, 2018. Both of them were severely weakened. They were transferred to Evin prison on May 10, 2018, which was a symbolic victory on their part against the Islamic Regime. The fear of their deaths must have played a role in the change of attitude on the part of the authorities, who feared international focus on its human rights violations if famous female human rights activists died in its jails.

On May 25, 2018, Daemi sent a letter from Evin prison condemning the death penalty and discussing the situation of a political prisoner on death row, Ramin Hossein-Panahi.

On October 10, 2018, World Day Against the Death Penalty, Daemi, Golrokh Ebrahimi Iraee, and Maryam Akbari Monfared signed a public appeal to Javaid Rehman, then UN Special Rapporteur, denouncing human rights violations in Iran, including the widespread use of the death penalty.

In December 2018, she was one of ten cases defended by Amnesty International in the "10 Days to Sign" campaign with other human rights defenders around the world.

Atena Daemi was released on the evening of January 24, 2022. She can be expected to be arrested on new charges soon. Her case is being replicated by other young women.

Leila Hosseinzadeh

Leila was born in 1991, a student who became a leftist feminist and human rights activist. She was arrested and put in prison in January 2018 for participating in the December 2017 protest movement at the university. She was sentenced to five years in prison for illegal assembly and conspiracy against national security. She was subjected to all the mistreatments inflicted on activists who demand an open political system and an end to gender inequality. She has gone on hunger strikes that endanger her fragile health and has refused to wear the compulsory veil while meeting her relatives. Due to her chronic illnesses, she was released. Then in 2021, she was arrested in Shiraz and was transferred to Evin prison.

Once again, we witness the dialectic of imprisonment, parole, re-imprisonment, and the attempt by the Islamic Regime to destroy the mental and physical capacities of political prisoners.

Atena Farghadani

Atena Farghadani, born on January 29, 1987 in Tehran, is an Iranian artist and activist, considered a prisoner of conscience by Amnesty International.[12] Through her caricatures and cartoons she denounces the Islamic Regime by depicting the Iranian authorities, members of parliament, and the Supreme Leader in an offensive manner. Her art not only desecrates the authorities, through it she ridicules them and denies them the "transcendence" (the inviolability) bestowed upon the Supreme Leader and those close to him. Her drawings are a denial of sacredness, it puts into question their untouchability, particularly that of the Supreme Leader.

As an arts student at Al-Zahra University in Tehran, she was arrested for the first time in August 2014 and held in solitary confinement for a fortnight. Released on bail, she denounced her prison conditions in a video and was imprisoned again in January 2015. Three weeks later, she went on hunger strike and was hospitalized after suffering a heart attack.

Her charges included propaganda against the regime, activities against national security, collusion with counter-revolutionaries, insulting members of parliament and particularly, the Supreme Leader.

These charges were directly linked to her exhibition *Parandegan-e Khak* (Birds of the Earth), held in tribute to the victims of the repression of the 2009 Green Movement demonstrations, and to the publication of a cartoon depicting Iranian MPs as animals. The cartoon denounced two government bills penalizing contraception and voluntary sterilization, and strengthening the rights of husbands in divorce proceedings.

Her trial began on May 19, 2015 and ended a week later with a twelve year and nine months' prison sentence, which was reduced to eighteen months at the Court of Appeal.

She was released from prison in the summer of 2015, through the efforts of the International Cartoonist Rights Protection Network. After her release, she told the *Washington Post* newspaper that she would not leave Iran and planned to continue her activities because her work has the greatest impact in Iran.

In October 2014, the Justice for Iran organization published news of a mandatory virginity test having been performed on Atena Farghadani in August 2014. This action was denounced by her lawyer and by Amnesty International.

Since September 2021 and the beginning of nationwide protests following the killing of Mahsa Amini in the custody of the Vice Squads, the arrests of protesting artists, journalists, and political activists have intensified. Atena Farghadani was summoned once again to the court on charges of insulting the Leadership. She refused to pay the bail, declaring: "I have not committed a crime," and that the summons and her charges were illegal and arbitrary.[13] She was arrested on June 7, 2023, and imprisoned.

What distinguishes Iran's young feminists is their lack of fear vis-à-vis an unscrupulous state that seeks to crush the individual by denying them their most basic rights. Armed only with their convictions, these women dare not only to confront the State but also to mock its supreme authority, which is also the "supreme male," by challenging patriarchy in the very person of those in power within the Islamic Regime. They are not afraid of years in prison, violence to their bodies, denial of medical care (Farghadani had a heart attack in prison as a young woman) and the courage to sacrifice their lives to their feminist beliefs.

Young female activists in the September 2022 protests

The Mahsa Movement has seen the emergence of a new type of social activist, one that is young, even very young (many are teenagers), who challenges the Islamic government on gender equality and political freedom. These young women have not hesitated to step up against a regime that only cares about its survival, not its legitimacy, and therefore does not hesitate to kill, regardless of its image in society. They have become the symbols of the struggle for women's rights.

Mahsa Amini

Mahsa Amini was born in 2000 in Saqez, a city in Iranian Kurdistan. Her Kurdish first name is Jina. At the time of her arrest, she was on vacation in Tehran with her brother and family members. She was hoping to attend university in West Azerbaijan, northwest of Iran. On September 13, 2022, she was arrested by the Vice Squad for her defective veil ("wearing inappropriate clothing"). She was transferred the same day to the hospital where she fell into a coma. On September 16, she died. In keeping with their practice of inventing accidental causes for the death of those killed by the security forces, the Iranian authorities attributed her death to sudden heart failure. The young woman is said to have collapsed after being interrogated by a female officer. Her father refutes this version, maintaining that his daughter was in perfect health before her arrest.

The London-based Iran International news channel broadcast on September 19, 2022, images showing a scan of Mahsa Amini's skull, revealing a bone fracture and other signs of injury that invalidate the official version. In such circumstances, the Iranian authorities give an "accidental" explanation of the death to clear themselves of the suspicion of having inflicted it. This is the case of the official medical report of October 7, which puts forward the idea of a brain disease. This report has been contradicted on the web by more than 800 doctors, who accused the medical examiner of complicity with the Islamic Republic.[14] It should be noted that the recourse to lying about state violence and attributing it to external circumstances (accidental death or health problems) has been systematically used in the statements about the deaths of demonstrators throughout the protests that took place from September 2022 to February 2023.

On October 26, large demonstrations were staged in dozens of Iranian cities on the fortieth day of mourning for Mahsa Amini. Many people walked to the Aichi cemetery in Saqez, the Kurdish town where Mahsa Amini was born and buried. The day began with a large march and rally, with demonstrators demanding the end of the Islamic Republic. Security forces had blocked the roads leading to the cemetery to prevent the rally but failed to achieve that goal and a large crowd made their way through side roads along the local river and on to the cemetery, chanting slogans against the Islamic Regime. Among the chants were "Kurdistan, Kurdistan, the cemetery for Fascists" and "Death to the dictator." According to eye witnesses the riot police opened fire on those gathered, and arrested dozens. The human rights organization Hengaw reported that people were shot by security forces.

The number of demonstrators on that day was much higher than on any other day since the protests began. There were also reports that the strikes in the bazaar in some cities (closing the stores as a sign of protest) and industries had spread. To make communication difficult, the government cut off the internet in Saqez.

Mahsa Amini became the most powerful symbol of the movement, launched after her tragic death mid-September 2022. Her name has appeared in hashtags, Roman and Persian, in social networks that informed about the movement and its repression by the Regime. Many commentators have called this movement the Mahsa Movement.

Nika Shakarami

Nika Shakarami was born on October 2, 2005, in Lorestan province in western Iran. She lived with her aunt in Tehran after the death of her father and worked as a waitress in a café. She participated in the demonstrations, on the death of Mahsa Amini in September 2022. She disappeared after demonstrating on Keshavarz Boulevard in Tehran on September 20. According to her family, her last communication was a message sent to one of her friends in which she claimed she was being stalked by the security forces. Apparently, she had been separated from her friends as the protesters dispersed to escape the crackdown. On the night of September 20, her Telegram and Instagram accounts and phone numbers were deactivated.

After losing touch with her, the family began contacting police stations and hospitals. They also posted her photos on social media in hopes that they would get information. Ten days later, they were informed that a body looking like Nika had been found during a forensic investigation of dead protesters. Her body was eventually found in the Kahrizak morgue located in a detention center near Tehran. Shakarami's family members were not allowed to see the body, only to look at her face for a few seconds for identification purposes. The authorities informed them that she had died by falling from a terrace. In what has become a customary excuse, the government cleared itself of blame for the killing. A photo of her lifeless body on the sidewalk sent to the family looked suspicious. In an interview on social media, her aunt said that her skull had been broken by multiple blows from a hard object, similar to a baton or stick, as well as her nose.

The family took her body to her hometown of Khorramabad for burial, to hold the mourning ceremony on October 2, her seventeenth birthday. Security forces pressured them to hold the burial privately and without ceremony. Shakarami's aunt objected and invited the public via Twitter to join the celebration of the girl's "last birthday." She was arrested on October 2 and other family members were threatened with reprisals if they participated in the protests. To neutralize the mourning ceremonies and reduce the influx of people to the cemetery, the authorities stole her body and buried it in Veysian, about forty kilometers from the cemetery.

Despite these abuses, hundreds of protesters gathered at the Khorramabad cemetery on the day Shakarami's funeral was scheduled to take place. Militants accused the government of abuse, torture, and the death of the young girl. News of her death led to large numbers of high school girls joining anti-government protests on October 4.

A video of Shakarami went viral on Twitter. She was seen unveiled on a stage, singing and laughing. This attitude, a testimony to a secular "joie de vivre," expressed her opposition to the Theocratic Regime in bodily, existential terms.

Shakarami's death and the authorities' seizure of her body were widely reported on social networks. Her name became a hashtag used by women's rights activists in Iran.

Hadith Najafi

Hadith Najafi, a twenty-year-old girl, had joined the crowd of protesters and was shot dead by the security forces in Karaj, a satellite city of Tehran on September 21, 2022. Bullets hit her face, neck, heart, and hand.

According to her friends, she had been heartbroken by the death of Mahsa Amini and was angry. She reportedly said that she was not going to stop there, that she would go all the way, even if it meant suffering the same fate as her heroine.

The fortieth day after Hadith Najafi's death turned into a solemn occasion to denounce the predatory Regime. In the videos posted on social media on that date, from along the paths leading to Behesht Sakineh cemetery in Karaj, demonstrators threw stones at a police car causing it to crash in the middle of the street. Meanwhile, according to eyewitnesses, deafening stun grenades were dropped from helicopters onto the protesters.

For a long time after the victory of the 1979 Revolution, the Islamic Republic's TV channel condemned the Shah's regime for attempting to fly over the demonstrators in helicopters

– a symbol of a repressive machine that treated citizens with contempt. The demonstrators emphasized in their social media messages the even more repressive nature of the Islamic Regime compared to that of the Shah. Whereas the latter's helicopters merely flew over the demonstrators, the Islamic Regime threw stun grenades at them, shocking them to the core. They vowed that the Regime would share the same fate as the old regime and would be overthrown by the current uprising.

Mahsa Mogouee

An eighteen-year-old girl named Mahsa Mogouee was killed in Fuladshahr in the province of Isfahan, western Iran, on September 24, 2022, by government forces who later denied as usual any role in her killing.

On the fortieth day of her mourning ceremonies on November 3, 2022, in Isfahan, Shahinshahr, and Fuladshahr cities, several protest rallies were held not only to commemorate her death but also to renew the vigor of the anti-Regime protests. Demonstrators chanted slogans calling for the overthrow of the Supreme Leader Ali Khamenei and the Islamic Republic.

Yalda Aqa Fazli

The tragic case of Yalda Aqa Fazli, a young woman of nineteen, inaugurates a series of deaths by suicide of young women and men who, under torture, lost their zest for life and on leaving prison, deeply traumatized, committed suicide – assuming that this version is true and that it was not the Regime that directly put them to death. Yalda was arrested on October 26, 2022, in the Enqelab Avenue protests in Tehran and detained in Qarchak prison, not far from the capital. Five days after her release, according to official reports, she committed suicide.

Yalda had reported being beaten while in detention and mistreated by her inquisitors. She had refused to obey the orders of self-denunciation that her torturers intended to impose on her. Her possible rape and other physical abuses are suspected.

The Islamic feminists

There is also a group of women who could be described as Islamic feminists, such as Azam Taleghani and Faezeh Hashemi, both daughters of prominent members of the political elite of the Islamic Republic of Iran.

Born in Iran in 1943, Taleghani was the daughter of Ayatollah Mahmoud Taleghani, one of the spiritual leaders of the 1979 Revolution. She served time in prison during the Pahlavi regime. After the Iranian Revolution she was a member of the Iranian parliament, founded Jame'e Zanan Mosalman (Society of Muslim Women), and published *Payam e Hajar*, a weekly Islamic journal about women and women's rights. In 2003 she protested against the death in custody of photojournalist Zahra Kazemi. Both in 2001 and 2009, Taleghani submitted her candidacy for Iran's presidential elections, but, like all women candidacies, it was rejected by Iran's Guardian Council.[15]

Faezeh Hashemi, born in 1963, is an Iranian women's rights activist, politician, and former journalist who served as a member of the Iranian parliament from 1996 to 2000. She is also president of the Executives of Construction Party women's league and the former editor-in-chief of the women's newspaper *Zan*. She is furthermore the daughter of the former president, Akbar Hashemi Rafsanjani.

She founded *Zan* in 1998, which was closed down in April 1999 by the Islamic Regime. She was sentenced to many prison terms due to her activism. On July 3, 2022, she was charged with carrying out propaganda activity against the country and blasphemy. She was arrested again in late September 2022 during the Mahsa Movement. Herself a veiled woman, she defended the right of the women to appear unveiled in public. She criticized the Talibanesque view of the Islamic Regime towards women. In 2023, she was sentenced to five years in jail.[16]

Islamic feminists have had no tangible impact on women's rights within the Regime. Either they let themselves be crushed by the Regime, or they became its opponents and endured, admittedly less harshly, the fate of Iranian feminists, with multiple imprisonments and the denial of the expression of their opinion.

The pop singers and sportsmen and women as the new intellectuals

For the new generation, immersed in modern music (blues, hip-hop, pop, rap), the highbrow intellectuals have little significance. The young singers who understand their anguish and frustrations without using sophisticated terminology have become their "intellectuals." Before the Mahsa Movement, which untied tongues, music was used to express ambivalently the rejection of the government and the denunciation of its repression not only through words and music but also through specific gestures. Rappers and pop singers have often paid a heavy price for their confrontation with a predatory Regime that often blurs the boundaries between intimidation, imprisonment, and violent killing.

Blues and rap have become the preferred means of expressing despair, oppression, and revolt against the Islamic Regime by youth. Desperation, the grim cry of revolt without directly naming the Theocratic State (before the Mahsa Movement), the yearning for a peaceful, secular life free from want, and suffocation living under a theocracy denying the simple "joie de vivre," are the social content of this music. It denounces the sectarian and prudish standards of the Islamic Regime, and its corrupt ruling elite. All this gives the musicians an intellectual, vanguard position in the revolt against an iniquitous political system. Before the Mahsa Movement, these singers brooded in an attitude that constantly swung between manifest resentment and inward anger. During the Mahsa Movement, their voices were heard as much as singers as activists with an individual commitment to the protest movement and new songs that incited revolt in an explicit or implicit fashion. Many of them have been arrested, tortured, and threatened with death.

These musicians fulfill the role of organic intellectuals within a movement of young people who do not recognize themselves in the highbrow intellectuals, detached from their existential concerns. They long for a secular "joie de vivre," free from a repressive theocracy – a political system that would recognize them as citizens with full rights.

Shervin Hajipour

Shervin Hajipour was born on March 30, 1997 in Babol, northern Iran. He studied mathematics in high school and economics at university. Hajipour started training in music at the age of eight. He entered the flagship Iranian TV talent show, "The New Era" (*asré jadid*), and reached the finals by the unanimous vote of the four judges.

In October 2022, after the death of Mahsa Amini and during the national protests in Iran, Hajipour wrote the song "For" (*Baraye*), based on users' protest tweets that began with the word "For." The video of this song was only on his personal Instagram page. In three days, it went viral and recorded almost 40 million hits. The song "For" became the main symbol of the protest movement of 2022 and won the Grammy Award. It became the anthem of the Mahsa Movement. In it he tackles themes that would later be taken up by the movement: the denunciation of the culture of sorrow and tears ("For the endless crying"), the aspiration to smile ("For a smiling face"), the lifting of religious prohibitions and the demand for social, not private, joy for men and women, and dancing and singing in public ("For being able to dance in the street"), for a decent life that remains unattainable under Islamic rule ("For the unattainable desire of a decent life"), for unpolluted air ("For this polluted air"), for a human economy not dominated by a tiny minority ("For this command economy from above"). Hajipour denounces a society where children cry because they have nothing to eat and rummage in the garbage for food, and the lack of freedom for men and women. He calls for a society where young people have confidence in the future, and echoes the Mahsa Movement's leitmotif of "Woman, life, freedom."

The word "For" (*baraye*) has many meanings in Persian. It can alternatively mean "for," "in view of," but also "because of," "in order to," or even "against." The singer reiterates the slogan that has become the watchword of the street protests, namely "Woman, life, freedom." Most of the themes that have been at the root of the decade's harshly repressed protests appear in this song: that of the girls who are denied the right to gender equality; that of an ecology polluted by the Regime through its negligence; that of the class injustice while a despondent youth dreams of another future, inaccessible to them; that of an anxious mental state while people swallow pills for depression to get a restful sleep within a morose life, without future, without a minimum of economic security; that of an existence enslaved to the commands of a government indifferent to the people.

On September 29, 2022, Hajipour was arrested. He was released on bail five days later, the government fearing that his imprisonment would increase national outrage and add fuel to the protests.

Hamri Saman

One of the rappers accused of fighting against the Islamic Regime is Saman Seyedi, nicknamed Hamri Saman Yasin. A rap singer from the Kurdish town of Kermanshah, he is known as a protest singer. In his songs, he refers to social problems and attempts to give voice to the oppressed.

His songs reveal that it is not only the women who must revolt, against a body subjugated by a compulsory veil, but also the men who are denied freedom and joy of life. Young men feel their bodies broken by a gloomy and killjoy Regime that neutralizes their capacity of resistance. In one of his songs, which he performs in Kurdish (Kalhori dialect), Hamri Saman speaks of voices choked in the throat. He denounces the prohibition of joy among the people (the theme of the Islamic Regime as a killjoy is common among young musicians). Referring to the violent arrests, he sings: *"They turned me upside down like an animal, but I won't shut up."* And then he speaks of the deep wounds that cover his emaciated body like hair and yet, it won't break. He intones, *"They built a wall all around me/ Whoever passes by will break off a part of me (my body)."* This body nonetheless continues to resist.

He was arrested on October 10, 2022, and charged by Tehran's Revolutionary Court with participating in anti-Regime protests. His family and relatives had no information about him and feared the worst.

On November 7, 2022, a hearing was held for several arrested protesters, including Hamri Saman, who was accused of "war against God" (*moharebeh*), which could lead to the death sentence. On the same day, government media published the footage of the rapper's forced confession and called his act a "war" and "collusion with the intention of acting against the country's security." He was denied access to a lawyer of his own choosing and was also barred from communication with his family. The Kurdistan Human Rights Network stressed that the rapper was subjected to pressure and severe physical and psychological torture to make a forced confession. He was sentenced to death.[17] A new trial was ordered for him by the Iranian Supreme Court on December 24, 2022, following international mobilization.

Like many political prisoners in Iran, to break his mental resistance the authorities alternatively threatened him with execution, them offered him release. He conveys his anguish in his song "Freedom" (*azadi*):

> *The prison has made me crazy,*
> *It has made me a stranger to the outside world*
> *One day in my flat, one day in solitary confinement*
> *One night dreaming of execution, one night dreaming of freedom.*

Before the Mahsa Movement, his songs manifest despair, like a choked cry in his throat. He tries to forget his distress in a pair of Adidas shoes or in rap where he shows the lack of horizon for a youth destroyed by a murderous Regime. His Kurdish identity, repressed tenfold, is also exhibited in some of his sung poems where he alternates between the Kurdish idiom and Persian.

In his song "Twice Nothing" (*hitch o putch*), he tries to acquire some kudos by buying cheap suits that he passes off as made to measure (he thinks he gains importance in the eyes of others by this childish ploy as well as by wearing Adidas sneakers). He recognizes that he has wasted his life completely, letting out his cry of despair in the rap song he sings while calling out "the yellow color of [his] pain."

The only meaning he finds in his life is to give himself a derisory relevance in the eyes of his friends and acquaintances by pretending his clothes are expensive while being acutely aware of having missed out on his life (*"I buy street clothes that are not tailor-made. I will come to you and bluff about its price"*). The only reference to the predatory state in this poem is indirect, that of the meaning of the rap which is "protest and shout."

Before the movement of September 2022 as a rule the singers do not name the Islamic State. There are allusions to its evil presence, but the fear of censorship and imprisonment, even torture, prevents them from clearly indicating their opposition to the Theocratic State. This is notably the case of Saman Yasin.

On December 20, 2022 he attempted suicide in prison.

Toomaj Salehi

Toomaj Salehi is a militant Iranian rapper. In his lyrics, he evokes social problems and urges mobilization against the Islamic Republic. He was arrested on September 12, 2021, and later released on bail. In the Mahsa Movement Toomaj became one of the major musical voices of protest. On his Instagram and Twitter accounts, he encouraged people to take to the streets to protect protesters attacked by security forces. He was arrested again on October 30, 2022. His relatives fear he is a victim of torture. He faces the death penalty as a "corrupter of the earth" (*mofsed fil arz*), a term that means in judicial Islamic jargon, the opponent of the Theocratic Regime, liable to capital punishment. He is being prosecuted behind closed doors with no lawyer of his choice.

Toomaj was born on December 3, 1990, in Chaharmahal in southwest Iran. His family later moved to Shahinshahr, a district of Isfahan where he grew up. His family's financial situation gradually deteriorated due to his father's imprisonment for his political activities.

Toomaj started as a political rapper in 2007, at the age of twenty-six. But professionally, his songs came to prominence in 2016. In his 2021 song "Rat Hole" (*soorakh moosh*), he criticized those who, out of fear or self-interest, remain silent in the face of oppression (*"If you see cruelty being carried out on the oppressed, and you go on your way [without reacting], [. . .] you are guilty"*). He refers to the protests that had taken place on several occasions and had been suppressed (*"If you mind your own business, while they take the lives of the young [. . .], you are a traitor"*). For him, it is not possible to remain neutral in the fight against the Islamic Republic (*"Know that there is no neutral vote. There is no neutral position in this fight"*), and silence is tantamount to complicity.

Salehi is outraged by society's indifference when the predatory state arrests, tortures, and puts innocent people to death, and he accuses of connivance those who pretend to ignore its abuses. His art consists in combining song and poetry in denouncing a regime that represses its citizens with the tacit complicity of a part of the population that pretends to ignore its evil, to lead a quiet life. During the demonstrations of September 2022, in addition to his artistic activities, he committed to informing people of the locations of the protests on social networks. He was followed by 500,000 people on Instagram and 380,000 on Twitter.

Security forces first arrested Toomaj Salehi on September 12, 2021, at his home in Isfahan. He was charged with propaganda against the Regime and insulting the supreme authority of the state. Nine days later, on September 21, 2021, he was released on bail, pending trial. During his arrest, the rapper Hichkas (Soroush Lashkari), one of the founding fathers of Iranian rap, tweeted support for Salehi, from London where he resides. On January 23, 2022, the Islamic Revolutionary Court of Shahinshahr sentenced him to six months in prison and a heavy fine. After the death of Mahsa Jina Amini, triggering the great protest movement of September 2022, Toomaj became one of the major voices of the social uprising. He took advantage of a network of supporters and technical tools to circumvent internet censorship and distribute his dissident music. He was arrested again in October 2022.

The Fars News Agency, affiliated to the Islamic Regime, described him as one of the "leaders of the riots which incited violence." According to the Isfahan prosecutor's office, Toomaj played a key role in the protests in Isfahan province and the city of Shahinshahr. His family and many activists on social networks feared for his life and believed that he was being subjected to the most severe torture to confess. Famous footballer Ali Karimi, who was also active in supporting the protesters, warned that the rapper's life was in danger. In April 2023, in prison and in urgent need of medical care, he faced the death sentence according to human rights organizations.[18] Media reported that Salehi was tortured in Isfahan prison to make him confess on television. They broke four of his fingers.[19] Ye-One Rhie, member of the German parliament, has become his sponsor, in a move to prevent his execution.

Vahid Moussavi

Vahid Moussavi, a singer from Lorestan, was arrested on November 9, 2022, by the security forces who raided his home in the city of Khorramabad. The Revolutionary Guard-affiliated Tasnim News Agency announced his release on bail four days after his arrest, releasing a video of his forced confession, in which the singer admitted provoking anxiety among people whom he had urged to participate in the street demonstrations.

The public know that these confessions are not voluntary, that they are extracted under torture. The authorities seek to show that they are capable of forcing confessions from the prisoners and make them submit to the State's views. This proves their omnipotence and their ability to crush the resistance of opponents by subjecting them to harsh physical and mental pain. The prisoners also know what their confessions might imply, namely condemnation to severe penalties, sometimes death, but under torture they usually prefer to put an end to their sufferings, even at the price of their future execution. The government thus stages sessions of self-incrimination by the accused to send a message of intimidation to the demonstrators, and more generally, the public, warning them that an identical fate awaits them if they engage in the protest movement. This strategy sometimes backfires and leads to increased indignation and a more determined commitment on the part of the opponents to stage more demonstrations.

The biographies of some of these pop singers reveal their secular mind, and their opposition to a theocratic state that intimidates and represses with no horizon of hope for its youth. It is a state experienced as proscriptive, sowing fear, and killing – in brief, a thanatocracy.

Hichkas

Soroush Lashkari, born on May 10, 1985, better known as Hichkas (meaning "nobody") is one of the pioneers of Iranian rap. He is from a well-off family and grew up in a residential area of Tehran. Using his father's fortune, he recorded all kinds of rap music in a well-equipped music recording studio in Tehran, which he also rented to other musicians.

In 2003, with another rapper, Salomeh MC, he released the song "*Cheshma Ro Man.*" In 2003, he formed a rap group called 021 with the slogan "Tehran forever," which gradually moved to social themes. After some time, the group 021 became a new group called Samet with the cooperation of Reza Phoror, who changed the direction of their art.

Hichkas came to fame in 2006 when he was twenty-one years old with the album *Jang Asphalt* (Tar War), and he quickly became the most famous rapper in Iran.

He left Iran for Britain in 2010 when he was twenty-five, and in his own words, not to stay there forever but to pave the musical way for the youth of Tehran.

His songs are full of idioms and references, and the use of street language has made his music understandable and appealing to a young audience. Through his songs he intends to serve the oppressed Iranian people.

In December 2019, Soroush Lashkari composed the song "He Clenched His Fist" (*dastasho mosht karde*) in support of that year's protests and put it on the social networks. The song went viral. Nine days after its release, it was accessed by nearly 250,000 listeners and retweeted almost 8,000 times.[20]

Hichkas denounces the oppressive Regime. *"They slaughter everyone behind locked doors,"* he sang of the experiences of the protesters of 2019, and of those of 2022, more than two years after his song was written. He speaks of *mardom*, which in Persian can mean both "people" and "the people" and points to the corruption of the predatory Regime and its cruelty that leaves only corpses on the ground. He sings of a kleptocratic Regime that appropriates the country's resources by excluding the people. The Regime bases its repression on the fact that "the life of the people is worthless." The association between its corruption (it is a government of thieves) and its thanatocratic cruelty (it leaves only corpses behind), is explicitly stated in the verse: *"They have exploited all the natural mines and taken them for themselves and only corpses remain on the ground."*

The acute sense of oppression goes hand in hand with the class disparity that has turned into a bottomless abyss. His words echo the demands of the 2019 movement in Iran against poverty and the recklessness and repression of the Islamic Regime. The rapper denounces in passing the opulence of the "sons of the new rich of the Regime" (*agha-zadegan*). They show off their lavish lifestyles in Iran and especially in the West, far from the undue restrictions imposed on the poor: *"The tulips are crushed under their boots and the blood-stained clothes become carpets under the feet of the sons of the rich people of this Regime."* The cry against oppression is coupled, at the end, with the call for a popular uprising against a bloodthirsty government that not only kills but also plunders the nation by robbing it of its resources and creating miserable living conditions for the people, who are put to death if they protest.

Emad Qavidel

Emad Qavidel is an Iranian rapper born in 1982 in Rasht, northern Iran. While attending university, he met the rapper Yas, a Persian poet known for his hit single "The Battle for Homs." Inspired by rap's style of political and social protest, he released his songs via a variety of streaming services, including Spotify and Apple Music.

He began participating in freestyle rap battles with his friends in the early 1990s. In 2009, he started to study music in college. His songs reflect the despair and resentment of a sacrificed generation whose tormentor is clearly identified as the predatory state. He describes his distress in his song "My Generation" (*naslé man*), recorded in 2018. In it he sums up the desperate mood of an entire generation that seeks to rid itself of the misery caused by what it calls Fate (*zamaneh* or its colloquial form, *zamuneh*). It is the desperate situation created by a predatory state that the rapper cannot name before the Mahsa Movement, under penalty of a ban on singing and imprisonment, even torture and death.

This song reveals the disarray of this generation that had not yet revolted and was afraid of insurrection because their parents and grandparents had experienced the revolution against the Shah in 1979. His overthrow, instead of opening new vistas, had devastating consequences. They saw their situation worsen under a more inquisitorial regime in which economic and social decline went hand in hand with the harshest repression (the numerous street protests that were cruelly crushed since 2009). Moreover, it is a generation tired of war (the long Iran–Iraq war, waged by the Iraqi Regime in the midst of the Iranian Revolution in 1980, lasted for eight years and resulted in more than half a million deaths on both sides and several hundred thousand wounded[21]). They cannot live in genuine peace since the Islamic Regime is at loggerheads with most of the world. The various Western sanctions and the ineptitude of the Islamic Regime, undermined by corruption, negligence, and a lack of responsibility towards society, have reduced a large part of the once prosperous Iranian middle classes to destitution (more than one-third of the Iranian population lives below the UN poverty line, 60 percent are poor by international norms, and Iran ranks 183 in terms of the ratio of wages to living expenses in the world[22]). This youth has no grudge against anyone, including the West, but the Islamic Regime uses its struggle against the Western world as a pretext for denying any autonomy to the citizens.

The singer states that his father and mother died after the Revolution and he is part of a lonely, parentless generation, who do not know how to give meaning to their lives and are driven by this sad refrain: *"Today I regret yesterday. Tomorrow I'll cry for today."* Hope has left their tired bodies, beaten by the real and symbolic blows of a predatory Regime.

He sings of how people must endure a life of misery (*"your family doesn't have enough to eat"*) and that he belongs to the burnt generation (*"I am from the burnt generation, let me stir the ashes"*). In this country, there is no joy for its young people, and life no longer has any meaning (*"When as a young person your joy of living (*zowq*) is dead, continuing to live makes you sick"*). However, he declares at the same time that there is no question of him remaining forever *"in the pram"* (to remain passive in the face of repression).

We understand all the more how the Mahsa Movement had a cathartic meaning for this lost generation who thought they had no future, did not know who to turn to, and found themselves regretting the past by suffering an inexorable destiny. The Mahsa Movement was a glimmer of hope, the joy of emerging from the dark night in which the hated Regime had locked them up – the revolt of women against the coercive veil, of men whose bodies were bruised by despair. Qavidel's ultimate message is: "Care about the living rather than the dead," which is a challenge to the Islamic Regime that has gradually become a thanatocracy, not shying away from killing and torture to uphold its despicable established order.

The Iranian rapper draws the mental landscape of this lost generation who found no relief before the movement of 2022. The rapper compares himself to the wild geese of northern Iran, near the Caspian Sea, who are shot by the hunter, personification of the bloodthirsty Regime. The revolt of 2022 is a salvation for this generation, which is not intimidated by death because it has lived with death in its soul throughout its desperate youth.

A desire for a peaceful and neutral relationship with the West, in contrast to the Theocratic Regime, is particularly visible in the rapper's words: "America and the devious England" have been replaced under the Islamic Regime by China and Russia, the new hegemonic powers. His attitude is reminiscent of the slogan chanted in the demonstrations: "Our enemy is here/They lie [the Islamic Regime's supporters] that it is America" (*dochmane ma haminjast/dorouq migan amrikast*). Singers often compare the predatory Regime to a colonial power that does not respect the people.

Security forces arrested several musicians and artists, including the two rappers involved in the protests – Emad Qavidel and Kurdish rapper Saman Yasin. Qavidel was released on bail and described in an Instagram post how he was tortured and had his teeth smashed. Saman Yasin, as described earlier, was subjected to severe mental and physical torture while in custody, according to the Iranian human rights group in Norway, Hengaw, and was sentenced to death in a show trial.[23] Under international pressure his sentence will be reviewed.

Despair in the depths of the soul is the most common feeling expressed by Iranian hip-hop singers. As with other rappers, engaging in the Mahsa Movement, with its promising beginnings, brought a sense of release to them and to all the youth who were not supported by their elders in the street protests.

Sportsmen and sportswomen as activists

Men largely outnumber the female victims of the Islamic Regime's physical violence; a high number of men have been abused, tortured, and killed for defending human rights under the Islamic Republic, and the fact remains that their deaths are in a long line of other men killed in the struggle against the powers that be throughout Iran's history. What is new now is that women too are acting massively as political activists and protesters in the streets in the name of their female identity, accepting the likelihood of being imprisoned, tortured, or even put to death. This fact distinguishes the Mahsa Movement from previous ones.

The revolt against the tyranny of the Islamic Regime has been supported by sportsmen and women. Their careers depend on the government's approval for them to participate in national and international sports events and they have paid a heavy price for the support of the Mahsa Movement. Soccer stars have played a significant role in supporting the demonstrators, at the risk of their privileges and sometimes at the price of their arrest and confiscation of their goods and properties.

Alongside Ali Dai (Iranian footballer), Ali Karimi, star of the Iranian national soccer team, has defended the Iranian protests, as well as Sardar Azmoun, a player on the national team. Belonging to the Turkmen ethnic minority, he supported his sister, herself a sportswoman in the national volleyball team.

Iranian archer Parmida Ghasemi publicly removed her veil on November 11, 2022, at an awards ceremony in Tehran. Threatened by the authorities, she later reneged on her decision in support of the protesters.

Niloufar Mardani, a roller skater in the Turkish games, came to the podium without a headscarf to receive her award on November 7, 2022. Similarly, in the Asian games, on a few occasions the sports teams refused to sing the Iranian national anthem in protest. At the 2022 World Cup in Qatar, Iranians were divided. Many refused to support their national soccer team because it did not side with the protesters.

Once the movement had ceased its collective mobilization, the Islamic State turned against the athletes and sanctioned them in multiple ways.

Human rights activists

Hundreds of human rights activists, lawyers, sports people, students, teachers have been put in prison and have died or had their lives shattered for resisting repression. One of the latest victims is Hossein Ronaqi, an activist for freedom of expression and free access to social networks, who was repeatedly arrested and imprisoned for many years, during which he lost one of his kidneys. The last time, after he managed to escape the Regime's plainclothes militia who abducted him, he announced in a video that he would freely surrender to the Evin prosecutor's office. On that day, the plainclothes militia violently stopped him before he could enter the office and took him to an undeclared prison in an ambulance (they often use ambulances to escape public scrutiny). The video of this incident was posted on social networks.

Two days after his arrest, in a brief phone call, he told his family that they had broken his legs (to show him that escaping was not an option). To denounce the abuse against him, he went on hunger strike for sixty-four days and according to the doctors, he was at risk of heart failure at any moment, as his kidney was not functioning properly, and infection could lead to his death. In view of the fame of this activist, the authorities released him under surveillance on November 26, 2022. He could return to prison at any time, should there be improvement in his health.

Another case is a little-known young man called Khodanoor Lajah, from the city of Zahedan in Baluchistan province. He was born in 1995 and died while confronting the security forces the day after the "Bloody Friday" protests in Zahedan on September 30, 2022, in which around 100 people were killed and injured.

According to his friends, he used to dance and sing and was active on social media. On his Instagram profile, there is a poem about *"I am tired of this prison called life."* Like many young Iranians, he felt that his life had no future under repression.

5

From a theocratic state to a totalitarian one

The state that was gradually rebuilt after the 1979 Revolution was clerical in its hierarchy, but also and progressively, plutocratic (a closed elite formed around the Supreme Leader and within the IRGC), and then kleptocratic (there was a lack of control by the legal institutions over the Supreme Leader's resources as well as those of the IRGC), and finally, thanatocratic (the widespread repression of society, first in 1988 – at least 2,500 executions – and then from 2016, the killing of thousands of protesters in the street demonstrations and in prison). In this State the Supreme Leader, the upper layer of the Revolutionary Guards as well as part of the clergy that dominates the judiciary and the major institutions of the Islamic Regime are the major actors of the Theocratic Regime. In this increasingly repressive state, Basij (an IRGC organization that supervises cities and neighborhoods and cracks down on protests) plays a key role. More than a dozen organizations share the task of repression, the most important being the IRGC and its subsidiaries, and especially Basij, which recruits young men of modest social origins, who patrol urban areas, particularly in the neighborhoods of the large cities, and enjoy various benefits. The militias dressed in civilian clothes (*lebas shakhsi ha*) are the agents of the Regime under the direct order of the Supreme Leader. They assault demonstrators with total impunity, without answering to official authorities. The cities have become increasingly the scene of protest movements while the government uses urban riot squads in conjunction with Basij, the police, and the militia.

The crackdown on protest movements as a central mission of the totalitarian state

In their great majority, protest movements fail, especially when they aim at the overthrow of states. But while failing, they open new vistas. Individuals who dared to confront the "monster" (the state, a repressive ruling class, and so on) gain experience, perceive themselves and others in a different light, and confront the powers that be with new challenges. Even those who refused or did not dare to take part in the movement might be influenced by the demonstrations. The government can become more repressive to prevent other movements, but society also learns not to have an inveterate fear of the state and dare to confront it in new, unpredictable ways.

The Mahsa Movement failed in its political aims (the overthrow of the Islamic Republic) but it culturally "won" insofar as women dared for the first time to assert themselves as citizens and continued to reject the repressive norms imposed on them in daily life. The movement revealed the crisis of legitimacy of the Islamic Republic, which it can no longer conceal. The conditions for future confrontations are gradually building up against a regime that neither adapts to nor recognizes society's evolution and which believes that any flexibility would weaken it and create the conditions for future challenges to its legitimacy. Blunt repression is the only means by which the Islamic Republic intends to subdue society: not to find a compromise acceptable to the people, but to declare itself the sole and exclusive power in the name of a totalitarian version of Islam. The repressive state hides behind the cloak of religion, but this does not fool the vast majority of citizens, who deny it legitimacy but remain powerless in the face of its brutality.

The aim of this type of state, which I call "soft totalitarianism," is to repress and eliminate the those in the vanguard of the protest movements, so that for a few years the government can remain unchallenged. With the advent of new protest groups after time, the solution is identical: behead the leadership groups once again, in order to neutralize social protest for another spell of time. In other words, from the viewpoint of this totalitarian state, nothing must be relinquished of the its absolute authority over society, and on each occasion, protest must be nipped in the bud by ferociously eliminating the groups at the fore. Protest movements are quashed, and the Regime remains steadfast in its crackdown of social activists who propel a non-organized movement (no organization is condoned by the predatory regime). As a result, social discontent counts for little.

Under Hafez al Asad, the Syrian state had no hesitation in ferociously repressing the opposition (1,000 executions in Palmyra prison on June 27, 1980, of members of the Muslim Brotherhood) or putting tens of thousands of people to death in the city of Hama in 1982. The Islamic Republic did the same in Iran in 1988, executing at least 2,500 political prisoners.[1] After 2016, the pattern of systematic repression was set in motion with the Supreme Leader's absolute grip on the state apparatus (with the reformists in 1997, there was a two-decade-long internecine struggle between the Supreme Leader and the President, and the former prevailed). Since then, the suppression of social protest by the most repressive means has become the rule, and the Mahsa Movement is no exception to this pattern of repression: decapitating the movement through mass arrests (more than 20,000 young people were arrested and tortured) and summary killings (more than 520 killed on the street).

The rupture between State and society being consummated, the catastrophic mismanagement of the crisis by the former lays the foundation for future social protests to occur, due to the lack of dialogue with society and its inability to entirely muzzle the people.

In Iran, civil society has been in part simply neutralized by the repression. The reigning theocracy has been totally discredited. It has no legitimacy, but continues to rule through sheer violence, in a society in which the vanguard of protest has been crushed in the streets of its cities.

Maybe one day society will find the ways to overthrow this state through new social mobilizations that will catch it off guard, or use its crisis to undermine it from within.

Forms of repression

Protest movements in Iran since the Green Movement of 2009 have followed one another at an accelerated pace not only because the socioeconomic and political situation has deteriorated, but also, and above all, because the Islamic State has become increasingly repressive. This can be seen in the increased number of prisoners and, since 2009, in the increasingly violent forms of control that have imitated the "Syrian model" of indiscriminate repression since 2015, when several hundred deaths were caused by the forces of law and order against demonstrators. These forms of repression include ethnic, ecological, religious, and imprisonment. In reality, they are intertwined.

Ethnic repression

The modern Iranian state, since its inception under Reza Shah in the 1920s, fought against the tribes and ethnic groups that refused to submit, and repressed them. During World War II, at the urging of the Soviet Union, a fringe of the Kurds formed an independent Iranian Kurdistan in 1943 and the Komala (the Democratic Party of Iran's Kurdistan) established the independent Republic of Mahabad in 1946, an attempt that failed after the Iranian–Soviet agreement. During the 1979 Kurdish rebellion after the establishment of the Islamic Republic, several thousand Kurds died in clashes with the Iranian army.

The Kurds have until recently pursued separatism, but in the Mahsa Movement in 2022, a new ethnic subjectivity emerged that no longer questioned national unity but aimed above all to join forces within Iranian civil society, to achieve social and political freedom by opposing the theocratic rule. At the end of November 2022, more than a hundred deaths among the Kurdish demonstrators were recorded of a population of 1.6 million, more than ten times the number of deaths compared to Iran *in toto*, with a population of 85 million and some 520 recorded deaths. The same can be observed among the Baluchis in southeastern Iran, who are Sunni Muslims. More than a hundred people died in this province during the demonstrations of September 2022, for a population of 2.3 million (around ten times more deaths than in the rest of the country).

The discrimination and denial of existence of ethnic groups did not trigger separatist tendencies during the Mahsa Movement; on the contrary, the demonstrators expressed their desire for unity with the Iranian people to regain freedom together and put an end to the autocratic Regime. This did not mean that the Kurds as an ethnic minority group did not still have demands, but that they did not express them during the Mahsa Movement so as not to weaken it, and to maintain a common front against the Theocratic State. The same holds true for the Baluchis.

Ecological repression

There is a serious environmental catastrophe unfolding in Iran, notably due to the ecocidal actions of the government in several regions where the fragile ecological balance is in the process of being irreversibly altered, not only because of global climate change, but also due to the destructive action of the State, particularly through the interventions of the IRGC's engineers.

The Iranian Regime has not only not acted to halt desertification due to climate change but has greatly intensified it in many ways. The lack of a comprehensive policy to combat desertification is particularly accentuated by the construction of numerous dams, mainly by the IRGC, the transfer of water from one basin to another for the establishment of industries run by its financial and technological branches, and the expansion of water-intensive agriculture to increase profits in the short term. This policy has accelerated deforestation, the shrinkage of marshes due to drought, and the decrease in soil fertility. The damaged ecology has in turn increased the migration to the cities of rural people whose agricultural land has been devasted by drought and salinization.[2]

Some of the many consequences of this environmental destruction can be mentioned. In Tehran, for example, the city is sinking by five centimeters per year, with areas where the level could even drop by 25 centimeters annually. The indiscriminate pumping of groundwater is causing the ground to sink.[3]

The city of Ahvaz in southwestern Iran, capital of Khuzestan, is one of the hottest cities in the world. The summer heat exacerbates the polluting fumes associated with large industrial activity (mass oil refining industries) and the many old and polluting cars. These fumes settle at a very low atmospheric level. This partly explains why, on June 29, 2017, the temperature reached 53.7°C.[4] This city is an ecological disaster, partly due to global warming, but largely due to the reckless and short-sighted pursuit of profit by the Islamic Republic's public sector, without regard for the fragility of the environment in this region. In 2013, Ahvaz topped the list of the most polluted cities in the world,[5] according to the World Health Organization. Ahvaz's average air quality index was 372 – the world average is about 71 – and was described as dangerous. It was the only city on the list with an average value above 300. According to the Unrepresented Nations and Peoples Organization (UNPO), "desertification caused by the detour of rivers and the draining of marshes, and by oil, petrochemical, metal, sugar and paper processing factories in Ahvaz and the surrounding area, are the contributing factors."[6]

More than four years later in 2017, the situation remained unchanged, and the people most affected were the city's indigenous Arabs, subject to "internal colonization" in the oil-rich part of Iran that produces much of the country's wealth. They are discriminated against and stigmatized because of their language and customs and are driven to economic destitution by the Islamic Republic, which continues and exacerbates the policy of social repression and economic domination initiated during the Pahlavi dynasty. Geographically, the city is located on the slopes of a basin on the edge of the Persian Gulf in which also lie other major oil refining centers (Iraqi, Iranian, Kuwaiti, and Saudi) such as Basra, Abadan, Kuwait City, the seaports of Bandar Mahshahr and Bandar Imam Khomeini, and petrochemical complex Khafji. This results in the accumulation of polluting gases over Ahvaz when the wind blows northwards, capturing the gases on the slopes of the Zagros Mountains. As a consequence, acid rain sometimes showers down on Ahvaz.[7]

In this city, as in many parts of Iran, accelerated desertification and the high levels of pollution are the result of the massive drying up of rivers and marshes due to the damming and river detour project launched since 1989, mainly under the aegis of the IRGC. The project diverted millions of cubic meters of water from the region's rivers to other parts of Iran and intensified the already high regional rates of pollution and environmental degradation. In addition to the oil refineries and petrochemical plants in the region, there is pollution from sugarcane burning caused by the expansion of its intensive agriculture started under the Pahlavi regime and accelerated under the Islamic Republic. These phenomena are at the origin of dust storms mixed with clouds of suffocating pollution caused by an absurd system in a fragile ecological environment. Local agriculture has suffered profoundly in Khuzestan, as in the rest of Iran.

Disregard for the ecology of semi-desert areas has led to droughts and the mass migration of villagers to the cities, where they have constituted an incompressible mass of unemployed as well as a growing discontent within swarming slum areas. The protests of 2018, in which environmental problems were one of the main issues, also included these peasant masses displaced to the cities among the protagonists. Iran has experienced fourteen years of drought this century, without any water saving or appropriate agriculture programs being put in place. Authorities, including then Energy Minister Hamid Chichian, acknowledged in 2016 the critical situation: 86 percent of water resources were being used instead of the 40 percent that is the international standard. Apart from climate change, the irrational increase in water-intensive agricultural production and control of water resources by the IRGC and power elites have been the cause of the country's critical ecological situation. This led to a 30 percent drop in wheat production in 2021.[8]

Iranian environmentalists have been trying to draw attention to the disaster unfolding in Iran, particularly in relation to the wildlife. A group of eight environmentalists, associated with the Persian Wildlife Heritage Foundation (PWHF), who tried to raise the alarm were arrested in January 2018 for "espionage" and "crimes against national security" and one of them, Kevous Seyed Emami, died in detention, most likely under torture, seventeen days after his arrest. According to UN experts, it was a criminal act by the Iranian state. Kaveh Madani, an expert on Iran's water resources, had left his academic position in London at the end of 2017 to help his country solve the problem of water shortage. A few months after his arrival, he was arrested and subjected to harsh interrogation by the IRGC. He fled Iran in April 2018. According to Human Rights Watch in Iran, more than forty environmentalists and some of their family members were arrested in May 2018 in the port of Bandar Langeh on the Persian Gulf and surrounding towns. They were working with the PWHF group.[9] The reasons for these arrests are the appropriation by the IRGC of wild areas of land for missile tests, but also the construction of dams that destroy the environment but are financially lucrative for its financial echelons. Environmentalists denounce the IRGC's utter disrespect for the environment in its economic activities.

Isfahan, Iran's third largest city, saw several days of street protests over water shortages in April 2018. The government had diverted water from Isfahan's rivers, not least the city's iconic river, Zayandeh Rud, which has now dried up, to the neighboring province of Yazd for so-called industrial purposes, again to the benefit of the military-economic conglomerate IRGC and its associates.

Similarly, in Khorramchahr in the south of Iran, the lack of water and water pollution have repeatedly driven the inhabitants onto the streets. People complained that the water flowing from their taps was murky and foul. The cause of this was known to environmentalists: the Gotvand Dam erected on the Karun River in 2004 despite warnings about its negative impact on the environment as it was situated on salt deposits that would be flooded and thus pollute its water. Since then, the high salinity of the river has damaged the once fertile agricultural land in the Khuzestan region.

A much mistaken and short-sighted policy, the lure of substantial gains even if only through the project funding paid by the government to the IRGC, and environmentally disrespectful agricultural policies promoted by the same actors always in search of short-term profits, are the causes of the ecological disasters in many provinces. Since the 1990s, under the aegis of the economic giant that has become the IRGC, Iran has built more than 650 dams (in 1979, before the Islamic Revolution, there were only thirteen dams on rivers in Iran), disrupting the ecological balance, and transferring huge sums of money to the IRGC at the expense of the farmers.[10] The projects carried out by the IRGC have resulted in the enrichment of its leaders, the impoverishment of the farmers, and the destruction of a fragile ecosystem. And when protests take place, it is with the violence of arms that they are dealt with. A breach has thus been progressively achieved between an autocratic regime and a society increasingly subjected to intolerable ecological and economic deterioration. In 2010 the country had the second worst rate of soil erosion in the world; in 2011 it was the worst, according to Esmail Kahrom, professor of ecology at Tehran University.[11]

The protests over environmental abuse often end in violence against the protesters, and sometimes, their deaths. One case among many can be cited. Hadi Bahmani, seventeen, was killed on the night of Tuesday, July 20, 2021 (more than a year before the September 2022 protests) during the demonstrations in the city of Izeh. Two bullets pierced his chest. The police shot with intent to kill, aiming at the upper body – which is especially their custom in ethnic provinces where deep rooted racism makes the police and militias even more violent than elsewhere.

Hadi was from the village of Sosan near the city of Izeh and came to Izeh in northeastern Khuzestan to work as a laborer.

On July 15, 2021, large-scale demonstrations were taking place in different cities in the Arabic-speaking areas of Khuzestan province to protest the lack of water and poor social and economic conditions, including poverty and discrimination. They soon spread to other cities in the region including Ahvaz, Susangard, Dezful, Behbahan, Mahshahr, and Abadan.[12] Hadi's body was buried on July 22 in Golal village in Sosan, accompanied by a large crowd. His family intended to bury him in Izeh, but for fear of anti-Regime protests, the security forces forced them to bury him in Sosan.

A week after the general protests in Khuzestan, other parts of Iran rose up, including parts of drought-ridden Isfahan, on July 21, 2021. According to videos released, protesters shouted, "An Iranian may die, but he does not accept humiliation" (*irani mimirad, zellat nemipazirad*).

In northwestern Iran, Lake Urmia has been reduced to one-fifth of its former size. It has been shrinking for a long time, with an annual evaporation rate of 0.6 to 1 meters. Although steps were taken to reverse the trend, the lake has shrunk by more than 60 percent and may disappear entirely. Only 5 percent of the lake's water remained in 2014 and the outlook is equally bleak in 2022.[13] There have been numerous protests since August 2011 over its gradual disappearance. Throughout the decade, there have been sporadic demonstrations in defense of the lake, which is also a symbol of the identity of Urmia city and even the Azerbaijan region. The last demonstrations took place two months before the Mahsa Movement began. Following the call of civil organizations and human rights groups, protesters gathered on July 16, 2022, in the main districts of the northwestern Iranian cities of Ardebil, Zanjan, Tabriz, and Urmia. Sixteen protesters were arrested. Dozens of civilian activists were summoned to security agencies afterwards (they had been covertly filmed).

Another example is the Kor River, which is the largest river in Fars province and one of the main sources of agricultural, industrial, and drinking water in the cities of Shiraz and Marvdasht. The dams built by the Ministry of Energy at the source of the Kor have stored water behind it. The profit-oriented vision of monopolistic groups within different institutions of the Islamic Regime has left the villagers without water and led to migration and the creation of slums around the major cities in the region.

The management of ecology in Iran is entirely subordinated to the organized exploitation of natural resources in the service of economic conglomerates constituted primarily by the IRGC, but also by monopolies dominated by Regime officials and often in collusion with it. The Islamic Republic and its power brokers have implemented a policy that systematically ignores the imperatives of a fragile ecology by promoting the short-term financial interests of dominant groups. Anyone who attempts to defend the environment comes into conflict with the economic mafia and is accused of endangering national security. The case of the arrested environmentalists (one of them killed in prison, as already mentioned) is exemplary in this respect. The environmental protests that have been suppressed for more than a decade point to the close link between the predatory state and environmental destruction, in short, its "ecocidal" nature.

The protests that began in September 2022 are an accumulation of grievances that are political (the muzzling of freedom), economic (the impoverishment of society and the monopolistic enrichment of a ruling mafia), ecological (the degradation of the environment), and gendered (women's inferiority).

Religious repression

Several groups are the targets of religious repression in Iran, to varying degrees: Sunnis (recognized but repressed as ethnic-religious minorities, Kurds, Baluchis, etc.), Sufi dervishes (Muslim mystics, including the Gonabadi dervishes),

Evangelists (Pentecostal converts), and above all, the Baha'is. The latter constitute a minority of some 300,000 people in Iran who refuse, because of their religious creed, to conceal their faith and therefore, are subject to systematic repression. The reason is that they believe in the prophet Baha'ullah, who proclaimed the new faith in 1863, and they deny that the Prophet of Islam was the last one. Since then, they have been treated as apostates and were persecuted by the Qajar and even Pahlavi dynasty. But it is especially since the Revolution of 1979 that their repression has become methodical and relentless.

The most elementary rights are denied them. The most brutal forms of repression, ranging from the arrest of their leaders, the denial of schooling for their children to expropriation and the death penalty under the pretext of espionage, have been imposed on them since the 1979 Revolution.[14]

Prison repression

Since its establishment in 1979, the prison has become one of the essential pillars of the Islamic Regime. Incarceration, torture, and capital punishment are the three main ways in which the Islamic Regime suppresses social opposition. The proliferation of jails (around three dozen undeclared in 2022,[15] many under the aegis of different repressive organizations) and the intolerable conditions within them such as the denial of medical care,[16] serve to break the resistance of the prisoners. There are human rights activists, feminists, bloggers, young people who refuse the arbitrary limitation of their secular freedom, and all those who reject the Regime's totalitarian political system in these prisons. Not only are convictions of political or civic activists commonplace, but also the designation as a crime of what in other societies would be a matter of social and health care policies, such as addiction (individuals have been sentenced to heavy prison terms for taking drugs). Certainly, prison is one of the privileged settings for suppressing political or civic activists, not only in Iran but in all tyrannical regimes. However, in Iran, repression is taking on increasingly harsh forms. As the government is losing legitimacy, espousing a "Syrian style" of harsh violence against its opponents has become commonplace.

In the tormented political landscape, Evin prison, built in 1972, has had an undeniable symbolic centrality as a place of detention and torture since the Shah's regime. Its evocation awakens in most Iranians the anguish of torture and death, not only among the former prisoners. Spread over a fifty-seven-hectare site north of Tehran, its premises have been greatly expanded under the Islamic Republic. A radical leftist activist, Monireh Baradaran, describes it as follows:

> Evin has never been without political prisoners. Subsequent generations have passed through it and are passing through it [still]. It is history; on the one hand, it contains the memory of five decades of struggle and protest, and on the other hand, it is a document of the repression by the governments of different eras, a document of the dark history of our country. No one, not even the best historical researcher, can write its history alone. Evin's history and memory are a chain and a collection of memories, memories recounted.[17]

In this prison, one section is most feared, that known as Section 2-A (*bande 2-aleph*), independent of the prison administration and directly under the command of the IRGC, which imprisons political and civic detainees, journalists, feminists, and bloggers among others. They are subjected to harsh interrogation and psychological and physical torture. This section began operating in 2009, after the crackdown on major street protests in Tehran and the arrest of thousands of people, who were contesting Ahmadinejad's fraudulent presidential election against Mir Hossein Moussavi. His election led to protests among young people and the chant of "Where is my vote?" (*ra'ye man koo?*), during the so-called Green Movement.[18]

Political activists and human rights defenders are subjected to severe mental and physical torture during their detention:[19] severe beatings by staff, sleep deprivation, endless and exhausting interrogations, several months in solitary confinement, prohibition of contact with family and lawyers, serious threats to family members of detainees in case they report to the foreign press, threat of long-term imprisonment, the use of electric truncheons, mock executions, rape, and arrest of family members are examples of the physical and mental torture that are ongoing against the prisoners. Many of them have subsequently described them in their memoirs, some of which are available on the web.[20]

Now feminist activists, internationally known or young women refusing the compulsory veil, are transferred to this section. One example is Yasman Ariani, an activist who was sentenced to more than sixteen years in prison for opposing the mandatory veil. She was transferred from the women's section of Evin to Section 2-A. She, her mother Munireh Arabshahi, and Mojgan Keshavarz were arrested and sentenced to more than fifty-five years in prison after a video, in which, unveiled, they are seen distributing flowers to passers-by on March 8, 2022, International Women's Day.[21]

On July 20, 2022, eighteen female political prisoners from Qarchak prison were transferred to Evin. Qarchak women's prison is in the deserts of eastern Tehran, whose location makes it difficult for families to visit the prisoners. The government exploits this fact to put under pressure those, like the feminist Nasrin Sotoudeh, who do not yield to intimidation. She was incarcerated there several times.

Following the protests in a district of Tehran, Golestan 7, by Gonabadi dervishes (see below), and the arrest of the protesters, several women were transferred to Evin.

The IRGC has several special prisons under its exclusive control that are not subject to any legal supervision. They are often located in the ethnic areas, in the northwest in Urmia (Turkish and Kurdish-speaking), Sanandaj (Kurdish-speaking), and Kermanshah (Kurdish-speaking), in addition to Tehran and prisons such as Evin.

Conditions in the women's ward of Khoy prison in northwest Iran are intolerable. Its female prisoners suffer from hunger. Red meat is not part of their diet. Chicken is rarely on the menu, and one chicken is the food quota for thirty-eight inmates. The guards distribute the precious meat to the prisoners who collaborate with them and do their "dirty work," often against other inmates, or by spying on the others or by attacking political prisoners. The hard labor unit is located next to Khoy prison.

Opened in 2009, Fashafouyeh prison has a capacity of 17,000, which makes it according to some experts the largest prison in the Middle East. It is located 12 kilometers from the Tehran–Qom highway. By comparison, France's largest prison, the Fleury-Mérogis remand prison, has a capacity of 2,850 inmates. More than half of the inmates appear to be drug addicts who should be in hospital and who are mistreated there, along with the Afghans, who are referred to as "cattle." Many prisoners suffer from infectious diseases without medical follow-up. In a practice that has become commonplace, political and civic prisoners are not separated from ordinary ones, and they often suffer from aggression on the part of the latter, encouraged by the authorities who put them under duress. Over 300 Gonabadi dervishes were arrested in late 2018. They were sent to Fashafouyeh and subjected to various mistreatment, including torture. On August 29, 2018, the imprisoned dervishes were beaten and some of them were seriously injured by the security agents. They had been on a sit-in for about two and a half months in support of the women dervishes imprisoned in Qarchak prison, to protest their mistreatment there. Human Rights Watch has condemned the ill-treatment of women by security agents.[22]

Alireza Shirmohammed-Ali, a political prisoner, died there from thirty stab wounds in June 2019. On September 21, 2021, the news of the suspicious death of Shahin Nasseri in the isolation cell of this prison was confirmed. He was a journalist and had witnessed the torture of Navid Afkari in Shiraz. On September 25, 2021, a prisoner named Amir Hossein Hatami died as a result of beatings in this prison.

Mehrdad Mohammadnejad, a social media activist, was imprisoned in Evin prison and transferred to Fashafouyeh on January 23, 2020. The twenty-three-year-old economics student is serving a three-year sentence for insulting officials and agents and spreading propaganda against the Regime. Mehrdad attended university three times a week and worked the rest of the week as a delivery boy for a Tehran restaurant to cover his tuition. He was arrested on October 21, 2018, after intelligence agents raided his home in Shahriar, a working-class town west of Tehran. They severely beat him before taking him into custody. They also confiscated his tablet, cell phone, books, and documents. For a few days, his family did not know his whereabouts, until Mehrdad called his older brother to tell him that he had been transferred to Evin prison.[23]

The case of Kurdish political prisoner Zainab Jalalian is a sad example of how the Regime treats ethnic activists in Iran. She was born in 1982 and is originally from the village Dim Qashlaq in the city of Makou in the northwestern Iranian province of Azerbaijan. She was arrested on February 26, 1998, and was subjected to severe physical and mental torture for about three months in the detention center of the Kermanshah intelligence department on charges of belonging to the Free Life Party of Kurdistan (Hayat Azad Kurdistan Party, Pajak).

On December 3, 2008, she was sentenced to death by the First Chamber of the Islamic Revolutionary Court of Kermanshah for belonging to Pajak and armed struggle against the Islamic

Republic of Iran. After appealing against this verdict, the case was sent back to the Court of Appeal of Kermanshah and the verdict was confirmed. It was ultimately approved by the Supreme Court in the winter of 2008. Following numerous efforts to overturn her death sentence by her family, lawyers, and human rights activists, her sentence was commuted to life imprisonment in November 2011 by the clemency of the Supreme Leader. She was transferred from Kermanshah prison to Ward 209 of Evin prison for common prisoners and where political prisoners are subjected to abuse, often at the encouragement of authorities. After five months in this prison, she was sent back to Dizelabad prison in Kermanshah. Frequent prison changes are meant to break inmates psychologically. In November 2014, she was transferred from Kermanshah to Khoy prison in northwestern Iran.

Amir Salar Davoudi, one of her defense lawyers who played an active role in her case, was in turn arrested on November 20, 2018 and sentenced to 111 lashes and thirty years in prison by Tehran's Revolutionary Court, including fifteen years of enforceable imprisonment for defending political prisoners.

Zainab Jalalian suffers from eye and skin diseases and since the summer of 2018, she has also suffered from severe migraines and digestive diseases. She attempted a medication strike in January 2017 to protest the lack of medical care.

In July 2019, when a delegation of inspectors from the Prison Organization visited Khoy prison, one of them told Zainab Jalalian that she would be denied treatment until she wrote a letter of repentance, which she rejected. Earlier, the Ministry of Information had announced the conditions for Zainab Jalalian's transfer to the hospital, namely a confession interview in which she would incriminate herself and her friends and make an act of repentance.

She entered the fifteenth year of her imprisonment in March 2022. In 2018, she published an open letter denouncing the denial of access to medical services by prison authorities. Subsequently, she was denied visitation rights with her family.

In 2020, she was suddenly transferred from Khoy to Qarchak prison near Tehran, then to Kerman prison (in the south of Iran, a thousand kilometers away from the first one), then to Kermanshah correctional center (in the west of Iran), and finally to Yazd prison (in the south of Iran) in October of the same year.[24] These frequent transfers were intended to destabilize her, not letting her take root, make contacts and acquaintances in detention.

Another case that highlights the use of imprisonment to punish civic detainees is that of the protesters in Golestan 7, a district in Tehran. A series of protests by the Gonabadi dervishes took place in March and April 2017 that denounced undue restrictions on their spiritual leader, Nour-Ali Tabandeh. They were suppressed by the security forces, particularly Basij. The repression was bloody. Six of them died, one was later executed, and hundreds were arrested and injured. Among the latter, a woman Shokoufeh Yadollahi lost her sense of smell due to severe beatings, and at least two people, Ahmad Barakouhi and Mohsen Norouzi, lost an eye after being hit by a bullet. During the Golestan 7 protests, about sixty women dervishes were arrested and eleven of them were transferred to the women's prison in Qarchak. Others were sent to Fashafouyeh. Gathering and collusion against national security, disturbing public order, and disobeying the police were the charges brought against them. After two years, most of the detainees, including women dervishes, had served their sentences and fifty of them had been released on amnesty. Behnam Mahjoubi, a protester, died in prison from drug poisoning and lack of medical care in January 2021. Five years later, four dervishes were still in prison. Three women, Shokoufeh Yadollahi, Sima Intisari, and Sepideh Moradi, were released after nearly two years in prison. In January 2021, Shokoufeh Yadollahi's two sons, Kasri and Amir Nouri, are among those still in prison.

From a theocratic state to a totalitarian one 191

In 2023 CNN produced an inquiry into the repressive prison system in Iran:

> In late February, CNN's international investigative unit published an investigation into secret detention centers used by the Iranian Regime, pinpointing more than three dozen clandestine jails, or black sites, many of which were undeclared and operated inside of government or Iranian Revolutionary Guard Corps (IRGC) facilities.
>
> Drawing on about two dozen testimonies from Iranian lawyers and survivors of the black sites, CNN found that the use of black sites – which exist outside of Iranian due process – was unprecedented in scale.
>
> Among the most severe forms of torture detailed in those testimonies were electrocutions, removal of nails, lashings and beatings that resulted in scars and broken limbs, and sexual violence.
>
> The findings paint a picture of a Regime meting out torture on an industrial scale, to crush an uprising that has posed the biggest domestic threat to the clerical elite in decades.[25]

Numerous biographies in Persian left by political prisoners show the perpetuation of mistreatment[26] and torture in Iranian prisons since the beginning of the Islamic Republic in 1979.

Mass imprisonment to break up dissent

The question that arises is the rationality of imprisonment against human rights activists (and especially feminists) in Iran. Often, the usual perception is that in repressive regimes, citizens transgress illegitimate norms and find themselves at the mercy of an unjust legal system. But the coercive logic of the Iranian Regime goes far beyond that. Often, an activist, male or female, finds themselves accused of fictitious breaches of the law and sentenced to long prison terms. But persecution does not stop there. Once imprisoned, they may wait until the end of their sentence to get out of prison, but the judiciary then concocts new charges against them that lead to the creation of one or more fictitious criminal cases and numerous prosecutions, resulting in the perpetuation of their imprisonment well beyond the original sentence. At the same time, everything is done to break the prisoner psychologically: they are denied access to medical services; their loved ones (especially spouse and children) are intimidated; the individual is placed in isolation and denied access to their family; they are sent to a remote common law prison where they are confronted with prisoners who are ready to assault them in exchange for various benefits (cigarette rations or various medical or food privileges in prison, in complicity with the authorities); they are forced to make fake confessions against themselves and friends in interviews recorded and broadcast on official TV.

In short, everything is designed to mentally break the male or female activists in prison. Threats are numerous, rape (women, even young men) and beating are common practices. Even when they are released from prison, they are pursued by the predatory state, which tries to discredit them among their own people, denying them privacy by tapping their phones, spying on them, and making it publicly known that they compromise anyone else they know by association. At the slightest act of protest (interview with the foreign press, participating in a demonstration, defending other civil rights activists as a lawyer, or transgressing Islamic norms, such as removing the veil), they are accused not only of their acts, but of a number of other fictitious ones, which the Islamic Republic cynically ascribes to them in order to compound their case and their sentence. They will be promptly sentenced and sent back to prison, unless they publicly acknowledge the fictitious charges against them. An unsubtle but effective way to create a criminal record that could lead to heavy prison sentences for the defendant is to accuse them of collusion with the reviled Western powers such as the United States, Israel, or Great Britain. Nasrin Sotoudeh, one of the leading figures of Iranian feminism, has experienced this and described it in her interviews.[27]

Another example is the detainees of the Tehran bazaar. One day after the bazaar was closed by shopkeepers for the anniversary of the November 2019 protests, as news of the strike spread throughout Iran, police announced the arrest of eleven people. They reportedly confessed to being on the payroll of foreign external enemies. Torture to make detainees confess is a common practice.

The spread of the coronavirus in 2020–1 worsened the situation of the prisoners. The absence of health and medical services, lack of soap, frequent water cuts, poor ventilation, overcrowding, poor nutrition, lack of vaccination, masks and care, and the abandoning of sick inmates to their sad fate have compounded the situation of the prisoners. However, the existence of luxurious cells for certain "privileged" prisoners showed a profound contempt for the others.[28]

Many unexplained deaths occur in Iranian prisons. According to Amnesty International since January 2010, at least seventy-two suspicious deaths have occurred in forty-two prisons and detention centers in sixteen provinces of Iran, in addition to the executions and deaths in December 2017 and October 2019 (those killed in the demonstrations). In 2021–2 alone, according to the Amnesty report, twenty-four people are believed to have died in detention under suspicious circumstances, amid allegations of torture and other ill-treatment, including deprivation of medical care.[29]

The case of Monireh Baradaran, a political activist already mentioned, is instructive in this regard for the 1980s. She was jailed several times. The first time, in June 1978 under the Shah, she was released six months later, just before the 1979 Revolution. Then in September 1981, she was incarcerated for nine years under the Islamic Republic. She was released in September 1990. Her comparison of the Shah's prison to that of the Islamic Republic describes the chasm between the two experiences:

> There was a good atmosphere in the common room of Evin [under the Shah]. We read hymns and books and did many things. It was more like a boarding house than a prison. It was not at all comparable to my experience in the 1980s [under the Islamic Republic].[30]

It is true that during that period the Shah was softening repressive measures and Evin was visited by human rights advocates.

To escape the abuses of the Islamic State, Baradaran chose exile and moved to Germany after her release. She published her prison memoirs. In December 1999, the German branch of the International Union of Human Rights awarded her and the writer Simine Behbahani the Carl von Ossietsky medal.

In her memoirs, she describes the abuse of male and female prisoners in Evin prison under the Islamic Republic. She notes in passing that lashes had left burn marks on the legs of some prisoners. She describes in detail the torture by flogging and its combination with being forced to hold postures that spread pain throughout the body. Like other inmates who recorded it in their prison memoirs, she describes the so-called "coffin" torture, called also "the tomb" or "the cage," invented in the prison Qezel Hesar, close to Tehran, by Davood Rahmani, its director from 1981 to 1984. The inmate was locked in a raised wooden coffin where they were forced to sit in absolute silence, while hearing during the entire day, for weeks and even months, the confessions of other inmates followed by sung readings from the Koran (*talaavat*). Some spent several months there and when they came out, they were severely psychologically damaged. One of the prisoners recounted later what Davood would say to her and many other political prisoners enduring this torture:

"You look like a dead skeleton. If you repent and confess in front of the microphone [to be recorded and then put on the TV shows of confession], you will come out of this coffin." This statement by Davood Rahmani, the head of Qezel Hesar prison at the time, was invariably heard by political prisoners of the early 1980s. He is the man whose name is associated with the most inhumane tortures and violence against political prisoners.[31]

Zia Nabavi, a civil activist in Iran, wrote on Twitter:

Haj Davood invented the "coffin" torture in 1983 (1362) when he was the head of Qezel Hesar prison. He would put the political prisoner blindfolded in a wooden and grave-like compartment with a length of two meters and a width and height of 80 centimeters, without having the right to speak until he repented.[32]

Many of those who were tortured in the coffin, generally after a period of several weeks to several months in the case of the most resistant, ended up confessing as required by the prison director. They retained the deep mental scars of this torture long afterwards and often described it in a horrifying way, even those who collaborated with the Islamic Regime and denounced their colleagues in their political party or association.[33]

As for Baradaran, she had to endure the torture of the coffin for two weeks and came out of it utterly exhausted. There are other variants described by other prisoners (they were laid in the coffin, and the lid was nailed down all day to increase the feeling of suffocation).

The torture during the interrogation period also left a lasting impression on her. She experienced a feeling of extreme humiliation and total powerlessness:

The absolute humiliation is when you realize that your body and mind are completely at the disposal of the torturer and that he will do whatever he wants with them. You are powerless in this situation. Of course, resisting and opposing it requires great strength.

In Baradaran's memoirs, the nightmarish reality behind bars in the Islamic Republic in the 1980s has a special place. The number of political prisoners reached very high figures in 1981. In the cells intended for a maximum of twenty people, the number of prisoners exceeded 100. From 1982, the construction of new cells began with more capacity. The cells were inhumanly overcrowded until the massacre of political prisoners in the summer of 1988, which was Iran's greatest crime against humanity in modern times and was later denounced by the United Nations[34] (at least 2,500 inmates were summarily put to death in that year, the estimates' upper limit being around 30,000, around 10 percent of them being women).

In the years that followed, she describes how she was tried twice in the courts of the Islamic Revolution:

> The Islamic judge had absolute power and I was alone in front of him, wrapped in a traditional veil [the black chador that envelops the entire body]. There was no semblance of a "court" there. Violence and injustice were brutally simple and exposed. He read the "crimes" [that I had committed] . . . I wanted to say a few words in my defense – "legal defense" – when the Islamic judge interrupted me and asked, "Are you interviewing [confessing]?" I wanted to give a reason for my refusal [to impute the crimes] when he interrupted me again. That was it [in my defense], just a few minutes. A few weeks later, they took me to sign my sentence. Three years [in prison]. I was lucky. How many thousands of death sentences have these Islamic judges handed down in these simple and ruthless courts?
>
> Three years later, I was not released, I was tried again. In the same building in Evin and in an empty room. The Islamic judge and me. This time the indictments were long. Everything

From a theocratic state to a totalitarian one

I had and had not done was charged as a crime. I was really scared. Would I be executed? I wanted to say that some of the facts mentioned did not concern me at all, and some of them that concerned me dated back to the early years of the revolution, when there was still some freedom left, and there was no [imputation of] secret political activity yet ... The Islamic judge interrupted me and casually asked if my future husband's family had given me gold [for the Islamic dowry]. This confused me and I kept quiet. Again [I wanted to speak and] he interrupted me asking me [if I wanted to do] an interview [where I would denounce what I had done and my accomplices, in a confession]. A few weeks later, they took me to sign my verdict. Ten years in prison, starting from the date of the trial. This time I was really lucky. It was early autumn 1984 and Ladjevardi [the director of Evin prison, known for his cruelty and the ease with which, as a revolutionary prosecutor, he had summarily sentenced many prisoners to death] had just been put aside, and they were supposed to reduce the death sentences and wait until 1988 to execute everyone at once [several thousand supporters of the People's Mojahedin were executed on the orders of Ayatollah Khomeini before his death in 1989]. I stayed in prison until 1987. In our area, all the women Mojahedin [belonging to the People's Mojahedin movement] were executed. The left-wing women were not. That year, the punishment for "apostate" women [like us] was lashes. They took some of us to court and ordered us to be flogged. Many did not get their turn, including me, and I was lucky.

Ladjevardi had said it many times in those years 1981 to 1984 when he was in charge of Evin prison, especially whenever he heard criticism about the lack of food – and his colleagues did not tire of repeating it later – that the dry bread was already too much for us; that we had all been sentenced to death and that we had survived thanks to the charity and mercy of Islam ... One year, we heard [in our cells] machine-gun fire twice a week, which was the sound of the executions. I heard those of the execution of my brother who was shot with 85 others on December 6 [1988].

I survived and walked through the door of Evin once more. It was autumn again, one of the last nights of October 1990. The last sound of the prisoner who accompanied me was the hoarse voice of a woman who said to the guard dragging her by her traditional veil [chador] in the corridor: "Why did you bring me here? Evin is for the communists!" The latter mockingly replied, "Don't worry, no one will confuse you with the communists!" The blue color of her face was indicative of her addiction.

The tools of torture that I saw in Evin in 1981 were only cables, handcuffs and ropes, and the absolute power of the torturer over his victim. The torturer was God's substitute, and the prisoner was a sinful slave. With these "simple" tools in the service of an unbridled power, they used the most violent tortures. A prisoner who can be put to death [always under threat of execution], if you are "lucky" and survive, you will have a scar – physical and mental – that will remain forever. All this happened in the modern concrete buildings of Evin ... It was on the upper floor of the same buildings that the Islamic "court" handed down thousands of death sentences in a matter of minutes. It was in this same garden full of flowers and old trees that people were shot and hanged. Parvaneh Alizadeh and other prisoners saw the bodies hanging from the trees in Evin and testified to it.[35]

The hellish life of prisons has been experienced in many autocratic countries and the novels of Alexander Solzhenitsyn and Vasily Grossman have described it in the Russian case under Stalin. In Iran, the Regime does not have a political party as omnipotent as the Russian Communist Party, but its extra-legal apparatus, its mafia-like economic power, and the collusion of the judiciary with the autocratic Regime are all conducive to the closure of the social and political scene. In

Russia, at least women and men were legally equal. Alcohol could be consumed and, above all, relations between women and men were free and unhindered. The Soviet Regime did not repress the "joie de vivre" of its citizens while denying them political freedom. The class gap did not exist with the same intensity as in Iran, where it has become a chasm. The corruption of the power elites goes hand in hand with their total impunity. Corruption worth tens or even hundreds of millions of dollars, if uncovered, attracts lenient prison sentences with non-execution clauses against the influential defendant, and extremely harsh sentences against his or her whistleblowers, if they are known. At the same time, a man or woman who advocates for human rights is sentenced to several years in prison and his or her life is permanently ruined.

The Islamic Regime's view on unveiled women and young protesters

On November 19, 2022, the Supreme Leader, in his commentary on the protests that rocked the country, threw insults at the protesters, and claimed they acted under the sway of the Islamic Regime's enemies, through deceit and malice:

> Until this hour, thank God, the Enemy [that is, the United States and Israel, more generally, the West] has been defeated, but the Enemy has each day more than one trick up his sleeve (*makr o kid*), and with his defeat today, he can go to different groups such as workers and women, although the dignity of women and honorable workers is too high for them to surrender to malicious people (*bad khahan*) and let themselves be deceived (*faribé anha ra bekhorand*).[36]

In his perception, the protests are not spontaneous but externally driven and they have no internal cause (poverty, lack of freedom, the Regime's corruption, a repressive political system).

In response to the young women denouncing the mandatory veil, Sardar Hossein Salami, the commander-in-chief of the IRGC, who adheres closely to the views of the Supreme Leader, said:

> They [our enemies] think that by staging a few whom they have more or less hoodwinked, they can weaken the glorious [Islamic] revolution. Whoever hears my voice knows that the cries of the Enemy are the cries of the Devil. They are at war with God and His Messenger [the Prophet of Islam]. They want our streets to be full of liquor stores and casinos and to make our women's faces look like those of Western women [without veils]. America likes to see our streets on fire and smoke so that we cannot send satellites into space ... America likes to see our youth killed in the street and people's faces withered, and [intends to] divide the nation and tear Iran apart, but these evil dreams of the Enemy will never come true, the Iranian nation is up and strong and resistant.[37]

He contrasts the fornication and corruption of Western women with the virtue of Muslim women and believes that the spontaneous protests of a whole generation of young people are engineered and concocted by America.

The mythical status of the Enemy, a devilish being, makes it a powerful one, likely to drag the youth in his wake, against the Islamic Republic. The deficiencies of the Regime are thus denied.

The Friday Imam of Karaj, honoring the week of the Basij organization, described the saint Zeynab (sister of the third Imam, Hossein) as symbolizing the greatness of Basij and as a role model for humanity:

> The pride of a woman in the Western world is that she exposes herself to the lustful eyes of men. The Western world has placed

women upside down in the social arena in the name of freedom and has taken away their motherhood, dignity and tranquility.

Western women are depraved, and the West wants to push Muslims in their wake to destroy Islam. This is exactly the view of Sunni jihadists who share the radicalized Shi'i perspective, while being their enemies. The cleric Ahmad Khatami, the Friday Imam of Tehran (who preaches on behalf of the Supreme Leader), stated during the period of the demonstrations that unveiled women and thieves shared the same values; they were on the same moral level:

> Some people say, "Why do you meddle with the few inches of a woman's hair that are out there, but you don't deal with theft and embezzlement?" To emphasize one sin is not to despise another sin, stealing and embezzling is certainly a sin, but being unveiled is also a sin; besides, many unveiled women and youth are of the same stock as the thieves.[38]

Similarly, the cleric Seyd Ahmad Alam-ol-Hoda, the Friday Imam of the city of Mechhed, stated bluntly a few days after the beginning of the protests, following the death of Mahsa Amini:

> A woman without a hijab depraves society, and a young man gets depraved in front of a half-naked woman [the official clergy identifies unveiled women with naked ones], with disheveled hair.[39]

The same cleric stated:

> Those who remove the headscarf and take off the hijab for America's pleasure should know that America regards them the same as the prostitutes of the 28 Mordad coup [August 19, 1953 when Mossadegh's government was overthrown by a coup

led by the United States and Great Britain]. Are you ready to give up your modesty to please America?[40]

The protest over the mandatory veil is thus identified as an American plot, and the woman who refuses to wear the hijab is called a prostitute, accomplice of this American conspiracy. The clerical representative of the Supreme Leader in Alborz province said:

> The West has nothing but humiliation for women, and today, the main demand of some rioters [the protesters of the Mahsa Movement] is a mixed university service. The issue of gender revolution and the [perverse] path taken in the West in this regard should be explained [to the youth, hoodwinked by these ideas].

Referring to the annual week-long celebration of Basij, the organization that suppresses peaceful urban protests, he continued:

> Imam Khomeini proposed the idea of Basij and the best children of the country accepted it, so it became a model for free people.[41]

The distortion of reality is at work in presenting Basij, the principal organization for the repression of urban protests, as the ideal of freedom for women and men. In his perspective, the Mahsa Movement is described as a perverse desire to copy the Western model that seeks to rob women of their Islamic femininity through fraternization with men that would pervert them, thus denying them dignity and motherhood.

Alongside this Manichean view of the Mahsa Movement, there are lower ranking leaders within the Islamic Republic who partly recognize the endogenous nature of the protests (as not purely dictated by America and Israel) and their grievances, but they go no further.

6

Secularization counter to the Theocratic State

Despite its domination of Iran for more than four decades, the Islamic State has failed to persuade the people to embrace its theocratic creed (*Velayat faqih*) – regardless of its total control over national education and the media and the Regime's ideological institutions, particularly since 2009. Indeed, for all this time, the ideological apparatus of the Islamic Republic has been working to convince the new generations of its legitimacy. The system needs to be analyzed in some of its major components to highlight its totalitarian character, not least its cult of the Supreme Leader (*rahbar*) and its concerted action to curtail political freedom and especially gender equality, but also its oppression of a secular culture of "joie de vivre," widespread among the youth.

According to estimates made by researchers, 70 percent of Iranian society in 2020 favored the separation of religion and politics.[1] This percentage is much higher among the youth.

The failure of the Islamic Regime, brought under the spotlight by the Mahsa Movement, is due to the following factors:

- The structure of the Iranian middle classes at the fall of the Shah and in particular, that of the Iranian family, especially in the large cities;
- The internet and its growing influence in Iran since the beginning of the twenty-first century;
- The influence of the Iranian diaspora;
- The university and its expansion after the 1979 Revolution;
- Leisure and the pursuit by youth of a joyful secular culture in contrast to the culture of mourning and martyrdom of the Islamic Regime that has transformed traditional Shi'i practices into a rigid, increasingly intolerant cult, experienced as depressive and killjoy.

The secularized family as a bulwark against the Islamic theocracy

The Iranian family has been and remains the pillar of social order, the primary source of identification for young people who do not trust any state authority and rely on family ties for their survival: to ensure the material necessities of life, to go to school, to have a stable social network, to live off their parents before marriage and even after. In the absence of a welfare state that would take care of the multiple needs of the individual (social security, employment assistance, unemployment coverage, etc.), the family is the focus of belonging and support in case of trouble or misfortune. Under the late Shah, the family was prolific (birth rate 4.21 per 1,000) and followed the traditional pattern (many births, many deaths). After the Revolution of 1979, the birth rate gradually declined to 1.79 in 2022,[2] which is not even sufficient for the reproduction of the population.[3] Iran has aligned itself with the developed world with regard to its birth rate. The worsening economic situation and distrust of a government that does not promote the future of the younger generations have created a Malthusian attitude towards the birth rate. Women have gradually taken possession of their bodies and refuse to follow the traditional model of the large family.[4] The divorce rate has been increasing, which shows the primacy of individual aspirations over the preservation of tradition. In 1980, a year after the Islamic Revolution in Iran, the divorce rate was around 6 percent. According to the Ministry of Youth, the divorce rate in 2020 had reached 32.9 percent.[5] The causes of divorce have been analyzed and among them, some scholars indicate the regression of religion (they call it "ignorance of religious issues" in order not to attract censorship on their studies) among others.[6] This means that family stability is no longer secure as it was in the past. Iran has also become massively urbanized during this period too, more than three-quarters of the population living in towns and cities (76.34 percent in 2021[7]).

Secularization is not only visible in the shrinking of the Iranian family in which women decide not to have more than two children (and men seem to agree with them) and the increasing divorce rate, but also in regard to sexuality. Research in Iran points to a new kind of "intimacy" (*samimiyat*) since the change in the mental outlook of the family. A new, widespread phenomenon, the "white marriage" (*ezdevaj sefid*)[8] or "life" (*zendegi*), has emerged where unmarried couples cohabit,[9] in spite of its illegality and the government repression in cases where it comes out in the open. According to research conducted in 2019, in June 2013, the Islamic Council published a report which noted the "worrying increase in illicit (*na-mashru'*) sexual relations and behaviors" in the country. According to this report, there were about 25,000 homosexual students in Iran. "Illicit" sexual relations between boys and girls had increased significantly (30 percent according to the sociologist Mohammad Sadat Mansoori; and according to the Ministry of Education's research (2018), by about 75 percent.[10] Many Iran based sociologists give a bleak picture of this phenomenon, describing it as a "social pathology" in order to conform to the

Islamic Regime's official viewpoint. Still, the fact of "free sexual relations" and "living together unmarried" is not exceptional in large cities, though no reliable statistics are available.

Iranian social scientists characterize the new youth as the "youth of the 80s and 90s" (*dahéyé hashtadi ha, navaid ha*), implying that by the Iranian calendar they were born in the 1380s and 1390s (i.e., the 2000s and 2010s) and were in their twenties at the time of the Mahsa Movement. In an interview on the 2000s generation (*dahé hashtadi ha*, those of the 1380s), Iranian sociologist Ali-Asqar Seyd-Abadi emphasized the profound change that had taken place within the Iranian family in which parents have become kinder and more open to their children than in the past. He pointed out too that girls used the internet more often than boys.[11]

Recent research shows that parents' attitudes toward children have indeed changed dramatically and they have become much closer to them emotionally than in the past. The cultural barriers between girls and boys have broken down due to girls' educational level and that of their mothers' over the past two decades. The internet has become essential for young Iranians with a high rate of use (59.16 million internet users out of a population of 84.51 million, more than 70 percent of the population[12]). The loss of parental authority is visible in the fact that they were not able to prevent their children from participating in the deadly Mahsa demonstrations in 2022–3. They went without parental permission, or worse, despite their proscription.

Cell phones are essential, especially for young people. In January 2021, there were 131 million cell phone connections, equivalent to 155 percent of the total population, meaning that many people had more than one. Against the inquisitive state, the encrypted channels like WhatsApp and Instagram, among others, are very popular. They are often censored, but ingenious young people manage to get around the ban, often aided by the service providers themselves.

In the family, revolving around just two children these days, paternal authority is not as sacred or removed as in the past. Iranian movies depict how children dodge their parents' authority, which is no longer as strict as it was. The tightening of affective ties within the family makes the once sacred and inaccessible character of the father obsolete, as he becomes much closer to his children than in the past. As for the mother, she is no longer the orthodox guardian of the patriarchal tradition, but the one who, by controlling her body (she refuses too many children) and by her involvement in the education of her children, gives them hope of a better life, notably by girls attending university, and by encouraging them to pursue a life abroad.

Secularization has undermined the influence of religion within the family and, at the same time, put into question the stability it enjoyed three decades ago. The new family places greater importance on the subjectivity and autonomy of children; the main concern is their well-being and future life in the world – a sharp departure from the idealism of the revolutionary youth of the 1970s. These new prevailing values of self-fulfillment and self-care contrast strongly with the revolutionary utopia of martyrdom and self-sacrifice. The family is the place where this new concept of the Self germinated, where dignity (*karamat*) and "joie de vivre" take absolute precedence over the religious values epitomized by sacred death and the denial of the Self in the 1979 Revolution. In this respect, Islamic family law defended by the Islamic Regime is obsolete, given the habits of the new generations. The rare instances of parental abuse of children, unpunished by existing Islamic law, draw media coverage and public outrage. Similarly, the early marriage of children, which allows families to marry off their daughters at the age of thirteen, or even younger, is denounced by public opinion as an archaic practice, though supported by the judiciary and proscribed by the clergy. Some poorer families consent to this custom of early marriage, to have fewer mouths to feed. Public opinion is appalled by this, but the Islamic Regime (often its clerical elites are octogenarians or older, like Ayatollah Khamenei) does not care: it is done in the name of the sacred Islamic laws.

The paradox of Iran is that it comprises an increasingly secularized society within a theocratic state that is less and less capable of understanding its citizens, and, consequently, more and more coercive in its norms and ruthlessly repressive when the complaints turn into social protest. The Islamic Republic has become a monster, not only because it represses senselessly, but also and above all because it is culturally out of step with the mindset of the younger generations. State and society are at loggerheads. Just as the traditional family in which the father was the sacred, transcendent authority is being questioned, so too is the Supreme Leader, in his image of patriarch of the nation, in turn attacked by the youth. The head of the state is no longer sacred (it had become so in the person of Khomeini in the first decade of the 1979 Revolution among his numerous followers), just as patriarchy is questioned within the family. The secularization of the family has undermined, in its turn, the social conservatism that supported the claim of the Supreme Leader to embody the absolute legitimacy of a fatherly figure in the name of patriarchal Islam. The Islamic Republic is increasingly more a kind of bogeyman, an accomplice of the sanctimonious grandfathers, insensitive to social ills, incapable of understanding the subjectivity of the young and the not-so-young, a prisoner of a fossilized version of religion and politics.

Forbidden leisure

A trend in sociology is to view dominant types of leisure as an alienation, as submission to mass society or "false culture," especially that based on consumerism. Examples include the

Frankfurt School or even, in postmodern thought, Baudrillard or Guy Debord. However, the case of leisure in Iran shows that it can become a motive in the fight against a totalitarian state. Leisure, even in its alienated forms, means in this context not so much alienation as emancipation, and that is what the Mahsa Movement is about.

The biggest killjoy in Iran is not the patriarchal family or the traditional Islamic mores (although they still play a significant role in the traditional strata, perhaps 10–15 percent of the population), but the leviathan Islamic State. It is the intention of the Regime, through a theocratic version of Islam that borrows many features from modern totalitarianism, to reduce individual freedom (traditional Islam was much more tolerant). It seeks at all costs to penetrate the depths of individual minds; it restricts relations between men and women, prohibits alcohol, makes it illegal for unveiled women to appear outside the home, and above all, imposes a segregation between men and women that makes it risky for young people to socialize freely in public, or even at home. The ban includes many kinds of music, for example that in which a woman sings solo or creates a sense of euphoria resulting in dancing. The Vice Squads cracked down on cases of flagrant offense, way before the 2022 protests.

The Islamic Regime is an ogre, but in face-to-face relations with its representatives, it is possible to soften it by bribing its agents, who have a shoddy sense of duty when it comes to kickbacks. This is the case with parties in which the Tehranis (the inhabitants of Tehran) celebrate a wedding or a get together with plenty of alcohol in the gardens of Karadj, for example, a few dozen kilometers from Tehran, and where the Revolutionary Guards who enforce the Islamic order have almost a semi-official rate of bribes to turn a blind eye to these breaches of Islamic prohibition. Corruption is thus the key word for these manifestations of joy, the qualifier "party pooper" is not merely metaphorical but very real in its effectiveness as well as its costs for increasingly impoverished families. But corruption can only be exercised if the financial stakes are sufficiently high to make it worthwhile for the security forces, and they are also still required to "perform." Otherwise, their hierarchy, which is corrupt too at higher levels, would call them to account. This means that the weakest, the most destitute (they cannot pay bribes) are the most abused. Repression and entitlement are thus the watchwords. Before the Mahsa Movement, when the Vice Squad arrested young people whose dress code was deficient in their eyes[13] – and especially young women – the space for negotiation was almost nil, insofar as they had to arrest a credible number of young girls per day to justify their salaries and publicize their surveillance over society.

The gap between the two, civil society and the Islamic Republic, has widened immeasurably over the past decade with the emergence of a new youth. Most of these young people no longer believe in the restrictions in place in the name of religion and, above all, they are not afraid to visibly transgress them, as a token of their inalienable right, an unwavering sign of their self-assertion. The new generations take pride in exposing themselves to the gaze of others as attractive and desirable, and above all, by cultivating a certain eccentricity in their appearance through a narcissism that seeks confirmation in the eyes of their peers, both on the street and on the web. The new magic of the gaze, the cult of the feminine as well as masculine beauty that the youth admire and want at all costs to emphasize within a transgressive voyeurism, none of this is understood by the gerontocratic, patriarchal Islamic State. It seeks to suppress these manifestations to legitimize itself in the eyes of the conservative fringe of the population that supports it and who denounces a sinful modernity. Modern leisure and the subjectivity that underlies it have become the worst enemies of the Islamic Republic, which yet does not perceive the extent of the cultural and social chasm that separates it from the subculture of the youth, even the sons and daughters of those same Islamist fathers who grabbed theocratic power. The Islamic Regime understands the youngsters all the less as it is corrupt and does not give them the opportunity to build a credible future by dreaming of a social and economic rise based on meritocracy. It widens the class divide disproportionately, with the poor and middle classes approaching destitution while the Regime's elites enrich themselves effortlessly. The Islamic Republic thus adds cultural misunderstanding to social injustice in the eyes of the people, especially the youth.

The Iranian diaspora and its cultural role in Iran

The new generations are in touch with the outside world through the web and the Iranian diaspora (as has been noted, more than 3 million Iranians live outside Iran), which has significantly contributed to the Mahsa Movement. The diaspora has mobilized Western public opinion by holding demonstrations of sometimes several tens of thousands of people in support of the young protesters, denouncing the numerous infringements of human rights by the Iranian Regime. We can cite those of Berlin, Montreal, London, Paris, and San Francisco on October 22, 2022 and on many other occasions in different cities in the West. As a sign of solidarity with Iranian women, those of the diaspora cut off their hair on the media, demonstrators chanted the slogan "Woman, life, freedom," as did "celebrities" in Iran, artists, movie stars, football players, scientists, and business people known in the West. The mobilization in the West has sealed once again, after the Green Movement of 2009, the close link between the Iranian diaspora and the democratic movements in Iran.

Considering the relative economic success of the Iranian diaspora in the West, another aspect of the government's policy, namely its antagonistic relations with the West, is at odds with their opinion and in many respects, with those of the

Iranian youth. The anti-Western stance of the Islamic Regime does not reflect that of Iranian society, which is neutral or even favorably disposed towards it, influenced by the attitude of the Iranian diaspora. The former accuses the international order (and particularly the West) for all the ills of the world and focuses on Israel and the United States as the mother of all vices. In their daily lives, Iranians do not target Israel, and the Palestinian issue is not paramount to them, although leftists might denounce the Israeli colonial attitude towards the Palestinians. Moreover, the Iranian government's position towards the West makes the social and material life of Iranians difficult. The dream of the Iranian youth is to migrate to the West, for lack of opportunity in Iran, but also to breathe the air of freedom on top of economic progress. The US sanctions are perceived as unfair (it hurts Iranians instead of targeting the Regime's elite), and the Iranian government is viewed as responsible for US retaliatory measures. As I have mentioned, one of the slogans heard in the streets was: "Our enemy is here/ They lie [Islamic Regime proponents] to say it is America" (*dochmane ma haminjast/dorouq migan amrikast*).

The Iran of the 2020s is a preponderantly secularized country, at least among most of its youth.[14] It aspires above all to a pluralistic and secular society where freedom of dress and political freedom go hand in hand, in a softened relationship with the outside world, especially the West.

After the collective protests in Iran ended, in February 2023, the diaspora continued to put pressure on Western governments over human rights violations and assaults on unveiled women in Iran. It acted as a sounding board for world opinion. It echoed individual women's resistance to veiling after the end of the collective mobilization in February 2023.

Manoto TV

Iranian radio and television suffer from a major disease: their boring, sanctimonious, and religious character. In 2021 more than one-fifth of the radio and TV programs produced in Iran were devoted to Islamic topics.[15] Islamic prohibitions apply to all programs, such as the ban on physical contact between men and women in movies, the compulsory veil, the ban on criticizing the Regime and its upper echelons, an atmosphere of censorship on joy perceived as suspicious and contrary to the martyrish culture of the Islamic Regime, an anti-Western vision that makes it difficult to have a balanced view on the outside world. For the new secularized generations, who are tired of litanies in the name of Islam and are looking for an openness to a secular world, switching to international channels, if possible in Persian, is the alternative.

Satellite TV channels in Persian have been set up by the Iranian diaspora in the West, to fill the void created by the absence of leisure time in Iran and to combat the Islamic Regime's view on life that smothers joy, and alienates the secularized middle classes, especially the younger generations, both poor and rich. Arab, Turkish, and Indian channels are also often switched to by Iranian viewers in search of something new. The satellite dishes through which these channels are accessed are illegal but largely available on the black market. They are placed on the rooftops and, from time to time, removed by the security forces in an endless game of cat-and-mouse. They get replaced by new ones almost immediately.

Iranians can get access to a variety of Persian-language channels, including Iran International, BBC, Voice of America, and others, which bring news from Iran and the world and offer them an alternative to the truncated and biased information provided by the Islamic Republic's state radio and television. But for leisure, the Manoto TV channel is probably the most watched. It was founded by two Iranians, Keyvan and Marjan

Abbassi, in 2010 in London. It is banned by the Iranian state, which regularly blocks its transmission as well the Persian news channels like BBC Persian, and CNN, among others.

Manoto has attracted many Iranians, so much so that to compete with it, the official channels in Iran had to relax their prohibitions and produce films in which the norms of segregation and Islamic prudishness were slightly loosened, which outraged the ayatollahs of Qom, who sounded the alarm in interviews. The Iranian public criticizes official state TV for being deadly boring, for programs and films that are soporific, and for making religion a principle of perpetual prohibition and lamentation (mourning martyrs, imams, authorities of the Regime killed heroically in the war on Iraq or recently by the Americans, such as General Soleimani assassinated in Iraq). Manoto is a leisure channel. It does not respect the Islamic veil, and the concern of its protagonists is to link Iran with the modern Western world by providing non-religiously oriented information and offering an alternative to the tedious programs of the Islamic Republic's broadcasters. It promotes a secular vision of Iran and the dismissal of the Theocratic Regime's culture of moroseness and anti-Western politics.

Iranian TV has to adhere to the puritanical morality of veiled women and forbidden bodily relations on camera, which has made it one of the most boring broadcasters in the Middle East. Many Iranians turn to Turkish or Emirati channels to escape the deadly monotony of national TV, or to the free satellite channels that broadcast movies in English. In this context, Manoto, which is broadcast in Persian, has become a very popular channel in Iran because of its shows, its series dubbed into Persian, its open debates and discussions, and above all, its jovial and festive tone, which contrasts with the doom and gloom of Iranian TV – where to be joyful is to be in breach of the Islamic Revolution. The tedium of theological discussions with obtuse clerics or debates where censorship makes it impossible to call a spade a spade often characterizes these long sessions that nobody watches anymore.

Manoto also has an investigative journalism aspect to it that is appreciated by the audiences in Iran. In 2013, on the twenty-fifth anniversary of the Islamic Republic's mass execution of political prisoners in 1988 on the orders of Ayatollah Khomeini (between 3,000 and 4,800 political prisoners summarily executed), Manoto aired the documentary *The Dream of Freedom*, which tells the story of women political prisoners in the 1980s in the Regime's infamous jails. For the first time, this documentary revealed the conditions and events of that time to a wider audience by interviewing the survivors among the prisoners, who had lost many friends in the prisons during this period. Some committed suicide, others died under atrocious physical and mental torture, others went insane, and many were summarily executed. The film, based on the words of these women, lays bare how the torturers tried to reshape their way of thinking by trampling their emotions and feelings, as well as destroying their psyche in their interrogations and physical and psychological torture.

The Iranian government has anathematized this channel. Unsurprisingly, it accuses it of being a pawn of Israel and the evil West, which seek to de-Islamize Iranian society and bring it back into the fold of godlessness by promoting a devious "cultural aggression" (*tahajome farhangi*). But beyond this attitude of sheer denunciation, the Islamic Republic's broadcasters have tried to imitate many of Manoto's programs. One example is the series *Please Have Dinner* (*befarmaeed chame*), the concept of which was acquired by Manoto from ITV and Channel 4 in the UK and which many foreign broadcasters have imitated in their turn. Each country adapts it according to its cultural orientations. Basically, the idea is that a group of people cook a dinner for each other, and vote for the best meal and host. Given its success in Iran, the Iranian channels were inspired to create a series called *Iranian Dinner* (*chamé irani*). The title is not insignificant, the reference to Iran being there to pander to Iranian nationalism, often abused by the political vision of the Islamic Republic, which officially claims to represent Islam and not a nation – that most infamous of Western inventions. In the last years, the Regime has fallen back on Iranian-ness to redeem a national legitimacy that it sorely lacks. Manoto broadcasts programs such as *The Grammy Awards, Miss World, Golden Club*, and many others that are very popular with young Iranians. Above all, women love the programs on this channel, in which men and women are equals, unlike the Islamic Republic's broadcaster.

Another attraction of Manoto lies in its Western allusions. On the eve of the Islamic Republic in Iran, a large part of the intellectuals and a significant part of Iranian society adopted an anti-Western attitude due to the complicity of the Western states with the Shah. Four decades later, a relaxed attitude towards the West, even a reserved Westernophilia, characterizes the new generations. Manoto, marked by an English and more generally, Western culture, opens new vistas to the imagination of Iranian youth, eager to enjoy life, tired of a macabre official culture that makes anti-Westernism a kind of revanchism not only towards the West, but more fundamentally, towards secular life. Eager to enjoy their earthly life, young people appreciate the West for its relaxed morals and cheerful sociability, free of religious constraints – not like the Islamic Republic, which imposes endless prohibitions on the people in the name of the martyrs and a morbid vision of existence.

Manoto offers Iranians modern life, without guilt. Under the reign of the late Shah in the 1960s, the new modernized classes that displayed "Westernized" attitudes and broke with traditional and Islamic norms felt a nameless malaise of uprootedness. They were ashamed to assume a Westernized stance that collided head-on with their pre-modern past. Iranian Third Worldist intellectuals expressed this sense of shame in their own way, pointing to the guilt of having abandoned traditional culture and embraced an extravert culture in which the West played not only role model, but also instructor and denier of Iranian-ness. Imitating the West for them was untenable and reflected a radical cultural uprooting. They branded these disembodied Westernized modes of behavior as servile imitations of an arrogant and contemptuous West. Jalal Al-Ahmad, along with the Iranian intellectual Ahmad Fardid, were the champions of this self-censure and self-deprecation. They coined the term "Westtoxification," saying modern Iranians were suffering from an insidious disease of which the symptoms were to abandon one's own culture and way of life and become uprooted, "de-Islamized," "de-Iranized" – at best second-rate Westernized individuals, neither Iranian nor Western.

According to these intellectuals, people should be ashamed of having espoused the secular habits of the West that reduce them to second-class beings. In short, the new modern Iranian (and also the Arab and to a lesser extent Turkish) middle classes felt a sense of guilt: they were unwillingly embodying a modern culture that was decried as imperialist and secular, and they were "disembodying" their ancestral culture, which castigated them by making them feel shame in their collective superego. Marxism, in its own way, contributed to the malaise: modern Iranians had become "Americanized" and thus betrayed, through their individualism, the communal solidarity that should bind them to the poor. According to this blend of Marxism and Third Worldism, the "underprivileged" were the only ones who embodied the legitimacy of class (Marxism) and of authenticity (Islam), as Ali Shariati argued. In the name of Marxism, the "dispossessed" (*mostaz'afeen*) were legitimized in the Islamic culture against the modernized middle classes who had adopted Western mores, and become the bearers of capitalist and imperialist secular oppression. Third Worldist intellectuals denounced Westernization not only as a pathology, but also as a double betrayal, of class and Iranian identity rooted in Islam. In short, everything coincided to make the modernized middle classes feel guilty. It heightened the psychic conflict between their modern ego and their superego that remained predominantly traditional, and clung to a nostalgic past. The superego became the more tyrannical as it lost hold on their secularized way of life. An important part of Islamism's attraction came from the mythical solutions of this brand of Islam, concocted by the intellectuals and Khomeini, to the identity malaise of modernized new generations in Iran.

The Islamic thinker Shariati advocated a revolutionary Islam, combining religion and modernity by blending eschatology and revolution. For him, Shi'ism was synonymous with revolution, and the classless society advocated by Marxism was in fact the same as the Islamic *qest*, where at the end of time in eschatological terms the Divine Oneness (*towhid*, the pillar of Islam) is in unison with the unity of the classes (the Marxist classless society). This mythical society married Marxism and Islam in a synthesis that was totally at odds with reality. Young Iranian Marxists justified Khomeini's religious fundamentalism as a step in the class struggle by rejecting the modernized culture of the middle classes, which was a slavish imitation of imperialist Western culture. They embraced Khomeini's fundamentalism, believing that they could then easily discard it and engage in the proletarian revolution.

The modernity dreamed of by these intellectuals magically reconciled Shi'ism (the guarantor of authenticity) and Marxism (the guarantor of social justice). The Marxist Jalal Al-Ahmad and the communist Gole-Sorkhi appealed to the "justice of Ali," the first Shi'i imam, to bring about the classless society. The Shi'ism authenticated by Ayatollah Khomeini was legitimized even among the hardened secularists because of his unyielding opposition to the Shah and the latter's pro-American despotism, an accomplice of imperialism in their eyes. The mythology of Islamo-Marxism made the youth of the 1970s overcome their identity malaise by reconciling social justice, the struggle against imperialism, and a culture of Shi'i authenticity. Islamic theocracy under the leadership of Ayatollah Khomeini became in fact the denial of both, the Islam of authenticity and the recovery of modernity and social justice through it.

After more than four decades of puritanical and repressive rule under the Islamic Republic, the sense of guilt has totally disappeared. Now, identifying with modernity liberates rather than poisons the minds of young people. They are not reluctant to declare their willingness to live their lives, to remove the veil, to relate freely to others, whatever gender, and to be free citizens in a world where standard relations with the West would go hand in hand with their willingness to reconcile with democracy. Manoto TV represents the aspirations of a large part of Iranian society to be at one with modernity, without fear of losing their soul or their identity.

According to various surveys, Manoto is particularly attractive among women, students, and other young people, regardless of their economic status. The egalitarian culture of men and women that it propagates, as well as its conception of a happy everyday life in contrast to the haggard gloom advocated by the state TV, are at the root of its success in the last decade. Recently, however, due to financial crisis, in November 2023 the channel announced it would be closing down.

This channel has had such a large audience in Iran because it embodied a West that was no longer antagonistic to Iran but showed a benevolent neutrality towards its people. The new Iranian youth do not seek to oppose the West, nor to follow it despite a sense of guilt that made joy impossible, or else against a bitter backdrop of nostalgia and a bad conscience, as was the case with the modern middle classes in the 1970s. The Iranian youth define themselves as being open to modernity and the West, without the terrified superego that prevailed among the new middle classes before the 1979 Revolution. The Islamic Regime is totally alien to the new generations, who see it as a usurper rather than a legitimate government. In this respect, Manoto was very much at one with Iranian youth.

Conclusion

The Mahsa Movement failed politically. The overthrow of the Islamic Regime did not happen, and for good reasons: on the one hand, the movement lacked organization because the Islamic State nipped it in the bud, and on the other hand, it lacked leadership, like many spontaneous movements in societies dominated by autocratic governments. The fact remains that up to September 2023 women continue to resist sporadically by not wearing the compulsory veil. Repressive acts such as the closure of stores that serve them and their intimidation in the street do not stop some of them from going out unveiled. The movement has revealed the political crisis of the Islamic Regime – and a part of its elite is convinced that it cannot survive by maintaining its repressive hold on society. This movement continues to have repercussions through its continuation in the Iranian diaspora in the West, where movements in support of Iranian women and citizens in general are ongoing. With the deterioration of the economic situation of the poor and middle classes, a high level of inflation affecting the price of basic essentials and food, and the unyielding attitude of the Islamic State, which refuses to take into account the culture of the new generations, further protest movements may follow in the future.

The youth culture of earthly joy, instead of gloomy martyrdom, introduces a form of recognition between men and women that is new to Iran, and much of the Muslim world. It is rooted in the growing secularization of Iranian society, not only among the middle classes but also among the substantial would-be middle classes. It is based on an intersubjective premise that demands the recognition of the reciprocal relationship between men and women, explicitly rejecting the strict limits imposed by traditional Islam. A new affectivity is evidenced that legitimizes socialization between men and women in the public space, rejecting the Islamic restrictions that segregate men from women. With the coercive introduction of secularism in Iran under Reza Shah, the fraternization of men and women and unveiling were imposed by the state, and it created a sense of unease and guilt because of the violation of Islamic norms, deeply rooted in the collective psyche. Now, the feeling of unease has disappeared and in the vast majority of the population, socialization among men and women is accompanied by a feeling of euphoria and well-being rather than unease and transgression of sacred laws. The prohibition of free inter-gender relationships inspires a feeling of revolt among the youth. They reject the traditional religious prohibitions and seek to open the way for gender equality in the future. The recognition is not between men on one side, and women on the other, but between both in their interactions without taboos, in a new existential configuration which ignores the Islamic interdicts.

Many protesters were killed during the demonstrations (some 520 documented by the human rights services, in fact more), others sentenced to death and executed. The Islamic Republic was expelled from the United Nations Commission on the Status of Women on December 15, 2022 and finds itself isolated internationally. A war of attrition has begun between the Theocratic State and society, mainly its youth. The former has multiple tools of repression: the IRGC and Basij, the police, the civilian militia (often the cruelest), and multiple repressive organizations, as well as its many prisons, legal and illegal. The Regime has a small percentage of support, perhaps 10 percent of the population, mostly its clientele, but also those who fear chaos if it collapses, or those who are financially dependent on it. However, in a society without autonomous political parties and trade unions (they have been suppressed), a unified and armed repressive force is able to subdue a people who are unable to respond other than by bare revolt, in most cases drenched in blood. The Mahsa Movement revealed the profound illegitimacy of the Islamic Republic. The refusal of Iranian society to bend to its yoke has shown its repressive, even thanatocratic nature (to rule over a society by imprisoning, torturing, or putting to death a significant part of its youth), following in the footsteps of the Syrian regime.

The movements in Iran since 2009 have one thing in common: the rejection of a hyper-repressive government that is incapable of ensuring social and economic development, and freedom for a secular society among its younger generations. In comparison, the Chinese regime ensures economic growth at the expense of political freedom, unlike the Iranian state, which combines political and bodily repression (of the unveiled or "badly veiled" woman, of men and women coming together, etc.) in conjunction with economic and social regression. In one word, in the eyes of the protesters, it is a "killjoy."

In summary, what distinguishes the Mahsa Movement from others, and in particular the 2006 Campaign for One Million Signatures and the 2009 Green Movement, is its relationship to the body on the one hand, and its taking place amid a culture of "joie de vivre" that is radically different from that of the older generations.[1]

Notes

Preface

1. Mehrdad Darvishpoor, "The spark of the explosion of a 'super movement' and 'women's revolution' in Iran?" (*Jaraqeh efejar "abar jonbesh" va "enqelab zananes" dar iran?*), BBC Persian, September 22, 2022.
2. Song by Amir Tataloo, "Peace Revolution" (*Enghelab solh*), https://www.youtube.com/watch?v=YuYvHaOF8Qw
3. I was one of those who called it by the date of when it began. See Farhad Khosrokhavar, *L'Iran: La jeunesse démocratique et l'Etat prédateur* [Iran: The democratic youth and the predator state], Fauve Publishers, Paris, 2023.

Chapter 1: The mindset of the younger generation

1. This view aligns with Alain Touraine's social movement theory.
2. See Farhad Khosrokhavar, "L'Etat chiite est un hymne à la mort," *L'Obs*, https://www.nouvelobs.com/moyen-orient/20221122.OBS66224/iran-l-etat-chiite-est-un-hymne-a-la-mort.html, October 22, 2022; *L'Iran: La jeunesse démocratique contre l'Etat prédateur* [Iran: The democratic youth against the predator state], Fauves Publishers, Paris, 2023.

3. According to unverifiable data and analysis, Iranians blamed the government for the major shortcomings of the economy. In the assessment of one specialist in 2020: "The public mistrust for the government's policies has increased over the past few years. This is reflected in frequent social uprisings that have led to the killing and imprisonment of many Iranian citizens by the authorities. The ongoing crisis will likely deepen the rift between the state and the citizens, possibly leading to more protests in the coming months. The loss of confidence in the government is visible in public discussions, social and broadcast media debates, and government polls. In 2015, 54% of those surveyed in a Ministry of Culture and Guidance poll believed that 'injustice in the government's policies' was the main cause for poverty in Iran," Sara Bazoobandi, "Deepening poverty threatens the social contract in Iran," The Arab Gulf States Institute in Washington, October 22, 2020, https://agsiw.org/deepening-poverty-threatens-the-social-contract-in-iran/
4. According to the latest unverifiable data, taking into account the very high rate of inflation, 60 percent of the population is poor. See Pooya Stone, "Iran: 60% of population is poor," *Iran Focus*, January 25, 2023, https://iranfocus.com/economy/49299-irans-population-is-poor/
5. The 2022 international Corruption Perceptions Index ranks Iran 147th out of 180. In comparison, Iran's neighbor Turkey is 101st, Saudi Arabia 54th, Tunisia 85th, and Egypt 130th. See https://www.transparency.org/en/cpi/2022
6. See Mansoor Moaddel, "Secular shift among Iranians: Findings from cross-national & longitudinal surveys," *Freedom of Thought Journal*, No. 12, Fall 2022. According to this study, "a reasonable expectation of the extent of the Iranian support for the separation of religion and politics is placed at 70%." For the youth, this figure should be much higher due to its revolt in the Mahsa Movement against the Theocratic State.
7. On the Iranian middle classes in historical perspective see H.E. Chehabi, "The rise of the middle class in Iran before the Second

World War," *The Global Bourgeoisie*, Princeton University Press, Princeton, NJ, 2019, https://doi.org/10.23943/princeton/9780691177342.003.0002. On the middle classes after the Iranian Revolution of 1979 see Farhad Khosrokhavar, "The Iranian middle classes between political failure and cultural supremacy," Sadighi Annual Lectures, Research Fund, International Institute of Social History, Amsterdam April 2015.

8. Deniz Kandioty, "Bargaining with patriarchy," *Gender and Society*, Vol. 2, No. 3, 1988.
9. See Saeed Mada Qahfarkhi, "Hundred years and hundred days" (*sad sal va sad rooz*), https://www.zeitoons.com/wp-content/uploads/2023/01/Mahsa-Saeid.pdf
10. Marie Ladier-Fouladi, *The Islamic Republic of Iran Seen from Within*, Google Books, 2022 (2020 French version).
11. https://www.amar.org.ir/statistical-information
12. See e.g., Farhad Khosrokhavar and Marie Ladier-Fouladi, "The 2009 presidential election in Iran: Fair or foul?" Working Paper, EUI RSCAS, 2012/2019, Mediterranean Program Series, https://hdl.handle.net/1814/22564
13. Rozalina Burkova for Human Rights Watch, "Iran: Women face bias in the workplace," May 25, 2017.
14. According to different sources Iran carried out at least 977 executions in 2015, at least 567 executions in 2016, and at least 507 executions in 2017. In 2018 there were at least 249 executions, at least 273 in 2019, at least 246 in 2020, at least 290 in 2021, at least 553 in 2022, and at least 309 so far in 2023 up to March 6 of that year (amnesty.org, Amnesty International, Iran Human Rights Watch). Per capita, Iran has the highest number of executions in the world. See for a summary Wikipedia, "Capital punishment in Iran," https://en.wikipedia.org/wiki/Capital_punishment_in_Iran
15. Noushin Ahmadi Khorasani, "Why the movement of the Girls of Enqelab Avenue has not extended to the entire society" (*tchera harekae dokhtarane khiabane enqelab gostarech nayaft*), December 18, 2018, https://www.radiozamaneh.com/425026?fb

clid=IwAR3_un4-R1g-pXP229xpFsBToOWLmrpKc73XIbq0yE
bc6rAXPPxWwVAzXFE
16. Ibid.
17. Under the Pahlavi regime, the modernization of a large part of society took place over half a century, with the unveiling of some women, promiscuity between women and men, the introduction of women into the state apparatus and urban modernization. But this took place against a diffuse background of committing sin against Islam, and this Islamic superego accompanied many men and women who believed that their modernization transgressed Islamic commandments.
18. Mahmoud Ayoub, *Redemptive Suffering in Islam: A Study of the Devotional Aspects of Ashura in Twelver Shi'ism*, Mouton de Gruyter, Berlin, 1978.
19. In his modernizing interpretation, Hamid Algar has given Shi'ism a revolutionary meaning through its eschatology and its sense of the twelfth Imam, Imam of Time (see Hamid Algar, *The Roots of the Islamic Revolution*, Open Press, 1983). In a similar vein, Ali Shariati tried to make Shi'ism the model of revolution by referring to the martyrdom of Hossein, the third Imam, the paragon of the revolutionary ready to sacrifice his life for a sacred cause that brings about the advent of the end of time (see Farhad Khosrokhavar, Mohsen Mottaghi, *L'Islam et le christianisme au défi de leurs théologies*, Rue de Seine, Paris, 2022). These authors make minority tendencies within Shi'ism the central one, denying the dominant Shi'ite propensity towards quietism.
20. In his book *Critique of the Foundations of the Fiqh and Kalam* (*naqd bonyad haye feqh va kalam*), aban 1396 (2017), http://mohammadmojtahedshabestari.com/, Mojtahed Shabestari underlined the similarities between Sunni jihadism and Shi'ite theocracy, inspired by the Islamic scholar Mohammad Moosavi Aqiqi, whose book he mentions: *Exclusivism in the Traditional Fiqh* (*enhesar garaee dar feqh sonnati*), Forums Human Coexistence, 1396 (2017).

21. See Farhad Khosrokhavar, *L'Islamisme et la mort, le martyre révolutionnaire en Iran* [Islamism and Death, the Revolutionary Martyrdom in Iran], L'Harmattan, Paris, 1995.
22. Seyd Mansur Majd'ol-ashrafi, "Innovation and bid'ah in the mourning ceremonies and mourning gatherings" (*no avari va bed'at dar majales aza-dari va sugavari*), January 21, 2007, https://www.armaneheyat.ir/issue/8602/
23. A clear sign of this marginality can be detected in the transient constitution of the opposition to the Islamic Regime in the Iranian diaspora. While many intellectuals reside abroad, none of them is listed among the popular figures who intend to form a government in exile based on an online petition whose signatories include Reza Pahlavi (the son of the last Iranian Shah), Shirin Ebadi (2003 Nobel Peace Prize winner), Hamed Esmaeeliun (novelist, defender of the rights of the families of the victims of the missile attack on the plane going from Tehran to Kiev on January 8, 2020), Golchifteh Farahani (actress), Nazanin Bonyadi (actress), Ali Karimi (soccer champion), Masih Alinejad (journalist and human rights activist). See https://rdi.org/people-of-iran/
24. "The attack of the government agents on the (festivities) of 2 April 2023" (*hamleh ma'muran hokumati beh marasem &3 Bedar*), April 2, 2023, https://news.gooya.com/2023/04/post-74727.php
25. For a succinct history of the Iranian middle classes see Farhad Khosrokhavar, "The Iranian middle classes between political failure and cultural supremacy," Sadighi Annual Lectures, Sadighi Research Fund, International Institute of Social History, Amsterdam April 2015. For a summary of some sociologists' viewpoints: Javad Heiran-Nia, "Iran's middle class has been eroding for some time. Now it's only getting worse," June 30, 2022, https://www.atlanticcouncil.org/blogs/iransource/irans-middle-class-has-been-eroding-for-some-time-now-its-only-getting-worse/
26. See Farhad Khosrokhavar and Mohsen Mottaghi, "La sécularisation en Iran sous la République Islamique" [Secularization in

Iran under the Islamic Republic], *Journal Raison Publique*, June 2015, http://www.raison-publique.fr/article755.html
27. "Special report: Iran's leader ordered crackdown on unrest – 'Do whatever it takes to end it,'" Reuters, December 23, 2019, https://www.reuters.com/article/idUSKBN1YR0QO/
28. Saeed Madani et al., "The extinguished fire: A look at the protest of aban 98" (Novembre 2019) (*atash khamush, negahi beh e'terazat aban 98*), Rahman Institue (mo'aseseh Rahman), 1399 (2020); "Hundred years and hundred days" (*sad sal o sad ruz*), January 31, 2023, https://www.zeitoons.com/wp-content/uploads/2023/01/Mahsa-Saeid.pdf. See for a synthesis of the theses on Iran, Saeed Paivandi, "The unaccomplished protest movements in Iran and the challenge of shaping the new political mindset in Iran" (*jonbesh haye e'terazee na'tamam va chalesh shekl dadan beh angareh siasi jam'I jaded dar iran*), *Azadi Andisheh Journal*, No. 13, Summer 1402 (2023).
29. Noushin Ahmadi Khorasani, "The mandatory veil, the Jina (Mahsa Amini) movement and the middle class" (*hejab ejbari, jonbesh jina va tabaqeh motevaset*), August 5, 2023, https://www.aasoo.org/fa/print/articles/4353
30. See Nazli Kamvari, "In the middle, on the edge, essays on Iran's middle class poor," *Radio Zamaneh*, March 2022. See also Asef Bayat, "The fire that fueled the Iran protests," *The Atlantic*, January 27, 2018, https://www.theatlantic.com/international/archive/2018/01/iran-protest-mashaad-green-class-labor-economy/551690/
31. I first developed this notion about the youth in the Arab revolutions of 2010–13. See Farhad Khosrokhavar, *The Arab Revolutions that Shook the World*, Paradigm Publishers, Boulder, CO, 2013.
32. Steve Hanke, "Hanke's 2022 Misery Index," May 18, 2023, https://www.nationalreview.com/2023/05/hankes-2022-misery-index/
33. For a summary of this report, see "Record-breaking '69% inflation' in April 2023" (*record shekani tavarrom 69 dar sadi" dar Farvardin*), VOA Persian, May 25, 2023.

34. "The beating heart of the labor movement in Iran," May 3, 2020, https://slingerscollective.net/the-beating-heart-of-the-labor-movement-in-iran/
35. Peyman Jafari, "Revolt with a revolutionary perspective," *Iranian Studies*, No. 56, 569–575, 2023.
36. Ibid.
37. Najmeh Bozorgmehr, "'Little readiness for general strikes': Iranians put jobs before pro-democracy protests," *Financial Times*, November 21, 2022.
38. Mowlavi Abdolhamid, "Even the Baha'is have the right to citizenship" (*bahaï ha ham haghe shahrvandi darand*), BBC Persian, December 30, 2022.
39. "Several killed as police shoots protesters in Southeastern Iran," Iran International, https://www.iranintl.com/en/202209306473 (retrieved October 2, 2022).
40. BBC Persian, November 20, 2022.

Chapter 2: Protest movements before the Mahsa Movement

1. Eliz Sanasarian, *The Women's Rights Movement in Iran: Mutiny, Appeasement, and Repression from 1900 to Khomeini*, Holitzbrinck, Stuttgart, 1982.
2. Parvin Ardalan and Noushin Ahmadi Khorasani, "Senator: The work of senator Mehrangiz Manouchehrian in the struggle for legal rights for women," Tose'e Publisher, Tehran, 1382 (2004).
3. See Farhad Khosrokhavar and Marie Ladier-Fouladi, "The 2009 presidential election in Iran: Fair or foul?" EUI Working Papers, Robert Schuman Centre for Advanced Studies, RCAS 2012/29.
4. See Mostafa Rahimi, "Why I am opposed to the Islamic Republic?" (*chera ba jomhuriye eslami mokhalefam?*), *Ayandegan*, January 15, 1979 (25 dey 1357).
5. There is a large body of literature on women in Iran and their social activism. See among others Janet Afary, *Sexual Politics in Modern Iran*, Cambridge University Press, Cambridge, 2009;

Nayereh Tohidi, "Women's rights and feminist movements in Iran," *International Journal on Human Rights*, December 2016; Azadeh Kian, *Femmes et pouvoir en islam*, Éditions Michalon, Paris, 2019.
6. https://www.unwomen.org/en/digital-library/multimedia/2019/12/infographic-human-rights
7. Ibid.
8. Islamic Republic oscillates between intimidation and belated law making and this "dialectic" is part and parcel of this Regime. Repression precedes legislation.
9. Shirin Ebadi and Azadeh Moaveni, *Iran Awakening: A Memoir of Revolution and Hope*, Random House, London, 2006.
10. See "Bahareh Hedayat," English Wikipedia.

Chapter 3: The Mahsa Movement: the first sweeping feminist movement in Iran

1. https://women.ncr-iran.org, December 19, 2018.
2. https://gamaan.org/wp-content/uploads/2020/09/GAMAAN-Iran-Religion-Survey-2020-English.pdf
3. "The confidential statistics of the Ministry of Islamic Guidance, 70% of the people are against the compulsory veil," *Independent Farsi*, September 17, 2020.
4. https://fr.wikipedia.org/wiki/Manifestations_cons%C3%A9cutives_%C3%A0_la_mort_de_Mahsa_Amini#cite_note-LMD0210-1
5. "Family house of Iranian climber Rekabi destroyed," Iranwire, December 2, 2022.
6. "The silent demonstrations of the protesters in Tehran and Isphahan" (*rahpeyma'i sokut mo'tarezan dar tehran va Esfahan*), BBC Persian, December 19, 2022.
7. HRANA, https://www.en-hrana.org/a-comprehensive-report-of-the-first-82-days-of-nationwide-protests-in-iran/
8. See "Iran protests – daily update, HRANA, https://twitter.com/HRANA_English/status/1614398173111357440?cxt=HHwWgMC8pbilv-csAAAA

9. The full slogan is: "If you can, put to death if you cannot, die!" (*agar mitavanee bemiran, agar nemitavanee bemir*). For a discussion of the slogan, see the article by Shariati's son, Ehsan Shariati, "Revisiting the philosophy of martyrdom" (*baz khani falsafeh shahadat*), January 2012, https://drshariati.org/?p=4941 #more-4941
10. See Nayereh Tohidi, "Iran in a transformative process by woman, life, freedom," *Freedom of Thought Journal*, No. 13, Summer 2023.
11. See Asef Bayat, "Is Iran on the verge of another revolution?" *Freedom of Thought Journal*, No. 13, Summer 2023 (in Persian).
12. For an analysis of this slogan, see Kamran Talattof, "The 'Women, life, freedom' movement in Iran: The anatomy of a slogan," *Freedom of Thought Journal*, No. 13, Summer 2023.
13. For a non-exhaustive list of these dances up to April 2023, see "The unique performance of a fighting woman in the Tajrish bazaar (near Tehran)" (*performance bi nazir yek zan mobarez, sar bazar-cheh tajrish*), https://news.gooya.com/2023/04/post-74866.php
14. See "Dancing and joy of men and women in Tehran" (*raqs o shadi zanan va mardan daar tehran*), Iran International, https://limportant.fr/contributeur/IranIntl/1911631
15. https://www.bbc.com/persian/world-64478195
16. "Judge Salavati's obscenity to Astiaj Haqiqi" (fahashi qazi salavati beh Astiaj Haqiqi), *Independent Farsi*, Iran International, February 5, 2023.
17. https://www.en-hrana.org/two-instagram-bloggers-sentenced-to-a-total-of-21-years-in-prison/
18. Annika Ganzeveld, Amin Soltani, Johanna Moore, and Nicholas Carl, Iran Update, March 10, 2023, https://www.criticalthreats.org/analysis/iran-update-march-10-2023
19. Prisoners of Conscience, Global Report 2021/2022, https://prisonersofconscience.org/wp-content/uploads/2022/11/Global-Report-PoC.pdf

20. "During the fight that happened yesterday between a group in Bagh Shazdeh in Mahan Kerman, a 59-year-old woman suffered a cardiac arrest and later died in the hospital. It is reported that some people were injured in this incident. A woman on the bus says loudly, 'Women should wear hijab.'" According to the "ruyedad 24" website this conflict occurred when a group of passengers on a bus strongly reminded veil-less women about the obligation to wear the hijab (*tazakkore hejab*), and people willing to support the women came and clashed with them. See "The mandatory hijab in Iran" (*hejab ejbari dar iran*), BBC Persian, April 24, 2023, https://www.bbc.com/persian/articles/c720lq59j4vo
21. https://observers.france24.com/fr/moyen-orient/20230526-femmes-iran-moto-voile-manifestation-permis
22. May 31, 2023, https://www.farsnews.ir/news/14010711000838/
23. "After a bloody May," Abdorrahman Boroumand Center, https://www.iranrights.org/attachments/library/doc_804.pdf
24. May 31, 2023 "Jamileh Kadivar explained: Why did sexually suggestive slogans become popular in the recent protests?" (*jamileh kadivar towzih dad: chera dar e'terazat akhir sho'ar haye mostahjane jensi ravaz peyda kard*) https://www.khabaronline.ir/news/1718828/
25. "Abbas Abdi, The fundamentalists introduced obscene and obscene words into political literature" (*now osulgarayan kalamata mostahjan va lowdegi ra vared adabiyat siasi lkardand*), May 31, 2023, https://fararu.com/fa/news/584455
26. "Two years' imprisonment for the maker of Emperor Kozko" (*do sal habs...*), Iranwire, December 4, 2022.
27. BBC Persian, October 26, 2022.
28. April 16, 2023, radiofarda.com
29. BBC Persian, December 31, 2022.
30. Jeffrey Alexander, *The Civil Sphere*, Oxford University Press, Oxford, 2006.
31. For a summary of Alain Touraine's concept of social movements in English see Alain Touraine, "An introduction to the study

of social movements," *Social Research*, Vol. 52, No. 4, Social Movements, winter 1985, 749–87.
32. https://cpj.org/2023/07/cpj-condemns-trials-of-iranian-journalists-niloofar-hamedi-and-elahe-mohammadi/
33. "Two Iranian women handed jail terms," Iranwire, July 31, 2023.
34. CDJ, December 14, 2022, https://cpj.org/reports/2022/12/number-of-jailed-journalists-spikes-to-new-global-record/#:~:text=The%20Committee%20to%20Protect%20Journalists,in%20a%20deteriorating%20media%20landscape

Chapter 4: The new intellectuals

1. This section has been written drawing on, among others, Wikipedia in English, French, and Persian.
2. See among others Ali Gheissari. *Iranian Intellectuals in the 20th Century*, University of Texas Press, Austin, 1998; Ali Mirsepassi, "Religious intellectuals and western critiques of secular modernity," *Comparative Studies of South Asia, Africa and the Middle East*, Vol. 26, No. 3, 2006; Farhad Khosrokhavar and Mohsen Mottaghi, "The Neo-Mutazilites in contemporary Iran," in Ramin Jahanbegloo (editor), *Mapping the Role of Intellectuals in Iranian Modern and Contemporary Hisrory*, Lexington Books, Lanham, MD, 2020.
3. Nahid Keshavarz defended a doctoral dissertation at the École des hautes études en sciences sociales that was published as a book, *Les nouveaux féminismes en Iran, le mouvement des femmes de 1989 à 2009* [The new feminisms in Iran, women's movement from 1989 to 2009], L'Harmattan, Paris, 2016.
4. For a biography of Iranian feminists up to 2017 see "Iranian women's rights activists," November 30, 2017, articles from Wikipedia or other sources online.
5. Shirin Ebadi and Azadeh Moaveni, *Iran Awakening: A Memoir of Revolution and Hope*, Random House, London, 2006.
6. See https://iranacademia.com/profile/mansoureh-shojaei/?lang=en

7. https://www.youtube.com/user/feministschool?
8. https://tavaana.org/en/content/noushin-ahmadi-khorasani-two-decades-struggle-womens-rights
9. https://www.amnesty.org/fr/wp-content/uploads/sites/8/2021/06/mde130242008fra.pdf
10. https://www.courrierinternational.com/article/peine-de-mort-en-iran-les-executions-sont-en-forte-hausse
11. Narges Mohammadi, *White Torture* (*chekanjehe séfid*), Baran Publishers, Stockholm, 2020.
12. "Iranian artist goes on trial for cartoon mocking draft law," BBC, May 19, 2015.
13. Atena Farghadani refused bail and was taken to prison; "I have not committed a crime" (*Atena Faraqdani az paziresh vasiqe khoddari kard...*), VOA Persian, June 9, 2023.
14. https://www.zeitoons.com/106140
15. See Wikipedia, "Azam Taleghani," https://en.wikipedia.org/wiki/Azam_Taleghani#cite_note-Farokhzad-3
16. See Wikipedia, "Faezeh Hashemi."
17. https://hengaw.net/en/news/2022/12/saman-yasin-a-kurdish-artist-sentenced-to-death-as-one-of-the-detainees-in-the-recent-protests
18. "Imprisoned dissident rapper Toomaj Salehi, voice of Iran's protests, faces possible execution," Center for Human Rights in Iran, April 6, 2023, https://iranhumanrights.org/2023/04/imprisoned-dissident-rapper-toomaj-salehi-voice-of-irans-protests-faces-possible-execution/
19. https://limportant.fr/infos-iran-/130/564740
20. Ghazal Golshiri, "Le rap et la révolution iranienne," *Le Monde*, January 14, 2020.
21. According to Iranian government sources, the war cost Iran an estimated 200,000–220,000 fatalities, or up to 262,000 according to conservative Western estimates; see Dilip Hiro, *The Longest War: The Iran–Iraq Military Conflict*, Routledge, 1991; Farhang Rajaee, *Iranian Perspectives on the Iran–Iraq War*, University Press of Florida, Gainesville, 1997.

22. Pooya Stone, "Iran: 60% of population is poor," https://iranfocus.com/economy/49299-irans-population-is-poor/, January 25, 2023.
23. Artemis Moshtaghian, "Family fears for life of rapper they say was violently arrested after encouraging Iranians to protest," CNN, November 6, 2022.

Chapter 5: From a theocratic state to a totalitarian one
1. See Henry Sorg, "Le massacre des prisonniers polititiques de 1988 en Iran: une mobilisation forclose ?" *Raisons Politiques*, 2008/2, No. 30.
2. One can consult the website Gostaresh News, May 2, 2021.
3. Marina Fabre, "San Francisco, Téhéran, Lagos... Ces métropoles qui s'enfoncent dangereusement," *Novethic.fr*, April 2, 2021.
4. https://magazine.meteocity.com/actualites/nouveau-record-caniculaire-53-degres-en-iran-le-29-juin-2017_5422/#bfjvDZwH1XoH4V2I.99
5. Noah Rayman, "The 10 most polluted cities in the world," *Time*, October 18, 2013.
6. "Ahwazi: Ahwaz city named most polluted on earth," Unrepresented Nations and Peoples Organization, March 8, 2013, https://unpo.org/article/15608
7. "À Ahvaz, les pluies acides empoisonnent les Iraniens," *observers.france24.com*, November 26, 2013.
8. "L'Iran achète un volume record de blé après la pire sécheresse depuis 50 ans" [Iran buys a record volume of wheat after the worst drought in 50 years], *L'Orient-Le Jour*, October 13, 2021.
9. Center for Human Rights in Iran, "Dozens of environmentalists arrested in southern Iran in widening crackdown," May 11, 2018, https://iranhumanrights.org/2018/05/dozens-of-environmentalists-arrested-in-southern-iran-in-widening-crackdown/
10. "Building dams is one of the largest state projects beset by huge embezzlement" *(Kahrom, sad sazi yeki az bozog tarine proje haye dolati ast kheh ekhtelas va davtalabe dar an ziad ast)* Entekhab.ir, 22 azar 1401(December 13, 2022).

11. "Iran ranked worst in the world for soil erosion: expert," Mehr News Agency, Tehran, April 16, 2012, www.payvand.com
12. The case of Khuzestan, the faulty management of water by the government and its relationship with the "water uprisings" has been studied by Saeed Madani Qahfarkhi and his colleagues in *Peaceful Protests* (*mozaherat salmiyeh*), Rahman Publishing, Tehran, 2022 (1401).
13. For an account, see Mehrnoush Cheragh Abadi, "Has Iran mismanaged its way into a water crisis?" *Equal Times*, March 22, 2017, https://www.equaltimes.org/has-iran-mismanaged-its-way-into-a?lang=en#.ZDu7BmQ6_qs
14. Some examples are reported by Amnesty International, see "Iran: Stop ruthless attacks on persecuted Baha'i religious minority," August 24, 2022, https://www.amnesty.org/en/latest/news/2022/08/iran-stop-ruthless-attacks-on-persecuted-bahai-religious-minority/
15. See the story of the protesters of the Mahsa Movement detained and tortured in this type of undeclared detention center in "How Iran used a network of secret torture centers to crush the protesters," CNN, February 21, 2023, https://edition.cnn.com/interactive/2023/02/middleeast/iran-torture-jails-black-sites-mahsa-amini-protests-cmd-intl/
16. "Deadly denial of medical care in Iran's prisons," Amnesty International, April 12, 2022, https://www.amnesty.org/en/latest/campaigns/2022/04/deadly-denial-of-medical-care-in-irans-prisons/
17. October 5, 2021, https://www.tribunezamaneh.com/archives/41776
18. Shadi Amin, "In the section 2-Aleph what is happening? Is it really the end of the world?" (*dar band do-alef cheh migozarad? Aya anja vaqe'an tahe doniast?*), March 7, 2012, https://justice4iran.org/persian/articles/aa/. This section is largely inspired by this article.
19. See Amnesty International, "Iran: Tortured prisoners at Evin prion are in urgent need of international protection," October

18, 2022, https://www.amnesty.org/en/documents/mde13/6129/2022/en/
20. See for instance the impressions of four former prisoners, Shiva Nazar-Ahari, Iraj Mesdaqi, Mehdieh Golru, and Asqar Izadi, "Evin, in the memories of its prisoners: 'The Bastille' of the Iranian Revolution" (*evin dar khatereh zendani hayash; "bastil enqelab iran"*), BBC Persian, October 17, 2022, https://www.bbc.com/persian/blog-viewpoints-63285116
21. "Yasman Ariani a été transférée à la section des renseignements de l'AP à la prison d'Evine" [Yasman Ariani has been transferred to the security section of the Army of the Revolutionary Guards in Evin Prison], October 31, 2022, Channel One HD, https://ch1.cc/iran/
22. "Iran: Crackdown on Dervish minority," Human Rights Watch, March 15, 2018, https://www.hrw.org/news/2018/03/15/iran-crackdown-dervish-minority
23. "Jailed Twitter activist transferred to notorious Fashafuye prison," January 23, 2020, https://www.ifmat.org/01/23/jailed-twitter-activist-transferred-notorious-fashafuye-prison/
24. Kurdistan Human Rights Network, November 14, 2019, https://kurdistanhumanrights.org/fa/?p=10371
25. https://edition.cnn.com/interactive/2023/02/middleeast/iran-torture-jails-black-sites-mahsa-amini-protests-cmd-intl/
26. On mistreatment and arbitrary imprisonment, see Mansoureh Shojaee, "We did not travel to India" (*ma be hend safar nakardim*), https://www.aasoo.org/fa/articles/4379?fbclid=IwAR3l3AzOaZpcCpCYO6vEH8oqoS03De3F-7qMASwvolApMIl5qtc_k_MLp44
27. See the section on Nasrin Sotoudeh in which her words are quoted.
28. https://datareportal.com/reports/digital-2021-iran
29. https://www.amnesty.org/en/location/middle-east-and-north-africa/iran/report-iran/
30. https://iranwire.com/fa/features/20788
31. See Ferechteh Qazi, "The death of Haj Davood Rahmani, inventor of the tortre 'coffin' or 'resurrection'" (*marg haj davood*

Rahmani, mokhtare' shekanjeh "tabut" or "Qiamat"), radiofarda .com, October 21, 2021.
32. Quoted in Ferechteh Qazi, op cit.
33. See Homa Kalhori, *The Coffin of the Living (tabut zendegan)*, Baran Publishers, Stockholm, 2020.
34. On 30 August 2017, the United Nations Human Rights Council referred to the 1988 massacre in Iran: "1988 executions of Iranian political prisoners," Wikipedia, https://en.wikipedia.org/wiki/1988_executions_of_Iranian_political_prisoners#:~:text=On%2030%20August%202017%2C%20the,Non%2DRecurrence%22%20The%20statement%20points
35. One can consult the weblog of Monireh Baradaran for her writings: https://bidaran.info
36. November 17, 2022, www.entekhab.ir/fa/news/703554/
37. November 17, 2022, www.entekhab.ir/fa/news/703554/
38. Roya Homayouni, "Loudspeakers to spread hatred; Ahmad Khatami: veil-less women are the wives of thieves" (*boland gou haye nefrat parakani; Ahmd Khamati: zanane bi hejab gamsarane dozd ha hastand*) Iranwire, December 18, 2022.
39. Seyd Ahmad Alam-ol-Hoda, "The female protesters are the prostitutes, deceived by America" (*mo'tarézan, rousapi haye farib khordeh ye Emrika*), Iranwire, December 13, 2022.
40. Ibid.
41. etemadonline.com, November 25, 2022.

Chapter 6: Secularization counter to the Theocratic State

1. Mansoor Moaddel, "Secular shift among Iranians: Findings from Cross-national & Longitudinal Surveys," *Freedom of Thought Journal*, No. 12, Autumn 2022.
2. https://www.worlddata.info/asia/iran/index.php
3. https://www.populationdata.net/pays/iran/
4. Marie Ladier-Fouladi, "Démographie, femme et famille: relations entre conjoints en Iran post-révolutionnaire," *Revue Tiers-Monde*, 2005/2, No. 182.

5. https://iranopendata.org/en/pages/the-drastic-increase-of-divorce-rates-in-iran-nearly-one-in-three-marriages-lead-to-divorce
6. See for the case of Tehran, Ismail Jahani Daulatabad and Seyed Hassan Hosseini, "A sociological study of the causes and contexts of marital conflicts in Tehran" (*motalé'ehjame'eh shenakhti elal va zamineh haye boruz ta'arozatzanashouee dar shahr Tehran*), *Barresi, masa'el ejtema'ee iran*, Fifth series, Autumn–Winter 2014 (1393).
7. https://www.statista.com/statistics/455841/urbanization-in-iran/
8. See Janet Afary and Jesilyn Faust (editors), *Iranian Romance in the Digital Age*, Bloomsbury, London, 2021.
9. Saeed Paivandi, "The emergence of the modern, tension-led sexuality in Iranian society: The experience of living together and sexual relationship outside the marriage" (*peidayesh portanesh sexualite jadeed dar jameeh iran: tajrobeh hamkhanegee va rabeteh jensi kharej az esdevaj*), *Journal nashriyeh azadi andisheh*, No. 7, 143–92, June 2019 (Tir 1398).
10. Abbas Lotfizadeh, Mohammad Javad Zahedi, and Fatemeh Pibari, "Thematic turn in explaining the relationship between men and women in the family: The emergence of the sociology of intimacy" (*charkhesh mazmuni dar tabyin ravabet zan o mard zohur jame'eh shenasi samimiyat*), *Zan dar Farhang va Honar*, year 11, No. 1, Spring 2019 (1398).
11. "The youth of the 1380s [the 2000s]: The advent of a new youth" (*daheh hashtadi ha; zohur nojavani jadid*), discussion with Ali-Asqar Seyd-Abadi and Mohsen Azmudeh, *Etemad newspaper*, https://www.iran-emrooz.net/index.php/news1/more/103483/
12. https://datareportal.com/reports/digital-2021-iran
13. Not only the veil but also other items of clothing were subject to repression: wearing short trousers; being barefoot, without socks; short coats (above the knee) with slits; short or rolled-up sleeves; open collars; tight-fitting outfits; thin scarf instead of hijab or balaclava; wearing makeup on face and hands. See Ali

Jafari, "Normes islamiques et répression sociale en République islamique d'Iran" [Dress standards and social repression in the Islamic Republic of Iran], *Outre-terre*, 2011/2, No. 28.
14. See Mansoor Moaddel, "Secular shift among Iranians: Findings from cross-national & longitudinal surveys," *Freedom of Thought Journal*, No. 12, Fall 2022. According to this study, "a reasonable expectation of the extent of the Iranian support for the separation of religion and politics is placed at 70%." For the youth, this figure should be much higher due to its revolt within the Mahsa Movement against the Theocratic State.
15. "Iran dedicates one-fifth of its broadcasts to 'Islamic teachings'," *Iran Open Data*, April 26, 2023, https://iranopendata.org/en/pages/iran-dedicates-one-fifth-of-its-broadcasts-to-islamic-teachings

Conclusion

1. One of the most prominent feminist intellectuals of the Campaign for One Million Signatures, Noushin Ahmadi Khorasani, "Why the movement of the 'Girls of Enqelab Avenue' has not extended to the entire society" (*tchera harekae dokhtarane khiabane enqelab gostarech nayaft*), December 18, 2018, https://www.radiozamaneh.com/425026?fbclid=IwAR3_un4-R1g-pXP229xpFsBToOWLmrpKc73XIbq0yEbc6rAXPPxWwVAzXFE

Index

Abbasid caliphate, 34, 36
Abbassi, Keyvan, 213–214
Abbassi, Marjan, 213–214
Abdi, Abbas, 113
Abdolhamid, Mowlavi, 65–66, 69
acid rain, 178
Adelkhah, Fariba, 108
Afghanistan, 39, 78, 100
Afkari, Navid, 188
Afkhami, Mahnaz, 108
agha-zadegan, 27, 165
agriculture, 177, 179, 181, 182
al-Ahmad, Jalal, 41, 74, 76, 217, 218
Ahmadi, Amir Mohammad, 102
Ahmadinejad, Mahmoud, 18, 19, 62, 72–73, 83, 138, 185–186
Ahvaz, 2, 136, 177–179, 182
Alam-ol-Hoda, Seyd Ahmad, 201–202
alcohol, 9, 29, 39, 52, 54, 104, 199, 200, 209
Alexander, Jeffrey, 120

Alexander Langer Prize, 144
Ali, Imam, 34, 218
Ali-Karami, Leyla, 138
alienation, 5, 11, 25, 49, 208–209
Alinejad, Masih, 108, 134
Alizadeh, Parvaneh, 198
Allameh University, 117
Alternative Nobel Prize, 141
American Physical Society, 144
Amini, Mahsa, 28, 87, 89–91, 114, 123, 125, 149, 150–151, 153
Amnesty International, 67–68, 82, 139, 142, 145–146, 147, 148, 149, 193
amputation, 73
Ansar-e Hezbollah, 132
anti-Westernism, 7–8, 11, 37–39, 41, 43, 57, 59, 92, 97, 167, 199–202, 211–213, 215–216
Arabs, 2, 26, 127, 178
Arabshahi, Munireh, 186
Ardalan, Parvin, 82–83, 130, 135, 137

Index

Ariani, Yasman, 186
arrests, 5, 17, 28, 42–43, 68, 72, 82–84, 89–93, 102, 116, 123–127, 138–140, 144–163, 168, 170, 174–175, 180, 183–190, 193
al-Asad, Hafez, 174
Asalouyeh, 92
Ashura, 35
Atatürk, Mustafa Kemal, 12, 70, 86
Australia, 13
authoritarianism, 12–14, 60, 71, 86
Azerbaijan province, 65, 182, 188
Azeris, 65, 69
Azmoun, Sardar, 169

Babiism, 85
Baha'is, 2, 127, 134, 184
Bahmani, Hadi, 181–182
Bahrami, Zahra, 139
Baluchis, 2, 67–68, 118, 127, 176–177, 183
Baluchistan *see* Sistan and Baluchistan
Bandar Iamam Khomeini, 178
Bandar Langeh, 180
Bandar Mahshahr, 178
Banisadr, Abolhassan, 50
Baradaran, Monireh, 185, 193–198
Barakouhi, Ahmad, 190
"*Baraye*" (Hajipour), 46, 91, 112, 157–158
Basij, 16, 40, 115–116, 172–173, 190, 200–201, 202, 223
Baudrillard, Jean, 25, 209
Bayat, Asef, 96
bazaaris, 13, 19, 63

Bazargan, Mehdi, 50
BBC, 213, 214
beatings, 28, 42, 82, 102, 130, 143, 155, 186–188, 190–192
beauty, 23–27, 210
Behbahani, Simine, 194
Beheshti, Sattar, 142
"*Bella ciao*," 112
birth rate, 204–205
Black Friday, 67–68, 171
Black Rewards hackers, 89
Bloody November (a*ban khuneen*), 54
blues music, 42, 45–46, 156
bodily freedom, 3, 23–25, 30–33, 45, 94–95, 98–104, 106, 108–109, 118, 205
Boko Haram, 78
Boroui, Mona, 91
bribery, 29, 209–210
business closures, 106, 221

Campaign for One Million Signatures, 33, 61, 72–73, 80–83, 87, 108, 109, 129, 135,–138, 223
Canada, 13, 27, 107, 123
capitalism, 62, 72, 75, 76, 217
Carl von Ossietsky medal, 194
cartoons, 148
catharsis, 35–37, 44, 167
celebrities, 93, 112, 113, 116, 119, 123, 211
censorship, 113, 124–125, 133, 135, 206, 214–215
charismatic leadership, 13, 15, 49, 77
Chichian, Hamid, 179
child abuse, 133, 138, 206
child marriage, 207–208

children, 18, 21, 70, 132, 133, 136, 138, 144, 204–205, 206–208
Children's Book Council of Iran, 136
China, 11, 38, 47, 143, 168, 223
citizenship, 1, 6, 31, 33, 62, 65, 101, 118, 157
civil disobedience, 111, 119
civil society, 51, 69, 73, 100–101, 102, 107, 118, 119–126, 175, 176, 210
clergy, 13, 14–16, 19, 63, 66, 72, 73–74, 77, 115, 172
climate change, 61, 177, 178, 179
clothing, 3, 8, 9, 22–24, 55, 66, 79, 210, 212; *see also* veil
CNN, 191, 214
"coffin" torture, 194–195
commemoration, 34–37
Committee to Protect Journalists (CPJ), 125, 126
communism, 12–13, 71, 76, 119, 218
confessions, 103, 159–160, 163–164, 189, 192–195, 197
conservatism, 1, 9, 19–20, 72, 208, 210
Constitutional Revolution, 70, 85
consumerism, 23, 25, 208–209
contraception, 148
contract workers, 63
corruption, 7, 60, 84, 117, 165, 167, 199, 209–210, 211
covert filming, 68, 106, 182
Covid-19 pandemic, 193
currency depreciation, 6, 53

Daemi, Atena, 130, 143, 144–147
Daesh, 39, 78, 116
Dai, Ali, 169
dams, 177, 179, 180–181, 183
dancing, 3, 32, 42, 46–47, 95, 97, 98, 99–105, 110, 118, 158, 171, 209
Darabi, Homa, 80
Darvishi, Farjad, 90
"Daughters of Cyrus, The" (Vaziri), 85–86
Davoudi, Amir Salar, 189
death sentences, 67–68, 76, 121, 139, 143–147, 159–163, 168, 184, 188–189, 197–198, 222
"Death to/Down with the dictator" slogan, 5, 56, 62, 90, 92, 98, 101, 116, 117, 130, 151
deaths
    in detention, 92, 115, 123, 142–143, 150, 172, 180, 183, 188, 190, 193, 215
    death sentences, 67–68, 76, 121, 139, 143–147, 159–163, 168, 184, 188–189, 197–198, 222
    executions, 20, 85, 112, 115, 121, 142–145, 172, 174, 190, 193, 197–198, 215, 222
    murders, 132, 133
    at protests, 53–54, 67–69, 90–93, 105, 115, 116, 132, 142, 150–55, 172, 175–176, 181–182, 190, 222
    prison massacres, 50, 172, 174, 196–198, 215
    suicide, 130, 132, 154–155, 161, 215
    under torture, 142–143, 180, 188, 193, 215
Debord, Guy, 25, 209

Defenders of Human Rights
  Center (DHRC), 133, 141
deforestation, 177
Dehghani, Ashraf, 71
democracy, 3, 25, 51, 60–63, 73,
  76, 81, 118, 121, 127, 128,
  132–134, 219
dervishes, 2, 183, 186, 187–188,
  190
desertification, 177, 178–179
desexualization, 3, 25–26, 45
"Dialogue to Save Iran"
  conference, 127
diaspora, 7–8, 24, 59, 107–108,
  112, 118, 126–127, 135–136,
  204, 211–213, 221; see also
  emigration
dignity, 6, 11, 23, 55, 57, 60, 62,
  64, 65, 96, 121, 207
divorce, 70, 133, 138, 148, 205
Dizelabad prison, 189
Dream of Freedom
  documentary, 215
dress *see* clothing
drought, 2–3, 177, 179, 182
drugs, 9, 184, 187
duality, 6, 8–11, 54–55
dust storms, 2, 179

Ebadi, Mohammad Ali, 131
Ebadi, Shirin, 81, 129, 130,
  131–134, 136, 138, 141
Ebrahim-Nejad, Ezzat, 132
Ebrahimi, Amir Farshad,
  132–133
Eco-Iran website, 58
ecological issues, 59, 61, 158,
  177–183
ecological movements, 61,
  179–183

economic development, 7,
  38–39, 223
education, 16, 18, 19, 56–57, 59,
  61, 70, 75, 80, 85, 86, 135,
  184, 203, 204, 206, 207
Egypt, 33, 100
election manipulation, 62, 73,
  185–186
Emami, Kevous Seyed, 180
Emami, Saeed, 132
emancipation, 25, 32, 61, 70–71,
  80, 85, 87, 99–101, 209
emigration, 8, 13, 15, 50, 77, 130,
  135, 136, 142, 164, 194; *see
  also* diaspora
employment, 18–19, 58, 59, 86,
  179
Entesari, Shahla, 82
equality *see* gender equality;
  political equality
Eskandari, Parvaneh, 132
ethnic minorities, 2, 65–9, 118,
  127, 169, 176–177, 181, 183,
  188–190
European Parliament, 141
Evangelism, 9, 184
Evin prison, 92, 138, 139, 140,
  142–143, 144–147, 185–187,
  188, 189, 194–198
executions, 20, 85, 112, 115, 121,
  142–145, 172, 174, 190, 193,
  197–198, 215, 222; *see also*
  death sentences; deaths
existential freedom, 11, 19,
  30–33, 44–45, 93, 202

Facebook, 142, 145; *see also*
  social media
family, 18, 19, 21, 29, 52–54, 78,
  82, 133, 204–208

family members, threats to, 83, 92, 130, 131, 134, 142, 143, 152, 186, 192
Fardid, Ahmad, 217
Farghadani, Atena, 147–149
Fars News Agency, 89, 112–113, 125, 163
Fashafouyeh prison, 187–188, 190
fasting, 9, 48, 55
Fazli, Yalda Aqa, 154–155
Fedayeen of the People, 49, 71
female body, 3, 19, 23–25, 30–33, 45, 94–95, 99–101, 108–109, 111, 118
female education, 16, 18, 19, 59, 61, 70, 80, 85, 86, 206, 207
female employment, 18–19, 59, 86
female intellectuals, 33, 71–72, 76, 85, 107–110, 113, 128–149
female rights *see* women's rights
female status, 3, 12, 14–21, 77–78, 80–83, 86, 107, 128
feminism, 3, 22–24, 60, 70–73, 80–87, 94–95, 104, 107–110, 118, 120, 123–124, 128–149, 155–156, 184–86, 192
Feminist School website, 136, 138
fertility, 3, 18, 204
festivities, 3, 30, 32, 43, 46–8, 59
fines, 28, 78, 79, 104, 162
flagellation, 34–35, 42–3
flogging, 73, 78, 79, 82, 83, 102, 104, 130, 140, 189, 191, 194, 197
Forouhar, Dariush, 132

France, 142, 187
Frankfurt School, 209
Free Life Party of Kurdistan, 188
freedom
  bodily freedom, 3, 23, 24–25, 30–33, 45, 94–95, 98–104, 106, 108–109, 118, 205
  denial of, 1, 5, 7, 11, 17, 159
  desire for, 1–4, 8, 21, 30, 59, 94–95, 103, 108–109
  existential freedom, 11, 19, 30–33, 44–45, 93, 202
  freedom from want, 60, 156
  freedom of dress, 8, 22–24, 212
  freedom of expression, 3, 60, 170
  freedom of the press, 91, 123
  individual freedoms, 29, 45, 59, 96, 209
  political freedom, 8, 11, 19, 21, 30–33, 45, 60–62, 80, 93–95, 103–104, 108–109, 176, 199, 203, 212, 223
Fuladshahr, 154
fundamentalism, 13, 14, 15, 20–21, 25, 41, 50, 75, 77, 218
"Future of Women and Minorities" conference, 127

Gamaan Institute, 88
gender equality, 3, 16, 18–19, 24, 31, 78, 81–83, 85, 87, 109, 120, 128–129, 133–135, 203, 222
gender segregation, 3, 4, 21, 59, 99, 103, 116, 209, 222
generational differences, 6–11, 17, 22–24, 29–30, 47, 52–54, 108–109, 206, 223

Germany, 144, 194
gestures, 111–12, 114, 156
Ghare-Hassanlou, Hamid, 68
Ghasemi, Parmida, 169
Ghavidel, Emad, 7
Gilan, 90–91
"Girls of Enqelab Avenue" movement, 84, 87, 154
global civil sphere (GCS), 119–124
Global Gender Gap report, 18
Gole-Sorkhi, Khosro, 76, 218
Golestan 7 protests, 186, 190
Golshani, Ariane, 133
Gonabadi dervishes, 2, 183, 186, 187–188, 190
Gotvand Dam, 180–181
graffiti tags, 93, 97, 112
Green Movement, 2, 5, 15, 30, 32, 33, 61–62, 73, 103, 109–110, 118, 121, 138–139, 148, 175, 186, 211, 223
grief, culture of, 34–37, 41–45, 93–94, 95, 118, 204; *see also* mourning
Grossman, Vasily, 198
guilt, 4, 24, 26, 35, 53, 75, 118, 216–219, 222

hair, 25, 27, 55, 59, 90, 101, 111–112, 123, 201, 211
hair cutting, 90, 111–12, 123, 211
Hajipour, Shervin, 46, 91, 157–158
Ham-Mihan, 123
Hama, 174
Hamedi, Niloofar, 91, 123, 125
Hamza, 40
Hanke, Steve, 57

Haqiqi, Astiaj, 102
Hashemi, Faezeh, 108, 155–156
Hatami, Amir Hossein, 188
health, 70, 137, 139–142, 146–148, 170–171, 189, 193; *see also* medical care
Hedayat, Bahareh, 82, 130
Heinrich Böll Foundation, 136
helicopters, 153–154
Hengaw, 151, 168
Hezbollahi, 78
Hichkas, 162, 164–166
higher education, 18, 19, 57, 59, 70, 80, 86, 204, 207
hijab *see* veil
hip-hop music, 10, 156, 168
homosexuality, 134, 205
honor, 22, 31, 97
Hossein, Imam, 34–35, 37, 39–40, 42–44, 45, 115
Hossein-Pouri, Azad, 68
Hosseini, Narges, 84
Hosseini, Ziba Mir, 108
Hosseinkhah, Maryam, 83
Hosseinzadeh, Leila, 147
housing, 179, 183
human rights, 20, 82, 120–121, 124, 131–134, 139–147, 170–171, 186, 194, 199, 211, 212
human rights activists, 129, 131, 142, 146–147, 170–171, 184, 186, 189, 191, 199
humiliation, 8, 10, 104, 195–196
hunger strikes, 123–124, 139, 140–141, 145–146, 147, 148, 170
hypocrisy, 9, 10, 29, 55, 87–88, 109, 115

identity, 12, 16, 22–25, 39, 40, 55, 74–75, 216–219
imperialism, 40, 71–72, 217, 218–219
imprisonment, 20, 42, 78–84, 91, 102, 104, 116, 120, 123–126, 130, 131, 135–149, 155–156, 162–163, 170, 175, 184–199, 215, 223
individual freedoms, 29, 45, 59, 96, 209
individual protest, 71, 80, 101, 105–106, 111, 126, 221
individualism, 22, 74, 205, 217
industrial action *see* strikes
industry, 62, 177–178, 180, 183
inflation, 2, 6, 7, 53, 58, 63, 221
Instagram, 90, 91, 92, 152, 157, 161–162, 168, 171, 206; *see also* social media
intellectuals
  in the diaspora, 107, 108, 135, 136
  female, 33, 71–72, 76, 85, 107–110, 113, 128–149
  feminist, 107–110, 123–124, 128–149; *see also* feminism
  Marxist, 74, 75–76, 217, 218–219; *see also* Marxism
  new intellectuals, 156–171
  reformist, 50–51, 81, 107, 110, 113, 128; *see also* reformism
  Third Worldist, 74, 76, 216–218
  Western, 23, 25, 128
internal colonization, 178
internalization, 8, 12, 26, 30, 74
international awards, 81, 82–83, 91, 123, 124, 133, 135, 137, 138, 141, 144, 194

International Campaign for Human Rights in Iran, 139
International Cartoonist Rights Protection Network, 148
International Freedom of the Press Award, 123
International Organization of Human Rights, 138
International Union of Human Rights,m 194
International Women's Day, 72, 93, 102, 186
internet, 5, 7, 30, 59, 65, 90, 97–99, 102–103, 112, 126–127, 151, 204, 206, 211; *see also* social media
intimidation, 2, 28, 52, 73, 78, 105–106, 116–117, 142, 186, 221
Intisari, Sima, 190
Iraee, Golrokh Ebrahimi, 146, 147
Iran Human Rights Watch, 91–92, 180, 188
Iran International, 67, 150, 213
Iran–Iraq War, 14, 15, 38, 39–40, 50, 79, 166–167, 214
Iran Women's Movement Documentation Center, 136
Iranian Center for Statistics, 18
Iranian Communist Party, 71
Iranian Dinner, 215–216
Iranian Parliament, 58, 88
Iraq, 14, 15, 38, 39–40, 50, 79, 166–167, 214
Isfahan, 3, 93, 117, 154, 161–163, 180, 182
ISIS *see* Daesh
Israel, 37, 38, 39, 92, 193, 199, 212, 215

Islamic feminists, 155–156
Islamic honor, 22, 97
Islamic laws, 12, 15, 21, 73–74, 100, 102, 133, 207–208; *see also* Sharia
Islamic patriarchal pact, 12–21, 30, 97–98
Islamic Republic News Agency (IRNA), 134
Islamic Republic of Iran Broadcasting (IRIB), 125
Islamic Revolution, 8, 12–17, 30, 33, 36–40, 49–50, 71–78, 80, 86–87, 95, 129, 131, 155, 166
Islamic Revolutionary Guards Corps (IRGC), 16, 56, 63, 89, 113, 125, 144–145, 163, 172, 177, 179–181, 183, 185, 187, 191, 200, 223
Islamic spiritualism, 51
Islamism *see* fundamentalism
Islamization, 15, 20, 73–74
Italy, 138
Izeh, 68, 116, 181–182

Jalalian, Zainab, 188–190
Jame'e Zanan Mosalman, 155
Javaheri, Jelveh, 83
jihadism, 37, 38, 39, 78, 201
job security, 63, 64
"joie de vivre," 6–7, 11, 17, 19, 24, 34, 44–46, 54, 94, 96, 99, 102, 109, 111, 118, 153, 156–157, 199, 203, 207, 223
journalists, 79, 82–83, 91–92, 108, 123–126, 135–138, 141–142, 155, 185, 188, 215; *see also* media; newspapers
joy, 1, 3, 7, 9, 11, 39, 43, 44–46, 48, 59, 93–105, 108–109, 111, 158, 159, 204, 213, 222
judiciary, 61–62, 70, 73–74, 83, 131–133, 135, 172, 192, 198
Justice for Iran, 149

Kadivar, Djamileh, 113
Kahrom, Esmail, 181
Kandioty, Deniz, 14, 15
Kar, Mehrangiz, 129
Karaj, 153
Karbala, 34–35, 37
Karimi, Ali, 163, 169
Karun River, 180–181
Kazemi, Zahra, 155
Kerman, 105, 190
Kermanshah, 159, 187, 188–189, 190
Keshavarz, Mojgan, 186
Keshavarz, Nahid, 83, 130
Keyhan, 88
Khamenei, Ayatollah, 92, 115, 154, 199–200, 208
Khandan, Reza, 140
Khash, 68–69
Khatami, Ahmad, 201
Khatami, Mohammad, 6, 21, 61, 79, 81, 83, 108, 132, 133, 135
Khomeini, Ayatollah, 12, 13–16, 23, 30, 37, 49–51, 72–79, 86–87, 129, 197, 202, 208, 215, 218–219
Khorasani, Javad Mousavi, 137
Khorasani, Noushin Ahmadi, 22, 24, 82, 130, 135, 136, 137–38
Khorramabad, 152–153, 163
Khorramchahr, 180
Khoy prison, 187, 189
Khuzestan, 2, 116, 177–179, 181–182

Kian, Azadeh, 108
Komala, 176
Kor River, 182–183
Kufa, 35
Kurdistan, 65–69, 89–90, 93, 105, 150, 151, 188
Kurdistan Human Rights Network, 159–160, 176
Kurds, 2, 65–66, 67, 89–90, 118, 127, 160, 176, 183, 188–190

labor laws, 63
labor market *see* employment
Ladier-Fouladi, Marie, 108
Ladjevardi, Asadollah, 197
Lajah, Khodanoor, 171
Lakan prison, 92
Lake Urmia, 2–3, 182
lakes, 2–3, 182
lashes *see* flogging
Lashkari, Soroush *see* Hichkas
Latifeh Yarshater Award, 137
leftism, 12–13, 15, 41, 49, 71, 72, 76, 147, 197, 212; *see also* Marxism
legal representation, denial of, 102, 145, 159, 161, 186
legal status, 3, 12, 21, 78, 81, 86, 107, 128, 132
Legam, 143
legitimacy
  crisis of, 119, 173–175
  cultural legitimacy, 52
  Islamic legitimacy, 19, 23
  of the patriarchal pact, 16
  of protest, 47, 122, 123–124
  of the regime, 6, 19, 20, 29, 38–39, 43–44, 47, 51, 52, 61–62, 93, 96–97, 107, 109, 129, 173–175, 185, 203, 210, 223
  of the Supreme Leader, 208
  symbolic legitimacy, 39, 96–97
leisure, 204, 208–211, 213
liberalism, 50, 132
live ammunition, 68, 90, 117
London, 150, 162, 214
Lorestan, 67, 112, 151, 163
lower classes, 6, 9, 13, 60, 211
Ludovic Trarieux Prize, 141
Lyons Award, 123

Madani, Kaveh, 180
Mahabad, 69, 176
Mahan, 105
Mahini, Hossein, 91
Mahjoubi, Behnam, 190
Mahsa Movement, 2–9, 11, 15–17, 19, 21, 25, 30–33, 39, 44–48, 52–65, 69, 85–127, 129, 149–177, 199–202, 206, 209, 211, 221–223
Majlis Research Center, 58
makeup, 23, 26–27, 55
Makou, 188
male gaze, 26, 27, 94
male honor, 31
Manoto TV, 213–220
Manouchehrian, Mehrangiz, 71, 137
Marcuse, Herbert, 25
Mardani, Niloufar, 170
marriage, 70, 135, 207–208
marshes, 177, 178, 179
martyrdom, 3, 34–45, 95, 97, 111, 115, 118, 204, 207, 213, 214
Marx, Karl, 41
Marxism, 15, 41, 49, 50, 62, 74,

75–76, 119, 217, 218–219; *see also* leftism
Mashhad, 68, 92
media, 61–62, 65, 79, 88–89, 108, 112–113, 123–126, 133–135, 153–154, 159, 163, 191, 203, 207, 211, 213–220; *see also* journalists; newspapers; radio; television
medical care, denial of, 130, 131, 142, 146, 149, 184, 187, 189–190, 192, 193; *see also* health
medication strikes, 189
men
  attitudes to appearance, 24, 210
  dancing with women, 3, 32, 46–47, 97, 98, 99, 103–105, 118
  machismo, 97
  male gaze, 26, 27, 94
  male honor, 31
  regime repression of, 20, 21, 55
  rejection of mandatory veiling, 88–89, 118
  rejection of theocratic constraints, 4, 16–17, 20, 21, 97–99, 101, 103–104, 118, 222
  repression of women by, 19–20, 97
  and sexuality, 23, 25–26, 27, 31, 45, 100
  social relationships with women, 3, 6, 9, 31, 39, 42, 46–47, 104–105, 209, 222
  solidarity with women, 3–4, 19, 24–25, 30–33, 55, 94–98, 103–104, 111
  support of Mahsa Movement, 3, 16–17, 19, 21, 30–33, 55, 60, 94–98, 103–104, 111, 117–118
middle classes, 6–8, 13–16, 20, 26, 49–64, 71, 74–75, 119, 129, 130, 167, 204, 211, 213, 217–218, 221–222
migration *see* emigration; rural–urban migration
Milani, Farzaneh, 108
minority groups *see* ethnic minorities; religious minorities
Misery Index, 57
mock executions, 186
modernity, 1, 20, 23, 26, 30, 110, 216–219
modernization, 12–16, 42–43, 50, 70, 74–75, 86
modesty, 19–20, 55
Moghadam, Valentine, 108
Mogouee, Mahsa, 154
Mohajer, Fariba Davoudi, 82
Mohammad Reza Shah, 12–15, 26, 49–50, 71, 75, 86, 153–154, 193–194, 204, 216, 218
Mohammadi, Elaheh, 91, 123, 125
Mohammadi, Narges, 123, 124, 130, 141–144
Mohammadnejad, Mehrdad, 188
Moharram, 34–36, 42
Mokhtari, Shadi, 108
Monfared, Maryam Akbari, 147
Moradi, Sepideh, 190

morality police, 27–29, 54–55; *see also* police; Vice Squad
Mossadegh, Mohammad, 80, 201–202
mostaz'afeen, 13–14, 15, 16, 20
"Mother, Mother, it's Time for War," 112
motorcycles, 106
mourning, 19, 34–38, 42–44, 96, 97, 151, 152, 204, 214; *see also* grief, culture of
Moussavi, Mir Hossein, 73, 185
Moussavi, Vahid, 163–164
Movahed, Vida, 84, 87
murders, 132, 133
music, 3, 28–29, 32, 36, 42–46, 66–67, 99, 112, 119, 144, 156–169, 209; *see also* dancing; singing
Muslim Brotherhood, 174
Muslim Student Followers of the Imam's Path, 50

Nabavi, Zia, 195
Najaf-Abad, 117
Najafi, Hadith, 153–154
Najafi, Shahin, 144
narcissism, 24, 25, 210
nasle khakestari, 17
Nasseri, Shahin, 188
Nassiri, Mehdi, 88–89
Nategh, Homa, 12, 71–72
National Front, 80
National Oil Company, 63
National Solidarity Day of Iranian Women, 82
nationalism, 41, 67, 216
Nazmi, Neda, 108
newspapers, 61–62, 79, 88–89, 113, 123, 144, 155; *see also* journalists; media
Nieman Journalism Foundation, 123
Nobel Peace Prize, 81, 133, 141, 144
Norouzi, Mohen, 190
nuclear treaty, 6

oil industry, 2, 6, 51, 62, 63, 177–179
oil workers, 2, 62, 63
Olof Palme Prize, 82–83, 135
Oneness of God (*towhid*), 41, 218
"oppressed" strata (*mostaz'afeen*), 13–14, 15, 16, 20
Osanloo, Arzoo, 108
Ottoman Empire, 33
"Our enemy is here" slogan, 8, 168, 212

Pahlavi, Reza, 134
Pahlavi dynasty, 8, 12–16, 26, 38, 49, 70–71, 73, 75, 86, 155, 178, 179, 184
Palestine, 212
Palmyra prison, 174
Panahi, Jafar, 140, 141
paramilitary groups, 52, 132
parties, 28–29, 39, 42, 59, 104, 209–210
patriarchy, 4, 12–21, 30, 61, 97–98, 129, 149, 207, 208, 210
Payam e Hajar, 155
People's Mojahedin, 49, 50, 71, 197
pepper spray, 82

Index

Per Anger Prize, 144
Persian Heritage Foundation, 137
Persian Wildlife Heritage Foundation (PWHF), 179–180
Peykar, 49, 71
phone-tapping, 192
Phoror, Reza, 164
Piramoon, Said, 111
Pirfalak, Kian, 116
"plumbing" (*polomb kardan*), 106
pluralism, 81, 107, 133, 212
poetry, 76, 85, 91
police, 26, 48, 52, 67, 72, 99, 106, 116–117, 134, 151, 153, 173, 181, 223; *see also* morality police; Vice Squad
political equality, 60
political freedom, 8, 11, 19, 21, 30–33, 45, 60–62, 80, 93–95, 103–104, 108–109, 176, 199, 203, 212, 223
political parties, 13, 71, 75, 223
pollution, 2, 61, 158, 177–179, 180–181
population growth, 19
populism, 18, 62, 72, 83
postmodernism, 209
poverty, 2, 6, 7, 13–14, 20, 52–60, 84, 97, 112, 117, 119, 165, 167, 182, 211, 221
prayers, 9, 54, 75, 91
prison fires, 92
prison massacres, 50, 172, 174, 196, 197–198, 215
prison transfers, 142, 143, 145–147, 150, 186, 188–190

private life, 8–11, 28–29, 51, 54–55
privatization, 63
processions, 34–35, 42
proletarian revolution, 41, 72, 74, 75–76
propaganda, 82, 125
prostitution, 84, 135
protest songs, 46, 112, 144, 157–161; *see also* music; singing
pro-Westernism, 7–8, 118, 211–212, 216
public life, 8–11, 29, 39, 51, 54–55, 71
puritanism, 25, 39, 59, 108, 118, 219

al-Qaeda, 78
Qajar dynasty, 184
Qarchak prison, 141, 154, 187, 190
Qavidel, Emad, 166–169
Qesel Hesar prison, 194–195
quietism, 37, 41, 49
Qom, 76, 78–79, 88, 89, 214

radicalization, 49, 50
radio, 213; *see also* media
Rafsanjani, Akbar Hashemi, 155
Rahimi, Mostafa, 76
Rahmani, Davood, 194–195
Rahmani, Taqi, 141–142
Rahnavard, Zahra, 108
Raissi, Ebrahim, 18
Rajavi, Maryam, 71
Rajavi, Mas'oud, 71
Ramadan, 9, 34, 48, 55
rap music, 7, 32, 45–46, 66–67, 119, 156, 159–69

rape, 67, 130, 133, 143, 155, 186, 192
Rasht, 92, 166
reformism, 6, 21, 50–51, 61–62, 73, 81, 107–108, 110, 113, 128, 132–133, 174
Rehman, Javaid, 147
Rekabi, Elnaz, 92
religious minorities, 2, 65–69, 127, 134, 176, 183–184
Reza Shah, 8, 12–15, 26, 70–71, 73, 86, 176, 222
Reuters news agency, 134
Rhie, Ye-One, 163
rights *see* human rights; women's rights
rivers, 3, 178–183
Ronaqi, Hossein, 170–171
Rouhani, Hassan, 134, 139
rubber bullets, 117
rural–urban migration, 177, 179, 183
Russia, 38, 168, 198–199; *see also* Soviet Union

sacrifice, sense of, 95
Safazadeh, Ronak, 82
Sakharov Prize, 141, 144
Salaam, 61–62, 79
Salahshuri, Parvaneh, 87–88
Salami, Sardar Hossein, 200
Salehi, Toomaj, 66–67, 161–163
salinization, 177
Salomeh MC, 164
Sanandaj, 65, 89, 187
sanctions, 167, 212
sandstorms, 2, 179
Saqaï, Reza, 112
Saqez, 65, 89, 150, 151
"Satanism," 37, 38, 104–105

Saudi Arabia, 39, 78
Second World War, 176
secular culture, 6–10, 16–17, 19, 24, 29, 44–46, 49–52, 54–60, 109–110, 203, 204, 214
secularization, 6, 8, 16–17, 24, 26, 32, 38–40, 51–52, 59, 62, 73–74, 99, 103, 109–110, 118, 204–208, 212, 222
selfie culture, 22, 23–24
Seyd-Abadi, Ali-Asqar, 206
sexuality, 3, 23, 25–26, 27, 31, 45, 97, 100, 205–206
Shabestari, Mohammad Mojtahed, 51
Shafiei, Saeedeh, 125–126
Shahinshahr, 154, 161–163
Shahkarami, Nika, 90
Shahr-e Rey prison, 146
Shakarami, Nika, 151–153
Sharia, 46, 73–74, 79, 133; *see also* Islamic laws
Shariati, Ali, 40–41, 51, 95, 217, 218
Sharif University, 91, 113
Sharq, 123
Sherkat, Shahla, 79, 108, 129
Shi'i Messiah, 34, 37
Shiraz, 147, 183, 188
Shirmohammed-Ali, Alireza, 188
Shojaee, Mansoureh, 130, 135–136
silent demonstrations, 93
singing, 3, 42–43, 46, 95, 100–101, 158, 171, 209; *see also* music
Sistan and Baluchistan, 2, 65–69, 93, 97, 105, 171, 176

Sizdah bedar festival, 47–48
sleep deprivation, 186
slogans
    "Death to/Down with the dictator," 5, 56, 62, 90, 92, 98, 101, 116, 117, 130, 151
    ecological movements, 182
    ethnic movements, 65, 66, 68–69
    Green Movement, 33, 73, 186
    Islamic Revolution, 33, 77, 95
    Mahsa Movement, 5, 8, 19, 31, 44–45, 56, 62, 87, 90–93, 98, 101, 111–117, 151, 154, 158, 211, 212
    "Our enemy is here," 8, 168, 212
    sexual and vulgar slogans, 112–114
    2016–2019 movements, 113
    "Where is my vote?" 73, 121, 186
    "Woman, life, freedom," 5, 19, 44–45, 56, 87, 90, 111, 117, 158, 211
slums, 179, 183
smartphones, 24, 206
social justice, 12, 61, 69, 75, 219
social media, 24, 84, 89–92, 103, 116, 119, 142–145, 151–154, 157, 161–163, 165, 168, 170, 171, 188, 206; *see also* internet
social mobility, 13
socialization, 3, 9, 42, 46–47, 110, 209, 222
Society for the Protection of Children's Rights (SPCR), 133
soft totalitarianism, 174

soil erosion, 181
soil fertility, 177
Soleimani, Qassem, 45, 214
solitary confinement, 131, 139, 145, 148, 186
Solzhenitsyn, Alexander, 198
Soroush, Abdolkarim, 51
Sosan, 181–182
Sotoudeh, Nasrin, 82, 84, 123–124, 130, 138–141, 186, 193
Soviet Union, 176, 198–199; *see also* Russia
spontaneity, 46, 55, 99–100
sportsmen and women, 91, 92, 111, 113, 163, 169–170, 211
Stalin, Joseph, 198
status *see* female status; legal status
stoning, 73, 146
street names, 116
strikes, 63–65, 68, 92, 151, 193
student protests, 3, 61–62, 72, 80, 116–117, 132, 141
Students' Movement, 61–62
stun grenades, 117, 153–154
submission, 10, 15, 19–20, 29, 44, 129
subversion, 25–28, 101
Sufism, 2, 183
sugar production, 2, 62, 178, 179
suicide, 130, 132, 154–155, 161, 215
Sultanbeigi, Nasim, 125–126
Sunni Islam, 2, 34, 36, 38, 65–66, 67–69, 176, 183, 201
superego, 24, 47, 118, 217–218
surveillance, 29, 54, 67–68, 170–171, 192
Sweden, 135, 144

symbolic legitimacy, 39, 96–97
symbolic protest, 59, 85, 93, 111–119, 123
Syria, 100, 174, 175

Tabandeh, Nour-Ali, 190
Tabriz, 68
Tahereh Ghorrat ol-Eyn, 85
Tahmasebi, Sussan, 82
Talattof, Kamran, 96
Taleghani, Azam, 155
Taleghani, Mahmoud, 155
Taliban, 39, 78, 100
talion law, 73
tasers, 117
Tasnim News Agency, 125, 163
Tasu'a, 35
Taxi Tehran (2016), 140
tear gas, 48, 92, 117
technology, 24, 206
Tehran, 2, 12, 27, 28, 31, 54, 68, 72–73, 76, 80, 82, 84, 89–93, 99, 102–103, 116–117, 131, 150–152, 164, 177, 185–186, 190, 193, 209
Tehran University, 31, 72, 80, 82, 89–90, 117, 131, 137
Telegram, 152; *see also* social media
television, 9, 29, 54, 88–89, 153–154, 163, 192, 195, 213–220; *see also* media
"10 Days to Sign" campaign, 147
thanatocracy, 164, 165, 168, 172, 223
theatrical performances (*ta'zieh*), 35
theocratic Shi'ism, 5, 37–45, 55, 59, 66, 93

Third Worldist intellectuals, 74, 76, 216–218
Time magazine, 123
Tohidi, Nayereh, 96, 108
torture, 20, 68, 83, 93, 102, 120, 123, 130–131, 142–145, 153–157, 160–164, 168–169, 175, 180, 184–188, 191–198, 215, 223
totalitarianism, 6, 37–44, 97, 173–175, 203, 209
Touraine, Alain, 120
trade unions, 64, 223
traditional Shi'ism, 3, 34–37, 43, 44, 204
transgression, 10, 27–29, 32, 39, 46–47, 55, 98, 99–102, 111, 210, 222
Trump, Donald, 6, 52–53
Tudeh Party, 71
Turkey, 12, 13, 50, 86, 214
Turkmen, 169
Turks, 26, 65, 90, 127
twelfth Imam, 34, 37
2016–2019 movements, 5, 11, 15, 30, 53–54, 60, 103, 113
Twitter, 91, 145, 152, 153, 161–162, 195; *see also* social media

Uighur Muslims, 38
Umayyad caliphate, 34, 36
UNESCO, 91, 123
UNICEF, 136
United Arab Emirates, 214
United Kingdom, 150, 162, 164, 168, 193, 202, 214
United Nations, 78, 121, 122, 147, 180, 196, 222

Index

United Nations Commission on the Status of Women, 222
United States, 6, 13, 27, 37, 38, 39, 45, 52–53, 80, 92, 107, 168, 193, 199–200, 201–202, 212
United States Embassy occupation, 50
universities, 18, 19, 57, 59, 70, 80, 86, 89–92, 116–117, 204, 207
Unrepresented Nations and Peoples Organization (ONPO), 178
upper classes, 71
urbanization, 205
Urmia, 90, 182, 187

Valiasr, 90
Vaziri, Qamar ol-Moluk, 85–86
veil
  "badly" veiled (*bad hejab*), 19, 25–28, 88, 89, 223
  banning of, 12, 16, 26, 73, 86, 222
  and desexualization, 3, 25–26, 45
  Islamic Regime views on, 199–202
  "loosely" veiled (*shol hejab*), 19, 25
  mandatory wearing of, 1, 9, 12–13, 19, 21–23, 72, 77–84, 85–93, 209
  numbers in favor of and against, 88–89
  penalties for not wearing or incorrect wearing, 19, 28, 78–79, 101–102, 186
  promotion of, 88
  public removal of, 47, 53, 55, 84–90, 92, 97, 100–106, 111, 118, 129, 140, 169–170
  setting fire to, 32, 47, 97, 111
  subversive approaches to wearing, 25–28, 101
  "thinly" veiled (*kam hejab*), 25
  in television programs, 213, 214
  unveiled, 12–13, 16, 25, 26, 72, 74–75, 78, 85–86, 97, 99–106, 116, 119, 186, 221, 223
  veiled female agents, 105–106
Velayat faqih, 51, 77, 107, 128, 203
Vice Squad, 26, 28, 87, 89, 96, 123, 149, 150, 209, 210; *see also* morality police; police
virginity tests, 149
Voice of America, 213

wages, 2, 61, 62, 63, 64, 167
Washington Post, 148
water supply, 3, 177–183
Weimar Human Rights Prize, 144
Western intellectuals, 23, 25, 128
Westernization, 38, 74, 95, 216–218
Westtoxification (*qarb-zadegi*), 41, 74, 217
WhatsApp, 90, 206, 206; *see also* social media
"Where is my vote?" slogan, 73, 121, 186
white torture, 142
wildlife, 179–180
witness, 101, 120, 122, 124, 188

"Woman, life, freedom" slogan, 5, 19, 44–45, 56, 87, 90, 111, 117, 158, 211
women's associations, 70–71
Women's Cultural Center, 135, 136, 137
women's rights, 6, 12–14, 19, 45, 70–73, 81–83, 86–87, 94–95, 120, 135–138, 141–142, 155–156
workers' protests, 2, 61, 62–65
working classes, 2, 9, 60–65, 129, 144
working conditions, 61, 63–64
World Day Against the Death Penalty, 147
World Economic Forum, 18, 78
World Health Organization, 178
World Press Freedom Prize, 91, 123
would-be middle class, 56–62, 64, 119, 222
Writers in Exile Program, 136

Yadollahi, Shokoufeh, 190
Yasin, Hamri Saman, 159–161, 168
Yazd prison, 190
Yazid, Caliph, 34–35, 40, 115

Zahedan, 67–68, 91, 171
al-Zahra University, 148
Zan, 155
Zanan magazine, 79, 108
Zanestan magazine, 135
Zanjan prison, 142
Zayandeh Rud river, 3, 180
Zeynab, 200–201